THE
FREEDOM
CODE

Simple Solutions
for Life's Major Challenges

MICHAEL J. RHODES

Ancient Elders Press
HUMBLE, TEXAS

THE FREEDOM CODE

Published by:

Ancient Elders Press
P.O. Box 2555
Humble, TX 77347
www.AncientEldersPress.com

ISBN 978 - 0 - 9825970 - 0 - 2
LCCN 2009909530

Edited by Cindy Carlone and Wendy Rhodes
Cover help by Dac Call and Merry Crain
Book Design by John Reinhardt Book Design
Printed and Bound by Central Plains Books

Orders can be obtained at www.AncientEldersPress.com

To my loving wife, Wendy

Make a Wish...
Then Believe!

Michael

CONTENTS

CONTENTS

PART TWO
MY FIRST WISH:
A ROADMAP FOR WORLD PEACE

ACKNOWLEDGMENTS

I THANK EVERYONE for your existence and contributions to this book. I took the best from my past, which was equally created by your thoughts, words, and deeds, and composed them in my own way to inspire hope and belief for the now and for our future. You have all taken part in this grand process of life, so this book was written for you.

In my mind, nothing is completely original. Every invention, building, poem, book, painting, and song owes its existence to all the events that led up to that wonderful day of creation and completion. We build upon each other's stones. Mozart could compose all of his forty-one wonderful symphonies because somebody else invented the violin. Michelangelo was able to paint the famous scenes from Genesis because someone else built the ceiling for the Sistine Chapel. Everything that you read, hear, dance to, and look at with awe, owes its creation to the events and knowledge that led up to it. I am building upon the stones of others with my shared knowledge and experiences. There is an unending cycle in which students create teachers, and teachers create students, and I have been fortunate to have learned from both. We are the builders and creators of life, and it is an honor to be the next stone in your palace of success because of all your wonderful contributions. Thank you.

In appreciation and gratitude, I placed my best efforts into this material to give you an option, another possible way to reach happiness. I am lucky to have learned many great lessons in life and to have learned from so many great teachers. Sometimes I had to hear the lessons presented over and over again, in many different ways, before that one eventful day when the planets aligned and I saw the light. In this book, you will undoubtedly hear some of the same lessons that you've heard before. Maybe today is the day you will hear it said at just the right moment to help you transform your blocks into successes. Maybe today is the day you will hear it said in a way that will bring clarity to life's major problems. And maybe this book will be the one step out of many that helps you move forward on your journey of transformation. In either case, congratulations! You have moved one step closer to your goal.

My thanks go to my parents, Jack and Elizabeth Rhodes, my brothers and sisters, Diana, John, Mary, and Jim, and to my relatives, both living and beyond the body. I thank my friends and teachers who have come into my life at just the right moment to share their wisdom and knowledge.

I thank Ed and Cheryl Martin, owners of The Path Foundation, for giving me a great introduction to hypnosis.

A special thanks goes to John Reinhardt at John Reinhardt Book Design for helping me with layout design; Dac Call and Merry Crain at Central Plains Book for helping me with my cover layout; Cindy Carlone and Wendy Rhodes for editing; and Melody Morris at Central Plains Book for being so kind to the new kid on the block.

My love and closest support for the last twenty-one years has come from a beautiful soul. She is not only my partner in life, she is my soul mate. My wife, Wendy Rhodes, deserves so much credit and appreciation for supporting my efforts to help the world. I would not have been able to write this book without her. Thank you, Wendy! Kisses.

DISCLAIMER

THE INTENT OF THIS BOOK is to give people hope, inspiration, techniques for enhanced cooperation, and suggestions for creating a peaceful and happier life. Use your best judgments when applying this material. If it doesn't feel right for you now, put it aside until you decide it is the right time. Consult with your parents, grandparents, children, grandchildren, relatives, doctors, priests, rabbis, gurus, teachers, principals, CEOs, your boss, employees, your pets, your named Deity, and anyone else that holds an important place in your life for permission to implement these ideas. Get a signed note of approval if you feel that is necessary.

Please do not treat this book like a bible or a religion. There are many ways to reach the North Pole. You can walk, swim, ride a bike, fly in a helicopter, fly in a plane, ride in a rocket ship, take a bus, ride on the back of a humpback whale, or jump in the back of Santa's sleigh. All of these modes of transportation will lead you to the final destination up north. Depending on what type of transportation you choose, some will take longer than others. Some of these choices will be more comfortable than others, and some you may not like at all. As you read this material, decide what you like most. Use the techniques from this book that resonate with you. If they resonate well inside you, you increase the chance they will work for you. You have the freedom to use some or all of these stories and techniques to reach your goal.

History is a story told through perception, and facts change as much as people do. If all of history were correct, finite, and factual, the world would still be flat, the Earth would still be the center of the Universe, and the smallest particle would be the atom. We know this is not true at this time. Use the facts presented in this material as a guideline. You will gain more if you focus on the message and not the numbers, places, or names. Our science is changing by the day, as is our perception, so it is possible that by the time you read this, the *facts and beliefs* may have shifted from their defined starting place.

PREFACE

WHAT IS A FREEDOM CODE? What secrets are hidden deep inside this code that could change the world and reinstate peace for all humankind? How could the Freedom Code help you achieve your dreams and desires? You currently hold in your hands a key that could transform your life and the lives of your loved ones. Within these pages, you have been given full access to a proven system that will help you achieve happiness, abundance, health, and success. You are invited to immerse yourself in the stories and techniques that can lead the way to a greater positive future.

Part of our purpose on Earth is to continue helping ourselves and others learn, grow, and find new ways to achieve success and happiness in life. With your continued success, you will inspire many people in many ways. When you look in the mirror, your reflection will beam with continued strength and appreciation for yourself and your natural abilities. You will be the one that will make the difference in your life. You are the new leader for your future. You begin to believe, and you find that you believe more with every passing breath.

When you are finished, you will have an unwavering resource that will enable you to transform your fears and release personal roadblocks time and again. Your natural abilities will have grown stronger, and your resolve to achieve your goals will strengthen beyond imagination. You will breathe life into your passions and resurrect the dreams you temporarily put aside as you encountered life's major challenges. It is time to bring peace and happiness into the world again. You will do this as you vibrate with joy resulting from your accomplishments and positive actions. You will be the one to make a difference. It only takes one step forward to start the process, and the rest will follow with ease.

The words and stories you are about to read were written to help you reach for the stars and live your passions without fear or judgment. Many have been looking for a roadmap to help them take one more step, a roadmap that will get them one inch closer to living their passions. A little bit of encouragement is all that is needed. You now have that roadmap in your hands. You believe again that your potential has been there all the time, and it's getting a little nudge right now. The energy of these pages is giving you that boost of encouragement and support. It is your natural right to be free to pursue life, to learn, and to love.

Because you are reading this book, you still have hope. You still have desire. You still believe there is a way. With this material in hand, you are already a success for making the effort to enrich your life and the lives of others.

TRANSFORMING CHALLENGES

I wrote this book to give you possible solutions for life's major challenges. Use as much or as little as you like. You may find yourself solving one or more of your problems while you read this material. Good for you! Finding your own solutions through the guidance and will of this content will be an added perk. Our greatest challenges, whatever they may be, will transform easily as you read and practice the techniques shared inside. Fear, ego, and denial will change day by day into courage, sharing, tolerance, and acceptance. Old programming will be understood from a new light. You will see your life's history with a brand new perspective. And once you understand the old programming, you can choose to keep it or release it for good. You have the *Freedom Code* to release your blocks and make room for new positive ideas, thoughts, and actions. You will be the one programming your mind and taking charge of your feelings and thoughts. As you live each day, you will be anchoring these new programs of success until they become natural habits in your daily life. A renewed spirit will move you forward as you experience subtle and major shifts in perception. You will find that you will be able to change your perceptions to meet your needs and desires and revitalize your potential.

By reading this book, the process has already begun. Continue seeking support, and you will be supported. As you encourage others, you will also be encouraged. When you give a helping hand, you will be helping yourself. Feed the cycle of life, and you will be fed forever.

KNOWLEDGE ON A COAT HANGER

When I teach a class or give a lecture, I help my students and audience receive new information with the aid of a short analogy. Let me share this with you.

Use your imagination and picture a coat in your mind. This will be a brand new coat that you would love to wear in the middle of winter. It looks fantastic on the hanger. It sparkles, it shines, and it's the best new coat you have ever seen. It peaks your desire and you can see yourself wearing it in your mind's eye. The color, size, and style are perfect. It's everything you could ever want in a coat.

You hold the coat in your hand. You feel the fabric, examine it, and you are ready to try it on without a second thought. With excitement you put one arm in, then the other. It slides on with ease. With one last adjustment, it's embracing your body. You can feel the warmth and protection already.

You walk over to the mirror to take a look. As you do, you remember how it hung perfectly on the hanger. It looked awesome on display. You say to yourself, "It must be a great fit." On the way to the mirror, though, you notice that the coat feels good, but it's not quite as perfect as you first thought. As you look in the mirror, you think, "Wow, it's a great coat, but it's not for me right now." Now because it didn't fit perfectly, you didn't walk over to a garbage can and throw it away. You didn't decide to destroy the coat or say that it was a terrible coat. You didn't shake your finger and ridicule the coat because it was new. You tried it on and noticed that it wasn't the right fit at that moment. It wasn't the right time for this coat in your life.

Information is like this new coat. Sometimes it fits, and sometimes it doesn't. If something doesn't fit in your belief system at this very moment, put it on the hanger in your mind. Place it in your vast memory storehouse until you need it again. If it doesn't help you now, it may help you later. It may be used to help a loved one. It may be the one piece of information that someone needs to transform his or her life. It may be the one piece of information that could lift someone's spirits. If you read something that doesn't fit your current belief system, put it in your mind's closet for later use. Who knows when it will change a life?

WHAT ARE YOUR THREE WISHES?

WHILE I WAS OUT TAKING A WALK the other morning, about a half block in front of me I noticed a car parked with its hood propped open. There was an older gentleman bent over the engine with a quizzical look on his face. He was tugging at belts, hoses, and connection lines. It was a telltale sign of a car in trouble.

"Hi there. What seems to be the problem?"

"Well, I think I left the lights on last night and drained the battery, but I'm not sure. I've been here for about an hour and you're the first person to offer any help. Thanks," said the smiling fellow.

"I'll be glad to try. Why don't you get in and start it one more time?"

"Sure, I'll give it another whirl, but I think it needs a jump. The battery seems pretty low."

He walked with a pronounced limp around the car door and gingerly crawled into the driver's seat. When he turned the key, the engine gave a little *rrr-rrr-rrr* sound.

"Yup, needs a jump," I said. "Listen, I live only two blocks away. When I get home, I'll drive over and give your battery a boost."

"That sounds great. There are a bunch of antique shops in the next town over that I want to visit today."

Within five minutes, my front bumper was inching up next to his. I popped the hood and attached the jumper cables. "Try it now. You should

1

have a good charge to get it going." It only took one turn of the key and his car started right away.

"Thanks, what was your name again?" I told him my name and gave him my business card.

"Let me know if you find anything interesting at the antique sales."

"I sure will. Thanks again for all your help."

I stepped back into my car and drove home. He followed behind me on his way out of town and waved as he passed by my driveway. I was glad I had been able to lend a hand.

AN EVENING VISIT

After dinner, I received a phone call on my business line. I usually don't answer after hours but decided to pick up the phone anyway. It was the older gentleman whom I helped earlier. He had finished his antiquing and told me he was on his way over to give me a special gift. I told him I didn't want anything in return for my deeds, but he wouldn't hear of it.

"I'll be there in ten minutes. You deserve this." And that was the last I heard from him until the doorbell rang.

When I opened the door, he had a smile that stretched from ear to ear.

"Here," he said, as he handed me a small white box. "You helped me in my time of need, and I always believed in sharing good fortune. Earlier today I was able to help a shop owner when his employee called in sick. He had no one else to run his store and he had a huge delivery coming in ten minutes. He didn't want to close his shop, so I offered to receive the shipment for him at his loading dock. I was inspired by your help earlier and didn't mind offering my time. He thanked me by giving me this gift."

"I'm glad you were inspired to help. By the way, I noticed you had a limp before, but you don't anymore. Did it get better?"

"Funny you should ask. That's why I wanted you to have this gift. I don't have a single bit of pain in my hips anymore. My arthritis is completely gone. I've never felt better." He walked a small circle to show me he had no more limp.

"Wow, that's fantastic. How did you heal yourself so quickly?"

He opened the box and handed me an old tarnished lamp and said, "You will know what to do with this when the time comes. Please enjoy this small token of my appreciation."

I didn't know what to say. I was completely caught off guard.

"Well, I have to be going," the man said. "Thank you again for helping me in my time of need. Best of luck to you and your future; I have a feeling it will be a good one." He practically skipped to the door and waved goodbye as he walked to his new car.

SERVICE OF THE BEST KIND

It had been weeks since I'd seen the man whose car needed a jump. My practice was going well, and my appointment book was full. One after another, my clients would come to my office and ask me to help them release old habits and find new solutions for their daily challenges. It's very rewarding work and I really enjoy doing it. I have a gift for teaching, helping people release unwanted habits, and showing them how to make tiny shifts in their perception that make a huge difference in their lives.

I love the individual interaction with my clients, and I love seeing them become successful and reach their goals even more. This made me realize it was time to take the next step. There are so many people in the world who are looking for another way, another possible solution, to a happier life. If I saw them one at a time, it would take me a thousand lifetimes to visit with every one of them. Way too long for my liking. I wanted to reach the masses quicker and still be able to help people on an individual basis. How was I going to do this?

I paced in my office for a few moments to gather my thoughts. After about the fifth lap, I bumped into the bookshelf and knocked over the old tarnished lamp. When I bent over to pick it up, I noticed there was a tiny inscription etched into the metal that I hadn't seen before. It said *Granted*. "'Granted,' I wonder what that means? Surely, this isn't…" I remembered back to the day I helped the older gentleman. His arthritis had been instantly healed, and he'd had a brand new car outside. I thought to myself, "Could he have found the magic lamp? Nah, it must be coincidence. Maybe he took a pain pill and had a second car at home." I was just about to put the lamp back on the shelf, but then I stopped. "It couldn't hurt. Let's give it a rub for luck."

Whoosh! A huge cloud of purple and gold smoke filled my office, and a human figure appeared right before my eyes. I had a genie in my office dressed in full traditional regalia. It was the most amazing thing I had ever seen. I rubbed my eyes to make sure I wasn't dreaming or hallucinating. But then I heard the genie say in a most convincing voice, "I am a servant among servants, and my lamp finds its way into the hands of those who perform good deeds. I assure you, you are not dreaming. How may I serve you today?"

I asked him, "Are you for real? Is this like the traditional storybook version where I get three wishes?"

"It is. Three is the number, no more, no less. Also, a wish may not be used to receive more wishes, so use them wisely."

"Wow, three wishes. I know what they are, but what happens to you when the three wishes are granted?"

"This will mark the end of my cycle in this dimension. I have performed my service, and it is time for others to maintain the process. I will pass on to another realm and observe the continuation of good deeds performed without the use of this special magic. The lamp will remain as a shell, a reminder of what can come from those who show kindness and compassion. There will be no return of my kind beyond this point to the planet you call Earth. I am glad to share the last of my powers with you. What is your first wish? How may I serve you?"

I thought to myself, "If this is the last time that these powers will ever be used on this planet, what could I wish for that would benefit everyone?" And not just everyone right now. I wanted something that would benefit everyone for generations to come. Finally, I said, "Genie, I know my first wish."

"Granted," is all he said.

"Granted? Don't you want to know what my first wish was?"

"I already knew. That is why I came to you for my last actions on Earth. But if you feel more comfortable telling me, you may do so now."

"Genie, I want to be able to help as many people as possible find peace in their lives. I want to help create *world peace*."

"As I said before, granted."

"But how will that be done, Genie? I don't want to become the next ruler, guru, or religious leader. Can you give me a hint, please?"

"You will pass along your knowledge in a book. You will reach millions of people and give them hope, encouragement, and inspiration. Your message will come across in entertaining stories and helpful techniques. Stories reach out to the subconscious in a very effective way. The conscious mind may read the words, but the subconscious understands and remembers the stories. You may have learned that stories speak to the subconscious with symbols, pictures, events, and emotions, just like we dream at night. This is the language the subconscious understands, and this will help your readers reach new levels of success."

"Wow, that's great. I've always wanted to write a book to help others. When will I start?"

"It is time for you to rest for the evening. When you wake, you will know more. Be prepared to ask for your second wish in the morning."

ONE DOWN, TWO TO GO

While I was sleeping, I dreamt about a story that had helped me when I was a child. "The genie's magic is working," I thought. "The story is a little different from the way I remember it, but it will encourage others for sure. I wonder if the Genie is ready for round two?"

I went to the lamp and rubbed my hand along the side. Whoosh! Another cloud of purple and gold smoke filled the room.

"How may I be of service?"

"Genie, your magic worked. Last night I dreamt of a story that helped me when I was a child. It gave me the inspiration to conquer my own fears and live with strength and courage. That was awesome, thanks."

"You will remember a number of fables that can be retold in this book to help your species move beyond fear, ego, and control. You will continue dreaming one story each night until you have enough for your book. Write them down when you wake and share your techniques for finding peace. This will bring peace not only to individuals, but to the entire world."

"Genie, what do others usually wish for? To inspire friends and clients, I've often asked them to make three wishes, and most of the time they are stumped. They often say that no one has ever asked them what they would wish for, or they were taught not to dream or ask for more. I ask them, 'If you don't know what will make you happy, how will you know to be happy when you get there?' You would think that everyone would know what they would wish for, if given a chance."

"It is true. Some of your belief systems teach guilt and shame for asking. It is OK to teach that it is better to give than to receive. But if everyone is giving, and no one accepts the gifts that are offered, which includes choice and wishes, then no one is receiving, either. This has becomes a block in the subconscious for your species and keeps people from asking for blessings and offerings. This guilt shows in the vibration of their thoughts when they pray and make requests. I certainly would not want to increase their guilt by giving them what they ask for, so it is better to let them be without until they are ready to receive happily and joyously."

"That makes perfect sense, Genie. It also explains why people become frustrated when their wishes and prayers sometimes go unanswered. So, what do most people ask for when they make their wishes?"

"Your people tend to wish for good health and financial security as two of their wishes. The third wish usually tells a lot about their personality and their true desires."

"I would think that if everyone had good health and all the money they wanted, they would ask for world peace. What good would those fortunes be if there is still war, anger, and hatred in the world?"

"A good thought. That is why your book will provide what so many are looking for. Your ideas will help people see the world from a new perspective. Your techniques will help people understand differences in perception, give them a way to shift their identities when they are ready, and establish a roadmap for peace amongst nations. What is your second wish?"

"Well, I can't make everyone rich, and I can't heal everyone. It wouldn't be right for me to do that anyway. Some people came here to hurt and be poor for the experience, and to use that experience as a reference point. Others came here to find their own wealth and heal their own minds and bodies in other ways. I also know there is no magic pill to create gold or good health. Genie, my second wish is to know how to teach others to become healthier and more abundant in their lives while creating a world of peace."

"Granted. You will share the techniques you have learned, and you will remember the ones you forgot from your Earthly teachers. Share this knowledge with your brothers and sisters all over the world. Allow them equally to find their own ways of creating abundance, good health, and world peace from other teachers. As you know, growth also comes from exploration. If you give people every possible answer, they might forget to seek on their own. You will receive what you need for this book, nothing more, and nothing less."

"Thanks, Genie. I'll write them down as they come to mind."

THREE IS A CHARM

"Genie, I don't have any other desires right now except to have the insight and ability to help others who are in great need. There will also be those whose belief system will not allow them to implement these ideas. I would like to help them if I can."

"I understand. Everyone is allowed to agree or not agree based on their upbringing. It would also not be wise to use your energy to change someone's viewpoints or beliefs just so they can implement your suggestions. People will accept this information when the time is right, and they may never accept these ideas. Help those who ask for help, and allow everyone their opinions. They will know when the time is right to make a change. With that being said, is that your third wish?"

"No, you are right. I will help those who ask for my help, and I will support those who choose to go in another direction."

"What is your third wish, then?"

"Genie, you have already helped me a great deal. I want you to have the magic from my third wish when you move to your new existence. Use it to make yourself happy in your next life beyond the lamp. That is my final wish."

"You are a kind soul. Thank you for this gift. I expect great things from your efforts to help the world."

"I will do my best, Genie. And thank you for the two wishes. We will both be helping the world with our combined efforts."

PART ONE

MY SECOND WISH: A ROADMAP FOR PERSONAL PEACE

CHAPTER ONE

THE FREEDOM CODE
DECODED

I WOULD LOVE FOR YOU, and everyone else in the world, to find your own magic lamp and receive your three wishes. It would be equally wonderful to see you attract whatever you desire and bring happiness into your life. Now I may not have found the magic lamp from the story in the Introduction, but I was given something just as rewarding. Through my life experiences, interactions with people, and knowledge gained from my teachers, I accumulated a bounty of useful information to help others move forward and increase their happiness. My experiences, both good and bad, have provided me with the needed tools to help others overcome their obstacles and challenges. I've also gathered a wealth of knowledge from reading, teaching, sharing, and listening, and I will give you the best techniques I've found for creating success, happiness, freedom, and abundance. I want you to be happy.

To start things off right, let me share a simple concept with you to prime the pump. If you want to live in peace, help others find peace. If you want to be happy, help someone else find happiness. If you want to be free, help others find freedom. That is what I am doing in this book. I am participating in the sacred hoop, the circle of life. (I was reminded about this great concept from one of our Native American elders.)

If you desire more peace and abundance to come into your future, please read on.

DEFINING FREEDOM

Freedom is such a great word. It means so many things to so many people. The vast majority of us want to be free so we can live our lives to the fullest. We want the freedom to speak our thoughts without judgment or reprisal. Many want to worship freely without the fear of subjugation, restriction, or persecution. Wouldn't it be great if we were free to express ourselves without being laughed at, ridiculed, or shunned by society? We can, we already are, and we are doing a better job of this each and every day. We can achieve this for everyone on the planet. We continue to create this positive change as we make simple adjustments in our lives and small shifts in our perception. This brings about peace and happiness for our brothers and sisters. As we continue growing and shifting fear into love, our ability to live in peace grows stronger minute by minute, day by day, and year after year.

As I alluded to in the last story, if you want to be free, it will help to know what freedom means to you. Do you know what freedom means to you? Have you thought about one of the most cherished gifts we can achieve as individuals and as a society? Let me share this example of how important those questions are. Instead of *freedom*, I will use *happiness* so you can still define your own meaning of freedom while reading the next three paragraphs.

During my sessions, I often ask my clients to tell me what would make them happy. The conversation usually goes something like this: "I'm glad you are here, and I know you came to my office with the intent to make an adjustment in your life. You want to improve your life in some way that will make you happy. Great! So tell me, what would make you happy?" You would be surprised at how many respond with, "Wow, I don't know," or "I don't have a clue." How do they know they are not happy already if they don't know what will make them happy? I know they are not completely happy because they are in my office, so now is the time to start the simple process.

You can probably see how this makes my job easier. The first thing we can do is establish what would make them happy and reinforce the importance of following through with their goal. I give them this analogy: Imagine you are a boat and we drop you in the middle of the ocean. You have no sails, no oars, and no rudders. You have no way of guiding yourself, and you don't know where you are going. The purpose of a boat is to float and take people and cargo places with the best possible speed and keep good direction while doing so. You want to be a good boat, but you still don't know where you want to go or how to get there. You are at the mercy of the currents and ocean waves. By giving yourself oars, rudders, and sails, you increase your ability to become a better boat and stay on course. Having a destination gives you the ability to celebrate confidently when you steer into your designated port or dock. Reaching your goal simply validates your happiness. Voilá. Instant success.

Just as a boat will be happy when it reaches the dock, so will you when you reach your definition of happiness and freedom. You can aid the process when you tell your conscious and subconscious mind what you desire. (We will talk about this in future chapters.) When you have defined your goals and firmly placed them in your mind, you will react happily instead of guessing how to respond when you get there. It reminds me of the familiar phrase from the backseat of the car: "Are we there yet? How much farther, Dad?" With your goals established, you will know when you arrive at the finish line so you can rejoice.

Have you been thinking about your definition of freedom yet? Have you defined freedom for yourself? Is freedom even important to you? Here's a good question to ask yourself: Would you rather be free—free to choose for yourself and make your own decisions—or would you rather be someone's slave, with no rights or privileges? If your answer is freedom, now is the time to define what freedom means to you so you will know if you have all the freedom you desire, or if you need to create solutions to gain more freedom.

Here is a quick bit of advice before we go any farther. When you define something, such as *freedom, happiness,* or *success,* it's OK to change your mind as time goes along. It's OK to make adjustments during the process. It may quicken the results, or it may set them back a little. But isn't it better to reach what you really want instead of settling for something else because you didn't change your mind? You are not locked into your first answer or response. You may find yourself changing your mind many times while you read this book. And I say, "Great!" Knowing what your true desires

13

are will give you increased focus and clarity. Focus and clarity speed up the process more than being at the mercy of the winds and ocean waves. And sometimes you won't know what you really want until you start the process.

EMPOWERING THE SELF

To me, freedom has many definitions. It can mean liberty, no laws, no restrictions, free will, self-determination, or choice. One of my favorite ways to describe freedom is self-empowerment. As you gather skills, knowledge, and ability, you free yourself from the need to depend on others. You open a world of opportunity to produce and accomplish on your own. Talk about creating satisfaction. This starts at a very early age, too. When we learn as young children how to tie our own shoes, we become empowered. We no longer have to wait for someone to tie our shoes before we can run outside to play with our friends. We empower ourselves with this knowledge and create more playtime. (And who doesn't like more playtime?) This process of empowerment continues all the way up until the time we decide to leave our bodies. As you look at your upbringing, you can probably think of many things you learned in life that gave you this type of freedom. What's even more exciting is that we get to decide how much empowerment we want from this point forward, and that is awesome.

In our quest for knowledge, the more you know and understand, the more you free yourself. You give yourself more options. The same can be said about developing skills. As you practice and maintain your ability to perform your own tasks, you increase your empowerment. This leads us to the next step that is created from self-empowerment. It is the freedom of *choice*. Choice is one of those things we wish we had more of, though sometimes we wish we had less of it when it causes confusion and indecision. Given a choice (no pun intended), I imagine that we all would welcome more choice over having no choice at all. That is one of the reasons we keep developing skills and seek greater knowledge.

The next question to ask yourself is how does choice empower you right now? Well, to put this in today's perspective, if you can change the oil in your car or replace your own timing belt, you now have a choice: you can do these things yourself, or you can take your car to a shop and have someone else do them for you. Without the knowledge to properly maintain your car, you are bound to someone else's abilities, time schedules, and fees. Your choice becomes limited. As we pursue freedom for all humankind, we are also creating choice and the freedom to choose.

Can you see how choice becomes one of the most important gifts of freedom and self-empowerment? You can choose who ties your shoes, who washes your clothes, who makes your dinner, who drives your car, who makes the money, who makes decisions in your life, and whom you can thank for creating more choices in your daily life. One of our greatest pursuits over the expanse of history has been to find ways to create more choice.

With so many talented and empowered people in the world, we have created a plethora of options for everyone to enjoy. Thank you for being self-empowered in so many ways. Thank you for using your gifts to give choice to your fellow kind without using it for power, greed, profit, and control.

You can probably already guess what I am going to ask next. What does self-empowerment mean to you? Are you self-empowered? What have you achieved that has empowered you? Everyone is capable of doing so many amazing things. I'll bet you can list at least ten things right now that you can do on your own. The more you realize what you can do and accomplish, the greater your freedom becomes. The more you realize what you can do, the greater your confidence grows. You are capable of accomplishing so much. It's time to pat yourself on the back. Realize how free you are this very moment.

Now it's time to stretch a little more. What can you do to empower yourself beyond where you are right now? What can you do that will increase your freedom of choice? Here are a few tips to help you on your way.

EMPOWERING PEOPLE

1. I believe we should start with this important question first. Do you want to be more self-empowered? You definitely don't want to do it just because we are talking about it. It should be a true desire. With knowledge and skill comes responsibility, and not everyone wants more responsibility. What was your initial response when you read the question? Do you want to increase your self-empowerment? Do you want to change your answer? Will you accept the responsibility with increased knowledge and skill for the betterment of yourself

and others? You are capable of empowering yourself as much as you want. Go for it!

2. Define what self-empowerment means to you. You might already be as self-empowered as you desire. If you seek more empowerment, you've just picked up a pair of oars and a rudder with this book and you are ready to start your journey.

3. Become a servant and not a slave. A servant has more choice than a slave. Choice is created with knowledge, skill, and ability. Pursue information and proficiency through life experiences that will bring you one step closer to your goal of self-empowerment. Serve others with your abilities. There are no masters if everyone is serving each other.

4. Know what makes you happy so you can celebrate when the time is right. Know your goals. Write them down. Say them every day. Find pictures that you can tape to your refrigerator. Do whatever it takes (morally) to make your goals known to your conscious and subconscious.

5. Release subconscious and conscious blocks, negative thoughts, and negative emotions that are keeping you from reaching your dreams. Continue releasing past beliefs and past experiences that make you feel unworthy of love, success, and abundance. (I will devote more to this in the coming chapters.)

6. Understand the difference between self-empowerment and ego. Creating choice by increasing knowledge and skills, and then sharing that knowledge with others, is considered a good characteristic of being self-empowered. When choice is restricted for the means of self gain, control, and creating fear in others, it is ego. Ego is unbalanced pride, desire, and an unbalanced need to control. Ego can stand for: Energy Going Overboard.

7. It's OK to be a follower instead of always being a leader. You can still live a very happy life if you never take the horse by the reigns. Being a follower also gives you an appreciation and broader perspective for leadership.

8. Be glad you make mistakes. Making mistakes increases your knowledge base. Every time you do something that doesn't get you to your goal, you can share this knowledge with others. You've just learned how *not* to complete your goal, so you have gained more knowledge.

9. You can become self-empowered by empowering others and helping

them reach their goals. When you help others and see them accomplish their dreams, this creates more confidence in yourself. Your abilities strengthen, and it feels great.

10. Continue transforming fear into courage. Continue transforming fear into acceptance. Continue transforming fear into love. Love, acceptance, and courage are all part of self-empowerment.

OTHER PERSPECTIVES ON SELF-EMPOWERMENT

I asked a few of my friends and colleagues to share their thoughts on self-empowerment. I'm glad I did because they reminded me of the vastness of perception. Their answers told me that self-empowerment means many different things to many different people. Here are a few of their responses.

Ed Sabo, co-publisher of *Natural Awakenings* magazine in Houston, TX, says that self-empowerment to him is "thriving in the major areas of life: financial, physical, relationship, mental, and spiritual." He described empowerment as being self-confident, willing to take risks, self-sustaining, independent, and capable. I asked him to share his motivational phrase, and he wrote, "All of life comes to me with ease, joy, and glory."

Many people find self-empowerment through prayer, religion, and faith. Teresa Leonard, my CPA, told me that her definition of self-empowerment is "the ability to handle life on my own. I do this with God's help through faith, prayer, study, and communication." Her motivational phrase is, "I can do all things through Christ, who strengthens me."

Along with prayer and religion, a great deal of people find empowerment through meditation, relaxation techniques, martial arts, yoga, tai chi, and self-hypnosis. Michael Schuman, a board-certified hypnotist in Houston, wrote that he would train others to become self-empowered with the use of self-hypnosis. "I would be sharing a technique that would give them the ability to overcome obstacles and achieve goals." He added a short, but powerful, motivational phrase that he uses: "I think, so I am."

Many others, including myself, are finding empowerment by other means in addition to what you have already read. We are releasing personal identities and the need for accumulating wealth. We are constantly transforming fear into courage and projecting love wherever possible. We are empowering ourselves by letting go. We are becoming empowered by needing less. We have shifted our focus from helping ourselves to helping others. We lend a helping hand to those in need. We give praise, positive thoughts, suggestions, ideas, and support. We are constantly releasing our old programming and taking charge of what we put into our minds and daily thoughts. We are teaching by example. We know that one of the best ways to help our society attain peace is by finding peace within ourselves. We are helping the masses with our positive outlook and good vibrations.

APPRECIATING FREEDOM

As we shift back from self-empowerment to freedom, a great way to realize how free we truly are is by appreciating all those things we are free from having to do on our own. Isn't it great that we don't have to make the sun rise or the planets revolve around the sun every day? Another perk is we don't have to create air for the entire planet so we can breathe. This gives us more freedom to explore and have fun. Plants grow naturally in the ground and change sunlight into energy without us lifting a finger. Birds migrate all over the world without us flapping their wings for them. Fish swim without us needing to give them swimming lessons. You and I did not have to discover fire, chocolate, or pizza. (Thank goodness! We just get to enjoy those.) Your body knows how to heal itself without you consciously telling it how. Your body knows how to rejuvenate without directing each cell to multiply and discard waste. Your blood circulates freely from your heart without you squeezing each artery and vein. These are just a few of the things you are free from that help you survive in your daily life.

If you made a list of all the things you do not have to create or control on your own, and made a list of all the things you are responsible for creating or completing, you would see how small the second list is when compared to the first. You would realize just how free you are to live and explore. You are so free right now. Do you realize this? Rediscover this appreciation. Appreciating what you have makes your life seem so much richer, fuller, and abundant. This is one of the shifts that can make a major difference in your life.

Take a moment now and think of all the things you can do naturally. If you can't think of any, here are a few more examples. What does your body do unconsciously for you every second, minute, and hour of the day that you don't have to do consciously? We breathe, metabolize food, perform cellular mitosis, we have a constant beating heart, automatic neural impulse, automatic glandular secretions, involuntary reflex, and so much more. This frees your mind to learn, create, experience emotion, and store vast amounts of information. You have huge amounts of free time because you don't have to consciously make these things happen to stay alive and function.

Think of what happens all around you in nature that you don't have to create or control. The entire food chain was set in motion long before you were born. You didn't have to decide who eats what, where, when, and how. This creates freedom in your life to enjoy the process of eating and being at the top of the food chain. Think of how free you are as the weather is set in motion daily for the entire planet. You are free to walk with confidence knowing that gravity is going to keep your feet firmly on the ground. You are free from making the seasons change. You don't have to fly to the sun on a daily basis to make sure that the nuclear fusion process of changing hydrogen nuclei into helium is still going on. Believe me, you will know when that happens. It will be lights out for everyone.

FREEDOM BEYOND DEFINITIONS

If you want someone to come up with a solution, sometimes all it takes is presenting a person with a goal or a challenge. I remember from my childhood hearing about the concept of infinity. I have heard so many people say that you cannot begin to fathom what infinity means or how infinity feels. Well, I took to that task like molasses sticks to BBQ ribs, and I came up with two possible ways you can begin to grasp infinity. Mind you, it doesn't mean you will understand infinity and everything found within, but it does give you a start for understanding this intricate concept.

The first one is simple. Let's start with distance. If you want to know how infinity works with distance, always add another inch. We know that our solar system is not the end of existence. But for example's sake, let's imagine that the farthest our mind can go to conceptualize infinity is to the edge of our solar system. You rent a rocket from NASA, start the engine, and off you go. You blink and miss Mars. You enjoy counting the sixty-three discovered moons of Jupiter. You pass the A, B, C, D, E, F, and other named rings of Saturn. As you continue, you pass Uranus, Neptune, and our once-recognized planet of Pluto. After you glide by Haumea, Makemake, and Eris, the other dwarf planets, you reach the edge of our solar system. But, you want to go beyond infinity. What do you do? Simple, don't stop there. Go another inch. Go a little farther and imagine what it would be like to keep going. Distance is only a concept of the mind. When you feel you've reached the end of your imagination, go a little farther. If the edge of infinity was the barrier of the known Universe, go another inch and cross into the next Universe. Every time you reach your destination in your mind— don't stop—go a little farther and add another inch. Distance will always be infinite as you learn how to use this expansion technique.

One of the reasons we don't spend too much time thinking about distance by way of infinity is that it gets too tiring. The mind gets bored. You just keep going, and going, and going. It's like watching a car race without a lap count and no finish line. It goes on forever. What we decide to do in the meantime is stop and smell the roses. We decide to spend some time on this planet as human beings. We might next decide to become an asteroid for another length of time. And when we are hungry, we spend time as a black hole and gobble up as much of the light and space matter as possible. When we make our decisions to stop and enjoy a pause in infinity, we call it a lifetime experience. It becomes the story of our life, much like we are doing right now.

For the second example of infinity (this is the one that reaches home with me the most), we will apply it to one of my favorite concepts—freedom. A great way to conceptualize infinity is to have unlimited freedom. Infinity is the freedom to create without constraint or restriction; the freedom to decide without lack of knowledge or understanding; the freedom to choose or not to choose; the freedom to live without laws, guidelines, or proclamations. It is also the freedom to know everything, and the freedom to forget everything at the same time; the freedom to do and not to do; the freedom to have responsibility or no responsibility; the freedom to live without ruling over another, or being ruled by another; freedom from taxes and financial obligations; the freedom to be in the now, the past, and the future—all at the same time consciously; the freedom to be consciously in your body and out of your body at the same time; the freedom to know life before you were conceived and after you leave your body—while you remain in the now; the freedom to be in multiple Universes at the same time, with full conscious awareness of each existence. I could go on for days. I could go on for infinity. You might say that I could go on for freedom. There is no end to freedom. And once you place a restriction on the imagination of freedom, it can no longer be considered pure 100% distilled freedom.

In my mind, the freer you become, the more infinite you become. The possibilities of freedom become infinite. We are only constrained by the limits of our own minds. As more people become free, we become closer as one infinite being.

If you ever feel bored, take some time to think of unlimited freedom. What would you do?

HIDDEN ABILITIES CREATING FREEDOM

I have been deciphering the Freedom Code and showing you all the benefits that are hidden inside this system. Part of this code is knowing what makes you happy, pursuing your dreams, and creating a peaceful environment so you can enjoy what you receive. Another part of the code is creating freedom through self-empowerment. You accomplish this as you gather knowledge, wisdom, and hone your skills and abilities. There is a third part of the Freedom Code that we will discuss in greater detail in Chapter 10. In this chapter we will unleash your hidden genie. Everybody has this genie inside themselves already. This is the part of your self that is waiting to help you at a moment's notice. It is an untapped resource just waiting to be called into service. I am talking about your subconscious. This powerful part of your mind is waiting patiently to give you what you desire. All you need to do is guide your subconscious with positive reinforcement and defined direction. You will learn a wealth of knowledge and techniques that you can use to bring life to your inner genie and create your own world of freedom and happiness. For now, we will move on to the next phase of the Freedom Code. What is in store for freedom in the coming years of our world? What can you do to help bring freedom to yourself and your neighbor's neighbor?

THE FUTURE OF FREEDOM

I believe that freedom is our natural birthright. We are born free from the moment we take our first breath. In a loving way, and sometimes in a not-so-loving way, we begin to grow up in a system where rules, guidelines, and restrictions slowly take away our freedom. (Sometimes this happens on the second breath of life and never stops until we die.) In time, as I have heard from others, we begin to feel trapped by the number of laws that bind our freedom simply because of where we were born or who is in power at the time. (We will talk about this in Chapter 15.)

I know this for a fact: We will find a way to gain freedom again for everyone who desires independence, even if it takes hundreds and thousands of years of growth, pain, and evolution. Freedom can be likened to a finish line for the human species. The human race will keep adapting and finding ways to reach beyond governments and laws that were created for control and power over the masses. The human race will continue to naturally gravitate towards its birthright of freedom. It is unstoppable. It is in our nature, our genetic coding, our destiny to live in complete freedom.

Here is how I know this will happen. With our incredible scientific advances, if a cure is found for a specific virus, and that virus is meant to remain on the planet for whatever reason, the virus will find a way to mutate and survive beyond the scientific ability to eradicate it from the face of the Earth. The virus will grow beyond the control of science. In time, the virus will revert to its natural birthright of freedom to remain a virus, even if it does not stay in its original form. The common cold and the flu are great examples.

Insects and weeds have learned to adapt to pesticides and sprays meant to control or kill their population. With the help of natural process and evolution, insects and weeds become accustomed to the harmful chemicals and sprays and they no longer die as easily. Sometimes they don't die at all. The effort to take away their freedom only strengthens their ability and resolve to survive. I think it is amazing that they have found a way to adapt and endure. They were put on the planet for a reason, and their birthright of survival, freedom, and identity as insects and plants remains intact.

People are equally gifted in this manner. People are born with a birthright of freedom. The human race continues to evolve and adapt in ways that will, in time, no longer need controlling governments, controlling religions, or laws based on fear. When the majority of people consciously decide to transform their fear and ego, and when people band together with peace as the underlying goal, we will have that freedom once again.

We are getting closer. We have so many people living peacefully with one another right now, it's inspiring beyond words. Look how large our planet has grown, yet the masses know how to get along naturally. It's true, there are still a few people in high political places, a few military leaders, and a few hidden behind the scenes who continue to draw the masses into war and conflict. Fear is their weapon of choice to keep control over the masses. Don't let them steal your dreams of freedom. Don't let them stop your ability to become self-empowered.

People are resilient and will find a way to live in peace without the need to control one another. People are always gravitating toward an existence with freedom as one of the main core values. It is happening, and this scares those who don't want to lose their power. The biggest fear for someone who desires control over another is losing that ability to rule. These are the people who govern with fear and create our world's conflicts for personal gain. But the people know this. They are waiting for the right time to move beyond this old way of living. They are waiting for the right roadmap, the right tipping point in society, the right *Freedom Code,* to accept a way of peace and cooperation. There are so many people who are ready to move beyond tyranny. There will be a point when these seekers of peace will be able to join together and give a rebirth of freedom for all.

YOUR THREE WISHES

How could I possibly send you on your journey without putting a huge gust of wind in your sails and giving you a port in which to dock your boat? What kind of genie would I be? This will be fun. For now, let's start with your first three wishes. You can always create more wishes later. Before we start, I also want you to temporarily put aside all your previous teachings that instill guilt or shame for wanting or accepting something in your life. Reach for the stars. There are no limits here. These are your personal wishes. What would you wish for that would bring you happiness? Get this firmly planted in your mind. Don't read any further until you get this first wish playing vividly in your mind like a movie. Stop here until your movie has played through at least once in your imagination.

Good. Now it's time to do the same thing for your second wish. What else do you want in your life that will bring you happiness and joy? This can be anything. There are no limits or restrictions. Once you have it, play the movie in your mind, and see yourself living with your wish coming true. Don't go any further in the book until you have played the movie at least once in your mind's eye. If it's a good movie, which I am sure it is, watch it again and again. Who doesn't like a good rerun?

Great! It's on to wish number three. Do the same thing you did for your first two wishes. Get your wish firmly in your mind. Then play the movie with your wish coming true. Play it over and over. You are doing wonderfully!

Now before you move on to the next chapter, I have three words for you. Take them deep inside your heart. Hear the words in your inner mind. Hear them spoken with confidence and truth. Know that they will come true. Hear the words now...

Wish Granted...

Believe...

CHAPTER TWO

———◆◆———

LIFETIME THEORY-TER

I THINK IT'S FANTASTIC that life is like a movie in which each one of us gets to be the main character. What kind of movie would best describe your life so far? Is it an inspirational movie, a love story, a melodrama, an action film, a scary movie, or a disaster film? Do you like the director and producer? Would you like to edit out parts of your film? Take some time and think about this next question before you move on. If you could start a new movie of your life from this very moment and play it forward, how would you write the screenplay for the sequel? What would you change in the second movie that would be different from the first part of your life? Once you have that picture playing in your mental theater, what would be the title for this sequel?

Wouldn't it be great if we all knew why we are here? Maybe if our lives were a foreign film with subtitles, we would understand life a little bit better. When I go shopping, and the checkout clerk asks if I have found everything OK, I sometimes reply, "I was looking for the meaning of life, but I couldn't find it. What aisle is it on?" That usually throws them for a loop because they don't know if I am asking a serious question or not. We laugh a little and share a passing smile.

For many people, the big question is this: Do we get to create our future, or are we bound to a script that was written long before we became movie stars? Are we able to renegotiate our contract and change production

25

companies? Do we get creative license? Do we get to choose who writes the screenplay for our sequel? Can we decide who will be our next supporting actors and actresses? There are as many theories and answers to these questions as there are people on the planet. I am going to share a belief that is growing stronger in my own theater of the mind as a possible answer. Grab some popcorn and ice cream and get yourself comfortable. Do you have the remote yet? It is now time to start *Lifetime Theory-ter.*

FROM THE BEGINNING
TO THE STORY WITH NO END

The best way to approach this is to bypass the question of how everything started and jump right into why things are the way they are. We can always spend time in another book discussing the seven-day creation story, the Big Bang, alien manipulation theories, Darwinism and natural selection, and of course, evolution from our furry cousins in the jungle. They all make great stories and belief systems, not to mention that they create excellent comfort zones and foundation stones for those who want to know how everything began.

As a species, we often want to know where we came from and how we got here. We want to know about our roots and our family tree. We want to know the answers to life. I, too, am curious about our origins and why things are as they are, and I do my best to remain open-minded to the many possibilities. I'm not ready to make a definitive decision yet. There are still too many unanswered questions. The facts keep changing and new discoveries are made all the time. Once I think I have a better grasp on our origins, something new comes into focus and I find myself adjusting my beliefs. For now, I enjoy gathering the facts at hand and building my temporary palace of belief. (I say *temporary* as all buildings can go through renovations to improve a living space.) Sometimes I remain neutral until more information is provided. I can tell you confidently that my views may have changed or grown stronger by the time you read this.

More than once, I have seen people cling to a belief system better than peanut butter sticks to the roof of their mouths. Their faith in their system is incredibly strong and unwavering. It gives them structure and a good foundation for making sense of the world. However, when someone presents a new piece of information that makes sense to that person, but the information goes against his or her belief system, that person becomes rather uncomfortable, defensive, and sometimes outright angry. Why is this?

People rely on their belief systems to be correct so they can have a calm grasp on reality. Belief systems are a foundation upon which people build their palace of life. If you rattle too many stones in a foundation, even if the new stones are solid and true, their palace can crumble and that person is left in unfamiliar territory. They are left homeless. Then they have to redefine part or all of their core beliefs and are left to rebuild their foundation. This can be very scary for some people. There are those who would rather live in denial and escape their fears instead of replacing stones and making a choice. Change is not scary for all people. We were taught to fear change and some people believed it. But this type of change can be so scary that some people won't change their beliefs, no matter what.

As an example, I was raised in a particular religion because my parents were raised in the same religion, and their parents were raised in that same religion, and so on. It was taught that the first inhabitants on the Earth were two human beings. OK, I can accept that for a start. Now comes along the discovery of fossils of other creatures that are older than the first two humans. They are scientifically dated millions and millions of years before our oldest ancestors. Now what? Do I say that those fossils were placed there by another being to test our faith, or do I adjust my beliefs to accept a new possible beginning to our existence? If you were taught the same concepts, what did you do? Was the book wrong? Did that part of the book get edited out? Whether you were taught that system or not, did you stick with the creation story you were first taught, or did you come up with one that fits your own personal beliefs?

I have been reading and studying a great deal of scientific, religious, and metaphysical material to gain more insight to why things work the way they do. Many of my foundation stones have been replaced more than once as I have grown in knowledge and experience. The best I can do at this time is to give you my interpretation. I am in no way making claims that it is perfected—yet. It can't be. We are all still learning, growing, and discovering.

For those who have never ventured this far it will be a great beginning for you to build a new foundation. But please, do your own research before you cement this as your basement. Don't just take my word for it. Use your gifted mind. That way you won't have to tear out the entire bottom floor if your belief system completely changes. For others, use these theories to solidify your own beliefs or to give you a new direction for change. There are many out there who love hearing options presented to them so they can redefine their own beliefs. These are the people who consider stagnation a dirty word. I have also talked with scores of people who accept the majority of their core values and beliefs, but they don't agree with all of the rules that were taught in that system. They are looking for a way to fill in the blanks. These theories could help provide a few possible answers for you. Use this material as it was intended. This book was written to provide options for your future, new possibilities of thought, and motivation and encouragement to become the best person you can possibly be. This is not a religion to follow word for word. It is a guideline, a roadmap for success. It's OK if you don't agree with what you read. It would be boring if we all shared the same thoughts and ideas. Stick with your beliefs and be open to change. That's the best advice I can give at this time.

TWO EXTREMES
AND EVERYTHING IN THE MIDDLE

I love talking to people about their perception of reality. There are more possibilities than there are galaxies in the observable Universe. That's more than 100 billion, or 10^{11} power. We will start with the two most opposite and work our way inward. As we go along, notice how you feel about each possibility and what emotions arise. Take note if these emotions occur as a result of your current belief system. Notice if the information makes sense to you or if it makes you feel a little unsettled. Then ask yourself why you feel that way. It will help bring clarity to your assessments. It will also help define your identity, which we will talk about in Chapter 9.

There is a theory that every possible action, every possible event in all of time—past, present, and future—has already been mapped down to the tiniest length of time. Our current smallest measurement of time is an attosecond, which is one quintillionth of a second. That's 10^{-18}. There is another proposed smaller length of time called Planck time, named after Max Planck, a German physicist who is regarded as the founder of the quantum theory of matter. Planck time is the amount of time it takes for light to travel one Planck length in a vacuum. (In theory, the Planck length is the smallest unit of measurement, or 1.616252(81) x 10^{-35} meters.) That's pretty small and amazing, especially if this theory where everything is pre-planned is the correct version.

In this grand idea, all things, from the smallest action to the largest events, were predetermined in our Universe before time came into existence. This means that every breath you have taken, or will ever take, has been pre-planned before the clock started. The length of every breath has been pre-set. The reason for every breath has been predetermined. Every cell in your body grows, divides, and dies at a specific time. All of your life choices were etched into the hall of records before you were born. All emotional responses were also pre-planned to coincide with every event.

If this is the case, I must say this was the work of one of the best event planners ever. Could you imagine seeing this Creator's résumé? Experience: I created all events and emotions for infinity. OK, you're hired.

That would take an awful lot of work to create, manage, and control. If you were the Creator for this theory of existence, you would have to make sure that every honeybee in every hive flew at just the right time; it took the exact same flight plan every day that was prearranged before bees were born; the bee had to land on every predetermined flower in every pre-planned field; this one particular bee had to take the perfect amount of pollen grains from each flower every single time; the bee had to wiggle its bee butt just the right number of times to communicate and do the bee dance; the bee had to create the exact number of honeycombs and drops of honey; and not to leave out emotional responses, the bee had to experience anger or fear to protect itself and sting the right person at the exact moment in time which caused the bee to die and go to bee heaven. And that is just one bee. Think of all the millions and billions of bees that have existed on this planet. Think of all the trillions and quadrillions of insects that have taken residence here. Each individual insect would have its entire life and emotions mapped from the beginning of its larval stage to becoming spider food or windshield decoration.

Let's look at another insect, something as simple as a butterfly. Every flap of a butterfly's wings has to be measured and calculated. Even the distance that they float on the breeze before they need to flap their wings again was written down somewhere in the butterfly's programming. This also means that the intensity of every breeze must have been pre-planned, which means that the weather for every attosecond has also been pre-planned.

The actions of every living and non-living being would have to be controlled because we all affect the environment with our actions, energy, and heat. It's tiring just thinking about it.

As we go back to humans again in this pre-planned theory, every emotional response would be perfectly matched to every event in life and last only as long as it was determined according to the grand plan. Tears would be numbered, including how far they would travel down your cheek. The evaporation rate would also need to be determined and controlled by a predetermined environment. Laughter would produce the exact amount of stress-releasing hormones into the body—no more, no less. Laughter would also have to produce the right amount of slurp to make milk go up your nose when you hear a good joke. Your skin pigment would change only as much as specified to show a little blush when you receive a compliment. Your facial muscles would have to be in prime condition from all your previous events to hold your beautiful smile while going on your first date. Each cell would have this programmed and coded into its memory to perform every action and emotional response when called for.

Think of all the wasted energy that would be used on making decisions if this theory is the correct one. Why worry? Stress would be a thing of the past. We would all be healthier and happier without stress. We wouldn't have to do anything except live the life that was carved out for us before time began. This is an amazing concept. Everything would have been designated for you. And let's not forget to add in all the animals, dinosaurs (both living and extinct), fish, bacteria and viruses, insects, birds, plants, and every other human in existence. Wow! What an accomplishment.

If this is true, we couldn't possibly deviate from this plan or else the entire structure would collapse. The entire Universe and its timeline could come to a massive halt, disappear, or fold in on itself. One small mistake or deviation, and the event that started as an attosecond in length could grow into a femtosecond's worth of disaster, which could grow exponentially into picoseconds, then nanoseconds, microseconds, milliseconds, seconds, minutes, and hours, and days, all spiraling out of control from a simple attosecond's worth of deviation from the master plan. It reminds me of the thought where a single flap of a butterfly's wings in Africa could create a massive hurricane crashing onto the Gulf Coast of Florida.

For those who crave choice, this system would be the worst possible reality. It would be a nightmare. There would be no freewill. There would be no need for options or possibilities. Options and possibilities would be an illusion. Life would just move along according to a master plan with no choice at all, making us nothing more than programmed androids with emotional capabilities.

Does this describe your belief system? How does this feel to you so far?

If you believe in the heaven and hell theory as well as this predetermined system, before you even had a chance to walk on this Earth, it was already planned and decided whether you were going to heaven or hell. No matter how good or bad you are, the decision has already been made. There can be no deviation from this decision, either, because it could cause a chain reaction to all future events. These are some of the thoughts that make you go, "Hmm…"

ONE STEP INWARD

There is another theory for reality that is built right on top of the one you've just read. Imagine that every event was once again mapped out before time started ticking on the big universal clock in the sky. As before, no single event can be changed, altered, or moved in the timeline. Everything must happen as pre-planned. It can't be lengthened or shortened for any reason. However—and here is the beginning to choice and freedom—a soul will get to experience a lifetime as a tree, a human being, a bug, a dolphin, a star, and be able to perceive each event and place an emotional value on the experience. Perception and emotional experience become the reason for living. Choice, however limited, is based solely on personal awareness, observation, and sensitivity to the moment. It is the beginning of judgment, discernment, and opinion.

How do you feel about this description of reality? I personally know a few people who strongly believe in this system. For me, at this moment in time, it still feels too robot-like. We fall because we had no choice. We were supposed to fall just to gain an emotional response. If you take this same concept and apply it to lessons of life, I have heard that we fall so we can get back up again. In this system of predetermined events, there is no chance of getting back up if it was already written for you to stay down. Does this provide an opportunity for personal growth and change if this system is *the one?*

Here is a good question. Are heroes created by their own actions? Or were our Earthly heroes, who overcame great obstacles and challenges to become heroes, only playing a part in a big screenplay? You decide.

I can hear this conversation forming in the back of my mind. A mother says to her child, "There is no choice. You have to be a hero whether you like it or not."

"But Mom, I don't want to be a hero."

"Now, now, eat your spinach so you can grow up big and strong. You don't have a choice. You have to face all the evil villains with courage and strength and die in the process of saving our town. You are supposed to be the most courageous hero of all time. That is how it is written."

"But Mom, I don't want to be the most courageous hero. What if I want to express fear? I can't be the most courageous hero of all time if I show people I am afraid. Everyone would call me Captain 'Fraidy Cat. If being a hero means always showing courage and confidence in the face of adversity, then I wouldn't have the freewill to choose and express my own emotions. I would still be locked into a system of predetermined emotions and actions."

More thoughts that make you go, "Hmm..." What do you think so far? But wait, there's more.

100% CHOICE:
THE OTHER WHITE MEAT

We now move to the opposite end of the spectrum of possibilities to explain why events come into our lives and why we act the way we do. There are two versions of the 100% choice theory. I will give you both so you can use them as reference points. To keep things simple, I will call one Choice A and the other Choice B.

In the Choice A theory, every action we experience in life was pre-planned by ourselves before we came into our physical bodies. We had complete freedom to choose every event we want to experience while existing in the spiritual realm. If we don't like what is currently going on in our life, we cannot blame anyone else because we were the ones who created our lessons in life. We are to take full responsibility for every good event and every bad action. Once again, nothing is left to chance because it was written in the records before we experienced the birth process. We had

100% freedom of choice in the beginning, but we don't get to change our choices on a conscious level while living out our screenplay of life.

In this system, we also have complete freedom to choose the emotional perception that coincides with every event. We have the ability to see the good in every situation, and we have the freedom to see the bad in every situation. How we react determines whether we are bound to repeat the lesson in another lifetime or in another realm of existence.

Does this feel right to you? I am not going to tell you if this system, or any other system, is right or wrong. That is for you to decide. I can only share with you why this system doesn't feel right to me at this time in my life—which may change by the time you read this sentence, and change back again before you take your next breath.

If we were given 100% choice, we would also get to choose the rules we get to play by. Anything less would negate the 100% freedom clause. It's the same as placing a restriction on freedom. Once you add a law, you take away a part of freedom. Now if this theory was the one we live by, we would get to choose the laws of gravity and how we interact with gravity. We would get to levitate whenever we wanted. That would be awesome. We would also get to decide if we can teleport instantly to distant lands, under-water, or appear on top of the Eiffel Tower with a fresh-baked croissant and a bottle of French wine. We would get to choose the strength and weakness of magnetism. We would get to play with the speed of light, which is a no-no to many physicists and scientists. We could turn lead into gold all day long. If you don't get to choose the rules or boundaries, can it be considered 100% choice? Maybe some clarification is needed with this theory.

Imagine that the world is one big amusement park. There are rules to the park so everyone can enjoy all the rides and attractions to their heart's content. To make everything fair and accessible, rules are put in place. There is supposed to be no line jumping, standing up in the middle of the rollercoaster ride, and you board the Ferris wheel at the bottom and not at the top. In order for everyone to enjoy their experience on Earth, we also have to follow the basic Universal Laws of gravity, magnetism, strong and weak forces, linear time, and so forth. If we don't get a choice about these laws, this negates 100% freedom of choice.

You can understand why, too. Not everyone is ready for a levitating group of tourists flying over the Great Pyramid of Giza, so gravity remains somewhat of a constant. It is also easier to get around town knowing that your car will not float off into space without you commanding it to follow gravity every time you get behind the wheel.

Here is another example of our current Universal Laws that must remain a constant with the opportunity for change. People might not like the idea of instant teleportation or the ability for someone to walk through walls. (Although, I think it would be cool.) Do I need to say much more about the possible negative side-effects of this if we all had these abilities? Privacy would be a thing of the past, not to mention fear running rampant because you would never know when your in-laws were going to pop in unexpectedly without a door or walls to form a barrier. I could go on for freedom/infinity on this one.

The more people become accustomed to the concept of possibility, or the possibility of Universal Laws changing and shifting, the more we increase our chance that new inventions or abilities become available for everyone to enjoy. Basically, fear is the underlying emotion that needs to shift. There seems to be a need for a certain percentage of people who are ready to accept a possibility before that possibility can become a new reality. At this time, I am not privy to that number. It just feels right based on my experience.

Let's go back in time for this example. Before airplanes and hot air balloons were invented, air travel was not accepted as a common ability. It was actually considered impossible and a waste of time to change the Universal Laws of nature. People are meant to stay on the ground. If not, we would have been born with wings. The ability to fly frightened a number of people. It still does to this day, but not nearly as many as before. Air travel seemed impossible a few hundred years ago, but now we have gone to the moon and sent satellites to the outer realms of our solar system. We have more satellites in space right now than you have popcorn in your movie theater popcorn bag. People barely blink an eye any more at our ability to fly heavy metal objects from New York to Los Angeles. In the beginning, though, you could hear the negative talk. "Oh, he'll never get that off the ground. How absurd," or "We will never reach outer space," or "We do not have any other planets or solar systems that could sustain life." All it took was enough belief in a possibility, a dream mixed with courage, fortitude, trial and error, and persistence, for a new ability to be born. We stretched what was once considered a Universal Law and made it a new possibility, a new reality for everyone to enjoy.

I have a dream that we will all be able to live peacefully together while pursuing our passions and growing beyond our current fear-based system of control and greed. As more people aspire to this possibility, the possibility will turn into a probability. A probability turns into a stronger belief. A stronger belief turns into an even stronger probability. This turns into a blueprint, a process, a *Freedom Code,* which creates a strong movement toward creating a new reality, a new ability, a new system. When people begin to live the possibility, it becomes a new existence, a new reality, a new constant. And this new constant becomes a new stepping-stone for the next possibility that is already in progress in another person's mind. And that's so cool!

CHOICE B:
THE OTHER WHITE MEAT
WITH A DIFFERENT WRAPPER

Choice B is a variation on the 100% choice theory. It's been said that our current experiences, and all of our future experiences, are completely controlled by our thoughts and emotions. I have seen this many times in metaphysical books and films. The concept behind this theory is simple: If we want to change or control our future, we have to change our thoughts and feelings. If we don't do this effectively, we can't blame anyone else but ourselves for our life experiences. Good thoughts and beliefs create happy futures and all possibilities. Bad thoughts or feelings create negative experiences and hold up our desires.

How do you feel about this theory? I agree with part of the theory, just as I can agree with parts of the other theories. But again, something just doesn't seem right. We have to go back to the amusement park analogy. I can believe all I want in my ability to levitate. I can feel it, see it in my mind, and create all the good thoughts needed to levitate. But if the masses are not ready for someone to have this ability, the odds of this happening are very slim. If someone developed this ability and the masses were not ready, that person would probably end up on the end of a BBQ skewer, just like they did to people a few hundred years ago. People may be ready to accept this ability from a magician, but they are not ready to accept this from every stranger they might pass walking along the street (or rather, levitating across the street). There is still too much fear in our society for that ability to become commonplace just yet. I am using an extreme example here, but it makes my point rather clearly. Belief and emotions do not create 100% freedom. There are Universal Laws and other factors to consider. For levitation to become possible, then a shift in the acceptance level for this ability must occur.

Here is a side point on levitation. You may believe that levitation will never happen. I ask you to consider the possibility. Levitation and the flight of a rocket or a plane are in the same category. We have already accomplished flight and space travel. The only difference between our current accomplishments and levitation are propellant, force, time spent off the ground, and the ability to shift gravity to achieve a common goal. I believe that levitation, or knowing how to work with gravity to achieve this great feat, is in our future. We reached outer space only decades after we had been using horses and buggies as our main mode of transportation. We can certainly find a way to work with gravity. Levitation has already been achieved to some extent with magnetism. We are on the cusp of this breakthrough, especially as more people release their fear and accept this new possibility.

We have one more factor to consider in this theory where we have 100% choice based upon our emotions and beliefs; we still must consider time. Our world makes sense and functions smoothly with the use of our current linear time system. There are many modes of time, such as subatomic time, subconscious time, no time, space time, time that stands still, time based on the speed of light, and more. One of the abilities that we are not privileged to as a race is instant manifestation. If we had 100% choice, we would also have the choice of when, where, and how our desired future would take place. I have not talked to every being on the planet, but 99.99% of the ones I have talked to do not have the conscious ability to instantly manifest their desires. So it is hard to agree with the statement that our actions and beliefs give us 100% choice of our present and future. I like to say that we have limited choice, and we have techniques that can stack the odds in our favor, but there are no guarantees. When the masses become ready for instant manifestation, this may become a new reality.

To wrap this up, with the information and data I have at this time, I do not believe we create 100% of our future by belief and emotions alone. There is more to consider here than just our own needs and desires. If we want to function and benefit from every living being on this planet, we still need to have Universal Laws that allow the masses to co-exist with some semblance of reality. The majority of people still need to grasp onto something like gravity and other universal constants. However primitive it may seem to some of us, this is how things are at the moment. Give it time. All things change and improve.

MY THOUGHTS ON THE GAME OF REALITY

I have shared the outer extremes for the possible creation theories that make up our current reality. There are many more, and there are many variations for those I have listed so far. I will share three or four short examples after I've painted my thoughts on what I believe is the best possibility for choice combined with Universal Law. Let's jump right in.

While in spirit, we get to decide all the major events that we wish to experience when we take on human form. These life experiences can be for growth, learning, or plain old fun. Some of these pre-planned experiences may even be painful at first, but can be looked at differently later on in life. Also, all of these life events are still bound to the Universal Laws with the possibility of change when the masses are ready to move forward.

There is a very strong possibility that these events will happen in our current life, but they are not guaranteed until we live events that will help solidify the probability factor. For a simple explanation, I will use W, X, Y, and Z to label events and to help paint a clearer picture of how this theory works. It will explain why things happen and why things don't happen in our desired timeline. Also, these events are not bound to a specific date or timeline in our life, but are based on generalities of time. There is a sliding scale for when each event can happen. They are not like pre-planned holidays that occur on a specific day.

Each of these major life events builds one on top of the other. Let's say that Z is the completion of this book. All of my life experiences have built upon each other so I could gather the right amount of information, data, and facts to create the content for each chapter. If I hadn't grown up in my current family, gone to school to be a teacher, moved to south Florida, got married, moved to Texas, learned about hypnosis, changed careers, and continued with my passion to help others, you probably would not be holding this book in your hands. You might hold a different book in your hands, but it would not be filled with the same words or content. If I hadn't lived my W event, my Z event may never have happened and could have created a different set of options or goals. For now, let's stay on this path and reach Z.

After W was completed, I may not have known why my X event was taking place. Let's assume that I wasn't completely happy at X and didn't know why I was experiencing that unpleasant event. But as I am at Z, I know why X and Y had to happen. X and Y make a lot more sense now that I am at Z. I learned from X, which enabled me to learn from Y, and those events helped crystallize Z, and now I am very grateful to be at Z. Have you experienced something similar?

Since Z was a major point in my life, that particular future event was crystallized stronger in the wave potential of matter and energy. The more I continued to unconsciously experience events that moved me toward Z, the more it strengthened and crystallized Z into my potential future. (In quantum mechanics, this is a theory known as a collapsing wave function. I will talk about this in the next chapter. Furthermore, my use of collapsing wave functions is not an exact mirror image to the concept presented in quantum physics. You will understand more as you continue reading this book.)

Interestingly, the mini events between X and Y could also change as long as they do not drastically move me away from Z. Those minor events would either speed up the process or slow it down. Z could happen today, tomorrow, or years from now. As long as I am living experiences that support Z's future, Z will crystallize into my reality. (Some people call these lessons in life, which is what brought us to this planet in the first place.) The great thing about these mini events is they create chance, choice, and room for unexpected surprises instead of everything being pre-planned.

So why don't things happen in life the way we want? As many people dream for a better life of financial security, one of those dreams might be to win the lottery. I, too, have dreamed of winning the lottery or creating abundant wealth early on in my life, long before Z was even in my conscious thought. I put my best efforts into all the techniques for the Law of Attraction (which we will talk about in Chapters 11 and 12), prayed, dreamed, changed my thoughts and feelings toward abundance and accepting, read positive and motivational books, believed I was a multi-millionaire, and more. No matter what I did, I didn't have a bank account with multiple zeroes early on in my alphabet of events. As you have probably figured out by now, if I had become a multi-millionaire before I went to graduate school, I would not have become a music teacher, eventually moved to Texas, and I would have changed my pre-planned Z event. Z was so strong in my pre-assigned list of events that I created while in spirit, my chances for becoming a multi-millionaire were pretty slim until I completed Z. However, I also believe that strong beliefs, emotions, and thoughts can alter a potential future, especially if reinforced by a group via meditation, prayer, focused intent, self-hypnosis, and other means.

I have also theorized that it is possible for a single life event to create such a massive amount of growth and enlightenment that some of the letters can be skipped or alleviated from the life path. This time let's use M, N, O, and P.

Let's say that your final goal at P is to learn how to share your abundance without fear. While at the M event, you decide to begin the process by increasing your self-empowerment and changing your actions as fast as possible. You make huge strides in changing your beliefs and releasing fear, so you donate a huge sum of your wealth to a worthy cause while living in the N event. There is no need for you to live through O and P because you have already accomplished your goal. You can now start a new set of goals at Q. Or, if the events after P are not crystallized as strongly as the previous events, you could change your future direction completely. You could start at a brand new alphabet, or even choose to leave the Earthly realm at that time. So many choices, so many possibilities. Isn't it wonderful?!

I want you to know that the techniques I listed three paragraphs earlier work really well. They help to increase the chance of success, especially if they do not conflict with a major pre-planned event made before you came to Earth. They also work very well if you don't have pre-programmed blocks of guilt, low self-worth, low self-love, and so forth. These techniques are very powerful if they are aligned with your major life events. These techniques can even help speed up the process of completing lifetime goals ahead of schedule. They are also excellent for creating positive mini-events in between major events. We will talk about all of those techniques in the coming chapters.

OTHER REALITY THEORIES

I've spent this entire chapter explaining possible reality theories based upon a belief that there is a higher soul system involving a Deity or a God.

It makes sense since the majority of the world believes in a God or supreme spiritual being of one type or another. It is equally easy to explain our reality without a higher entity directing at least part or all of our development and experiences. Without a spiritual influence, every event builds upon the other by natural selection. This is called determinism. There is also the theory that everything happens strictly by chance.

Another possible reality is the multiverse, but this one can exist with or without a spiritual influence. The multiverse theory states that there are multiple Universes existing all at the same time with infinite possible parallel dimensions found within each Universe.

What would it be like to experience a multiverse? Here is one potential explanation. Let's imagine that you were born seconds ago and you had the choice to cry or not to cry. With each choice you make, you create an alternate parallel self, splitting off into parallel dimensions, so you can experience life from every possible angle. One parallel dimension starts with you crying and moves forward to the next choice before it splits into another parallel dimension. The dimension in which you did not cry also continues until you make another choice, then the non-crying version would also split. One dimension continues with you taking your first step, and the other continues with you falling again, while a third continues where you didn't move at all. Every new choice would continue to create a new parallel dimension. This would continue until all of your selves would pass on in every dimension and you leave all of your bodies behind. When all your souls have rejoined in another realm of existence, they compare notes and decide whether you want to start the process all over again. It's a pretty amazing theory that can be combined with my theory and many others.

For some people with deep faith, and according to their religious beliefs, all of us are living according to God's plan. In this theory, people are living their lives based upon a master plan dictated by their version of a God that matches their religion. Another theory is that our reality is based upon the belief that we are already in heaven, hell, or purgatory trying to work our way into the afterlife. Your perceptions would create these temporary realities as you move from one event to the next. Any of these theories would impact how people make their choices and perceive all the events in their lives.

An offshoot of these reality theories is that there is no heaven or hell, but we can create the concept of a heaven or hell in any realm where we exist. There is a major shift going on right now regarding the heaven and hell theory. I have talked with many people who have decided that the concept of hell was created by the human race as a means for controlling the masses. Infinity seems like such a long time to only get one chance at life. This would lead to another theory of multiple lives, which creates past lives, which also becomes a reason for why things are as they are.

PAST LIVES AND THE INFINITE LIFE THEORY

In my profession, I have witnessed people who have made incredible changes in their habits and behavior. I have seen people transform fear into courage, release unwanted habits, and formulate new desires with the aid of imagery, belief, and self-hypnosis. Part of my experience—while helping others achieve success—has guided me on an incredible journey of possible theories for life after death. I've been presented with new questions that have created new foundation stones. (I already had numerous theories of what happens beyond our life on Earth. Past life regression just helped a little more.) To continue helping others, I pretty much had to define at least some of my own beliefs based on my theories and the theories of others. I asked myself, "What happens in the afterlife, and does this explain why we are here? Do our past and future lives dictate how events transpire in our current life? Do we only get one chance in all of eternity?" It is time to explore these questions and go a little deeper. Here is my theory on past and future lives.

I am going to relate this to something that everyone can understand—music and vibration. Everyone has experienced music and vibration at one point or another in his or her life. Even if someone is unable to hear, they can still perceive vibrations. We are surrounded by sound, silence, and music all day long. Even our everyday sounds of nature create music and vibration. Listen to the calming sounds of ocean waves breaking on the shore and notice how easily it relaxes the nerves. Sit next to an old chalkboard while listening to the grating sounds of nails scraping across the surface, and you will witness the ear-plugging and teeth-clenching reaction from those who hate this sound. Vibrations influence our reality and our reactions every moment of the day. Vibration also influences why things are as they are.

A fairly new theoretical science, called string theory, postulates that our smallest building blocks of matter are not the atom; they are not the protons, the neutrons, or the electrons; they are not the quarks, muons, and leptons; nor are they any of the newly discovered particles that continue to be revealed on a seemingly daily basis. But instead, they are individual single-dimensional strings. When these strings vibrate at a specific speed, frequency, or amplitude, they create the elemental building blocks that create all the matter that we see and experience today. (I list a few good books on string theory, quantum mechanics, and multi-verse possibilities in the next chapter.)

String theory has since grown from just strings to also seeking a solution to unifying quantum mechanics and Einstein's theory of relativity. We also have mention of an eleven-dimensional theory, multiple Universes in the form of membranes, and the holographic principle. In the mix of all these ingredients, string theory has led to five different string theories and also an M-theory.

I have spoken to many people who believe everything owes its existence to vibration. Light is a form of vibration, emotions are expressed and felt as vibrations, color has a vibration, and matter is made up entirely of vibrations. As human beings, we experience events and produce an emotional response for each event. These emotions carry a vibration that can be pleasing to others or as agitating as a stinging jellyfish caught in your bathing suit.

As we take our Coda back to the beginning of music (a musician's joke), we can see another structured system that creates a perceived reality. In our western musical system, a major scale is based upon eight notes. To keep this easy, I will use the C major scale—C, D, E, F, G, A, B, C.

Each note has a specific quality to it. Some notes of the scale make great resting points or vibrations of completion. These notes would be C, G, and C an octave higher. Other notes beg to move to certain places in the scale. If the 8th note of the scale (C) is a natural resting place, then the 7th note of the scale (B) was created to lead to the 8th note. B must lead to C in order to create a calm resolve, a good resting place. Anyone who has listened to western music has heard this resolution: Do, Re, Mi, Fa, Sol, La, Ti leads to Do.

Let's imagine that two people in life come together to share many experiences and learn lessons from each other. While life takes its many twists and turns—creating joy, happiness, and sorrow—if the events experienced between these two people were left in an unresolved state, then that vibration could carry over beyond death. The events, trauma, unresolved emotions, or fear could be so strong that the soul never gets to resolve the vibration, even in the afterlife. If I want to rest on C, the last thing I would like is to hear Ti, or B, for an eternity. Can you see where this is heading?

OK, now you are in spirit. Your soul life is a mess because you are not able to resolve your vibration because of previous life experiences. All the other souls want to help, so you sit down with your soul group or council of teachers and create a new life experience. You might be tired of coming back as a male because you did that for the last 100 lives in a row, so this time you choose to come back as a female and see how the other half lives. On top of choosing your sex, you choose your parents, your relatives, your friends, and you choose a number of your lessons in life that can help you resolve your current unresolved vibrations. You may also choose your occupations, your financial status, and what nationality you want to experience. You choose the major W, X, Y, and Z events.

The goal of this new life would be to resolve any past life issues with lessons and experiences in your new current life. You might even do this with the same person as before, but they may be in a different body. At the same time, your other main goal would be to make it all the way to the end of this current lifetime without creating any more unresolved issues. Your goal would be for every experience to rest on C when you reach the end of your life. You can always reach C many years after an event by releasing negative emotions, forgiving, and moving on. In theory, if you can accomplish this, you move up the soul ladder and become one of the new masters, teachers, and guides. Cool, huh?

In this past life theory, we can come back as many times as we want, in as many different forms as we want, in as many different time periods as we want, in as many dimensions, Universes, or species as we want, to continue learning, resolving, and experiencing all the pleasure and great amounts of variety that were created for everyone to enjoy.

OPEN MINDS, OPEN HEARTS

I want to thank you for being open-minded while reading these theories. I haven't even listed all of them yet. We could fill volume upon volume of books talking about all the great possibilities for reality. What conclusions have you drawn so far? Have you solidified your own beliefs and made them stronger than before? Has this material created any new possibilities for how life works? Do you have a new foundation stone that you would like to try out for a while? Remember, theories become reality when people believe enough in their thoughts and they take their theory and make it part of their daily life. Make your theory come to life today and have fun.

In the next chapter, we will cover how objects are formed to make our experiences a physical reality. We will combine quantum theory, metaphysics, and logic to paint an incredible world of possibility.

CHAPTER THREE

OBJECT THEORY-TER

I N THE LAST CHAPTER, we covered theories that explained the mac-
ro version of why our lives work the way they do. In this chapter, we
are going to cover theories based on the micro version of objects, matter, and anything that we may consider to be real. We will cover topics of
collapsing wave functions, potentiality of solid states, and the holographic
approach to our Universe. We will also discuss how objects come into our
lives through belief, intent, prayer, and focus. This will be presented as
theory blended with science and logic. Trust me; you don't have to be a
physicist to understand what I am going to cover in this chapter.

We are lucky that scientific information covering these vast topics
is abundant on the internet, in books, on TV programs, and in movies.
These media types do a great job of explaining the mathematical and
technical principles of quantum mechanics and string theory. One of the
best explanations that I have found to date is Brian Greene's *The Elegant
Universe: Superstrings, Hidden Dimensions, and the Quest for the Ultimate
Theory,* and his other work, *The Fabric of the Cosmos: Space, Time, and the
Texture of Reality.* His interpretations are scientific in nature but provide
a simple explanation for those who are not physicists and want to understand quantum mechanics and string theory. I also enjoyed Michio Kaku's
*Hyperspace: A Scientific Odyssey Through Parallel Universes, Time Warps,
and the 10ᵗʰ Dimension,* and Amit Goswani's *The Self-Aware Universe: How*

Consciousness Creates the Material World. Goswani's work begins to tackle the bridge between science and possibilities for creation through intent, a bridge not easily crossed when mixing science with metaphysics and spirituality.

Our greatest scientific minds are doing a fantastic job of defining how and why matter is created in the micro version of our Universe. Their continued efforts help to identify and classify the beginnings of our elemental building blocks. But even as science is still learning and making new discoveries, there is still no definitive answer to explain how matter exists in all of our realms of reality. We are still formulating our best theories about the creation of our Universe and how finite objects exist. Science has shown evidence to support a Big Bang theory, but we still don't know what caused the bang. There is talk about the bang occurring from colliding membrane-type Universes, but what created the membranes and where did they come from? These are some of our greatest questions, and they will lead us to our greatest discoveries. In time, we may come to the end of our search, but for now, we can only continue forming theories to explain why things are as they are.

It is time to watch another version of our reality unfold before your very eyes. (I am also very curious to find out how this will turn out.) Refill your popcorn bag if needed, and get ready to expand your mind. It is now time for *Object Theory-ter.*

QUANTUM THEORY

In the beginning of quantum mechanics, there was light. (I couldn't resist.) Right before the birth of quantum mechanics, a famous scientist, Thomas Young (1771–1829), performed an experiment that would forever change our viewpoint regarding the solid state of light. Young's experiment showed that projected light, when aimed at two slits in a piece of board, will create an image of interference patterns. These interference patterns demonstrate a wave-like quality that is very similar in imagery to the interference patterns water creates when waves of water interfere with each other. The most important result of this experiment shows that photons—the smallest particles of light—do not act entirely as solid particles as suggested by Newton and others. Light can travel and relay information in wave form and in particle form at the same time. That is amazing to me every time I read it.

Here is the concept behind Young's incredible findings. First, you take a board and cut two parallel slits near the middle. Next, place another surface behind the board that will catch any light that makes its way through the two slits. To start this experiment, and to define a reference point, we cover up the right slit and shine a beam of light at the board. As expected, you get an image of the left slit displaying on the back surface. For the sake of comparison, we cover up only the left slit and shine the light at the board. Again, as expected, we get an image of the right slit showing on the surface at the back. Everything is working normally up to this point.

Now we shine the light at both uncovered slits. Here is where things get interesting. If we polled 100 people who never heard about Young's double-slit experiment, I imagine the majority of people would say there would be an image of two slits projected on the back surface. This makes logical sense. However, that is not what happens, and something unexpected and mind-blowing occurs. Logic takes a long extended holiday. The projected image does not appear as two slits, but shows an interference pattern that looks like multiple bands of shaded bars, with the greatest wave intensity occurring between where the two slits would paint their shadow. (You can find pictures of this and a sketch of Thomas Young's double-slit experiment all over the internet.) Thomas Young presented these amazing facts in his paper entitled, "Experiments and Calculations Relative to Physical Optics" in 1803–4. His double-slit experiment, using light as the measuring force, has been duplicated many times over. His work has become a precursor to numerous other double-slit experiments that show light and other quantum particles share a wave-particle duality and can be in more than two places at the same time. It sounds like it should be impossible, but it has been proven again and again.

WAVE-PARTICLE DUALITY: A NEW BEGINNING TO STUFF

We jump forward to the early 1900s when Louis de Broglie postulated that all light and matter in motion has an associated wave pattern. His ideas created a new field of study in physics known as wave mechanics. Wave mechanics unites the characteristics of all solids with the same possible wave characteristics as photons. De Broglie claimed that if light can travel as a wave and as a particle, particles of matter can also exist and travel as a wave and as a solid at the same time. His theory also lends credence to the idea that everything in our world is made up of potential.

Louis de Broglie's theory was verified when Clinton Davisson and Lester Germer performed an amazing experiment at Bell Labs in 1927. Their work proved that electrons displayed wave-like characteristics, much like light does. In their experiment, Davisson and Germer fired electrons at a nickel target and noted the diffraction patterns. The results produced the exact same effect as photons being fired through Thomas Young's double-slit experiment. Our traditional belief that the elemental building blocks of the Universe act as solids has just been turned upside-down. Protons, neutrons, and electrons—oh my!

How does a photon, electron, or any other quantum particle know when to be a wave and when to be a solid? In other experiments using this double-slit format, when a particle is observed, it always acts like a particle of solid matter. When not observed, it is in a state of potential. Another genius took this finding a step further. Richard Feynman (1918–1988) proved that particles can act as waves, solids, take multiple paths at the same time and interfere with each other, or not go to the target at all. Hold on, there's more.

Things get really interesting when you add in the Heisenberg uncertainty principle. Werner Heisenberg (1901–1976) came up with a theory that shows we have the ability to know the location of a particle, but when we do this, we no longer have the ability to know the exact speed of the particle at the same time. When an observation is made of either one of these defining characteristics, it is said to collapse the wave function and display more of one result and less of the other.

Up to this point, we have seen mathematical and experimental proof that electrons and other elemental particles do not exist completely as solids. As I have further discovered from my research, electrons are not individual entities, but also have the potential for identical duals of each other with the possibility that all of existence is made up of one large field of one mass electron or one elemental particle/energy state. Other findings in the quantum history reveal that electrons and other particles can be in multiple places at the same time and transfer information instantaneously no matter how far apart they may be. Particles can travel as solids and as wave forms. Particles, or energy, can be unified, condensed, or remain in a field of potential until observed. And a particle can cease to exist here and instantly be over there.

When I was first introduced to this material, I was excited and confused. Based on what I was taught in school (with the exception of water and a few other elements), if something was a solid, and came into existence as a solid, it functioned as a solid. This solid would also remain a solid as long as it was not interfered with by outside influences. (If it squeaks like a mouse, it must be a mouse.) I was taught that electrons can bounce off each other much like a basketball bounces off a court. I was not even introduced to this idea of potential wave characteristics until I was in my 40s. My foundation stones were rattled for a microsecond and I thought there was going to be an earthquake that was destined to tear down my palace of life. What was once solid—something that I could rely on—was now potentially a wave. I must tell you that I am glad I learned about these amazing discoveries. A whole new world of potential opened before my very eyes, and it was beautiful.

HOLOGRAPHIC TIDBITS

I have heard many in the metaphysical and New Age realm talk about how our bodies, world, and Universes are created based on a holographic principle. Even science has delved into this expansive theory. (Look into the works of David Bohm and Karl Pribram.) According to these theories, we are supposed to be able to create images with our mind and thoughts alone. As we do this, the wave potential of matter collapses into our current reality. The holograms become real, and we are able to live in a world of possibility based on our emotions and belief systems. To take this a step further, we are also supposed to create everything as an individual entity while we are connected as one larger source of being. Some have suggested we are connected by threads of energy and thought, like a giant spider web of information.

We are still at the very beginning stages of understanding all the holographic principles that could be behind our everyday existence. A great book to introduce you to the subject is Michael Talbot's *The Holographic Universe*. I appreciate the ideas of a holographic reality. It gives us an even greater potential for creating a peaceful reality. As I gather more information on the potential of a holographic Universe, you can be sure I will share it with you.

HIDE AND SEEK OF MATTER

If quantum particles take on a solid form when observed, and our world as we know it is made up of these elemental building blocks, what happens to our world when we are no longer looking at it? Is what we are observing really there to begin with? Does our world revert to a wave form when we close our eyes, go to sleep, or turn our heads? These are the questions that pop into mind when you begin to grasp the concepts of quantum mechanics.

My mind has been stretched near to capacity at times with these ideas, but I am ready to ingest more and venture farther down the rabbit hole. Honestly, I really could go on indefinitely talking about quantum possibilities, and I believe it is important to know how objects can potentially come into your life. In fact, it will play a big role when we cover enhancement techniques later in this book. But for now, I will save my excitement for the quantum stuff and holograms for a future work. Science is already painting one good picture of how reality works. Let's explore another that combines science, logic, metaphysics, and spirituality.

TIME FOR LIFE AND FOCUS

When dealing with our current reality, time is a factor in our daily lives. There is a time for the sun to come up and for the sun to go down. There is a time for our bodies to rest and a time for us to explore and use our muscles. And depending on where you fall in the food chain, there is a time to eat, and a time to be eaten. Time is a measurement from one event to another, which can speed up, slow down, and come to a life-changing halt. We have heard the statement that time is money. Well, that is only true for those who covet money, power, and control. Time is really a shifting measurement system existing between major and minor events that occur in our daily lives. We are all granted 24 hours each day, so the initial measurement is equal for all people in the beginning. Then time begins to change when we are in conscious and subconscious states and begins to fluctuate even more based on how much we focus our thoughts.

From my work with hypnosis, I know that subconscious time is very different than conscious time. When we sleep, meditate, or use self-hypnosis, the conscious mind trades places with the subconscious self, and time shifts in duration. I ask my clients if their typical 8 hours of sleep feels the same as 8 hours of waking consciousness. They all tell me the same thing, "No, it never feels the same." After a hypnosis session (which is not sleep—hypnosis is a focused state of mind or an altered state of awareness), I ask my clients how much time they felt had elapsed during their session. Most often, they say about 15–20 minutes, but in reality it was 45–60 minutes. We do not lose time while in hypnosis or while sleeping; time is recognized differently in altered states of awareness, subconscious awareness, and states of intense focus.

I am aware that there are many belief systems to explain time and the stories of creation. It seems that every culture and religion has its own take on time and how it relates to our current reality. Some believe in a defined beginning with a defined ending to all of life, while others believe in a theory with no beginnings and no endings. The last example would be a revolving continuation of events with intermittent breaks and gaps between lifetimes. There is also a similar concept of time that takes on the shape of a tube torus.

A tube torus is a geometric figure that emulates the shape of a doughnut. Before you take a bite out of the tasty dough (preferably with chocolate icing and sprinkles), you find there is no beginning or end. If you trace a line from around the outside of the doughnut to the inside hole and back around again, you can go around, and around, and around, from the outside to the inside, for infinity. If you relate this to time, imagine that you are the size of a chocolate atom while you pass through the center hole of the doughnut. (I know; there is no such thing as a chocolate atom. There is in my world, though.) As you float through the space in the doughnut hole, you can see each and every crinkle, air pocket, and dimple in the dough. Each new segment can represent a part of an infinite life's experience. You can stop for a moment and sneak a small taste. It might be a sweet bite, a floury bite, a salty bite, an eggy bite, and more. Each new place on the torus/doughnut can provide a new life experience. It is a beginning without an ending, but with so many varied bites of life. Yum!

MORE ON TIME AND OBJECTS

You have probably heard the spiritual phrase, "In the beginning, there was light." I believe that should be the second or even third statement for creation. In my humble opinion, I think it should read, "In the beginning, there was a question," or "In the beginning, there was a desire for change," or "In the beginning, there was curiosity," or "In the beginning, there was an accident." In my experience, all events that occur in the future are a direct result of a question, a desire for change, curiosity, or an accident. Let me explain.

If you want to create a new experience in life, a question is usually posed in the mind either consciously or subconsciously. "I wonder what it would be like if we went to the Bahamas this spring? We always go to my grandmother's, but this year it's time for something different." Then the mind starts to formulate a process, or a series of events, that could take you to your final destination. You look at your budget, your schedule, your children's spring break, your other life obligations, where you can leave the dog and the goldfish, and you begin to formulate a thought, or a belief, that you can actually go to the Bahamas. If you think you can go, then the energy is set in motion to take you to the sandy beaches with an umbrella drink and braided hair. (Those of you who have been to the Bahamas know what I am talking about.) You make all the plans, and you constantly dream about sand between your toes, smells of suntan lotion and baking skin, and salty air blowing in your new braids. All of this started with a desire posed from a question, curiosity, and a need for change. Life needed a little change.

Here is another example. You are in your job. It's a good job and you are not really thinking about leaving. However, you start to wonder what it would be like to work in another position just for the reference point. You wonder whether a job change would be better or worse than where you are right now. Would it be better for you and your family if you stayed in your current position? Can you relate to this? Sometimes deciding to change, or not to change, comes from a question of relativity.

Another change comes by way of accident. On the way to your couch to watch *Lifetime Theory-ter,* you stop in the kitchen and grab a bowl of your favorite ice cream and a bag of chips. You didn't plan for the bag of chips to burst open and pour crispy potato wafers all over your delicious ice cream, it was an accident. You say to yourself, "Well, it's all going to the same place anyway; let's try it and see what it tastes like." A new opportunity arose from an accident, and you get to decide if you like it or not. (Who knows, it may have been a subconscious action set in motion from a future desire to taste potato chips and ice cream.) Your accident could also turn into the new flavor of the week—potato chip ice cream. If you like this combination, a new event was created by accident. Next time, try it with hot fudge and cherries and see what you think.

So, as we circle back to the micro version of reality, somewhere before time began, a question was posed. What would it be like to have a planet that could sustain life in orbit around a Sun? Think about it. If there is a Creator, and He/She/It knows everything and how everything feels, then why do it? Was He/She/It bored? Well, boredom creates a desire for change. Then a question is posed: "In the beginning, there was a question." If there is a Creator, and it didn't know what the outcome would be, well that explains a lot, too. In the beginning, there was a question—a question posed from a desire. Our world then became a fun playground for all forms of life to experience all the fantastic variations and possibilities.

Not to leave out the non-spiritual explanation, there is a benign approach that states there is a natural process of events that leads from one event to the next. These linear events also transfer to objects. One object's existence and interaction with its surrounding elements, including time, creates a potential for a new object. That's the simplest way to explain that theory. Well, the science part wasn't *simple*. I have a great appreciation for the scientific mind and the efforts that go into proving theories. And depending on which time period these scientists lived in, they sometimes sacrificed their lives and freedom for the pursuit of knowledge. My hat goes off to all the people who gather and share knowledge for the empowerment of everyone. Take a bow. You deserve it.

I presented both theories because not everyone believes in a Creator or spiritual being. As always, you decide. I respect all opinions. We now come to the last part of my theory on where objects and matter come from to give us our reality.

FABAL JUICE: A THEORY FOR MICRO REALITY

It's time to revisit the period before you took on solid form. So, you are in spirit form, and you are figuring out what to do to pass time in eternity. Playing tag with the other spirits is fun for a while, but it gets boring chasing other entities around the Crab Nebula. Inter-dimensional hide-and-seek is fun, too, but that also loses its appeal after a few millennia. While passing by the Earth, you see all the possible types of life you can

53

experience. You can also see the Earth from any different time period that might tickle your fancy. The Earth soon turns into the greatest commercial ever created. It's an advertising agency's dream come true. I can just hear the Earth now in that familiar infomercial voice: "Please come join us. You can experience a lifetime as a dinosaur, be an oak tree on an 1800s plantation, or become a grain of sand in a Japanese garden. Come experience all the variety and opportunities we have to offer. Live as a human, a puppy, or a piece of metal. Come back again and again and gain frequent soul miles. There is so much to explore for free. It doesn't even cost you any time, because time is different in the spirit realm than it is in human form. All you need to do is decide what physical shape you want, and the potential quantum particles will cooperate and give you the form you need when you are observed by others. *But wait!* There's more... If you come down today, we will give you a second personality for free!"

This commercial caught you at just the right moment. You saw other potential existences on Mars, Jupiter, and Venus, but this time you want to come down and be a part of the human experiment. So you pick up your celestial cell phone and dial the 800 number to make an appointment with your soul group. You approach your council again and establish a list of goals for this new life. One of your goals will be to experience a 25th wedding anniversary with your spouse. Your group also convinces you to pass on the multiple personalities this time around and stick with just one personality.

Before you take on human form, you have to forget what it is like to be a soul floating around the spirit realm. That's part of the whole package deal for becoming a human. This way you can experience life and give each new event a fresh perception without knowing what is going to happen next. It wouldn't be the same if you knew what was going to appear around every corner; it would ruin the overall surprise and effect. Also, forgetting and trying to remember all over again where you came from is one of the greatest ongoing games for all time.

Hours before you leave the spirit realm, you are given a surprise going-away party and your soul group takes you to the Last Stop Solaroon. You're given your list of goals and experiences to download into your unconscious, which will help guide you through this new life. Then your soul buddies hand you a drink for a toast. The last thing you do in spirit is take a sip of this non-alcoholic fruity drink to help start the process. (I hope you realize this is a story to present my theory, and not fact.)

54

The drink was originally called LABAF Juice, which stood for Liquid Amnesia Bicarbonate and Fear, but that name didn't have a good ring to it and didn't sell so well in the Solaroon. So, they changed the name to FABAL Juice: "Forget All But A Little" Juice. You won't have complete memory loss, but you will be able to remember certain things in life that will give you clues where your soul came from and how to get back home. Sometimes people go overboard on the FABAL Juice because it is very tasty, and they take a double or a triple shot. I think some people have drunk a whole gallon of it.

I asked if there was another reason for calling it FABAL Juice, and they told me it was because FABAL is very close to our word fable. A fable is a story told for entertainment. So it seemed natural to drink something that would help write a story of your life. When you leave the body and go back to spirit again, you get to tell all the other souls your fable. And believe me, they will all be listening intently. Nobody else will ever be able to duplicate all of your perceptions. So, you are incredibly unique, gifted, and special. All of your soul group will rejoin you for this campfire tale with tasty s'mores in hand. It's a very important event. Some will never come to Earth, so they are very curious to learn about your experiences. You become a star.

So, what about all the objects of matter we will encounter in our lifetime? How do they know to take solid form for us to enjoy and experience? If you remember, there is a 25th wedding anniversary coming up. You and your spouse will be receiving a silver platter to commemorate the occasion. Silver... platter... these items need to come into existence from wave form before your special event. How does this happen? The theory continues. Don't turn that dial. We'll be right back.

CONSCIOUSNESS IN EVERYTHING

The last two sections you read are only theories and possible explanations for how things work from spirit to your life on Earth. If any of it doesn't fit, remember to put it on your coat hanger in your mind.

Before we continue with my thoughts on life, we need to talk about some great discoveries made by others who have shown a consciousness in basic elements and life forms that are all around us on the planet. An eye-opening book that talks about the responses and interactions of plants was written by Peter Tompkins and Christopher Bird. Their book, *The Secret Life of Plants,* gives a wonderful account of scientific studies showing the consciousness of plants. They also have another book called *Secrets of the Soil: New Solutions for Restoring Our Planet.* The works of Masaru Emoto show water reacting to positive and negative intent projected through words, prayer, and music. In Emoto's book, *Messages from Water, Vol. 1,* he displays before-and-after photos of water crystals reacting to intent. This would also suggest water having a consciousness. We also know that animals and insects can feel emotions with a conscious level of awareness. If our soil, plants, water, animals, insects, and other inhabitants of the Earth can feel emotions as a conscious response to outside stimulus and intent, and if they are all made up of elemental particles, would it be safe to say that elemental particles also have a consciousness?

I am not stating this as a fact, but merely as a possibility for helping to understand how our subatomic particles may know when to be a solid or function as a wave form.

As we revisit our silver platter, silver, also recognized as Ag and atomic number 47, will need to take a solid form at some point to become a gift for the 25th wedding anniversary. You can trace the silver back to the point when it was a part of the Earth, or when it was discovered to be used in the platter. Either case will work.

For fun's sake, let's say that while in spirit form, you and a bunch of your friends put together a very elaborate journey of cause and effect. One person's desires and actions will have a direct influence on another person's life. You make your agreement and come to Earth, get married, and live a happy life. Your best friend knows your 25th wedding anniversary is coming up soon and he wants to give you a silver platter. He doesn't want to buy something from a store, so he plans to make this a very special one-of-a-kind gift. He finds someone who can make the design for him (also a soul friend), but now he needs the silver. He goes online to look for a silver supplier, and within minutes he finds out that one of his old schoolmates owns a mineral shop in another state. It just so happens that his old friend discovered a small pocket of silver a few years back and became a wholesale supplier. Everything is working as pre-planned.

The elements of silver, with a consciousness that we are not commonly aware of yet, nor able to prove scientifically, has a consciousness and a willingness to remain in a solid form for the schoolmate, the friend who is giving the gift, the person who gets paid to make the platter, all of the shipping people, and the couple on their 25th wedding anniversary. And let's not forget to add the Earth to the list. In my mind, all of the elemental building blocks for our Universe have a consciousness beyond our current understanding.

Now in this theory, the longer something stays in solid form, the harder it is to return to wave form. Think of objects as stage props for your fable. If a stage prop was only going to be used once and never again looked at by any conscious entity, then that prop could decide to stay in solid form or revert back to wave form. If your fable turns into the longest-running show on Earth, then that prop would sacrifice its ability to continually move back and forth from wave to solid so everyone could see the same object as a solid. What a great sacrifice from our everyday objects. If this is true, it gives a new appreciation for everything that is around us to help us live our fable.

While this is only one theory, all I can tell you is that this feels right to me at this time. I appreciate all that is around me and I thank my house for protecting my family from the elements. I thank my car for being a great car and taking me safely from place to place. I thank my computer, my food, my water, my chocolate, my clothes, fire, and everything that has contributed to my life story, my fable. And yes, I thank my version of the Creator and Universal Consciousness, too.

ELONGATING THE WAVE COLLAPSE

Back to some of the other questions posed earlier in this chapter. What happens to the moon when you don't look at it? Does it become a wave of potential, or does it remain the moon that we have all come to love and expect? It seems like a pretty easy answer based on the last section. As long as it's observed by something or someone, it will remain a solid. The moon has its own fable to write and has sacrificed its ability to revert to a wave form for the benefit of everyone else. I came up with my answer while flying back home from one of my classes a year or two ago. I couldn't see the Earth below me, but that doesn't mean that the Earth reverted to a wave function. The Earth was still being viewed by billions of other people. And, the Earth cooperated in the big picture to remain a solid planet and sustain life—The Big Experiment.

The next question that popped into my mind was, "OK, what if everyone on the planet no longer observed the Earth or the Moon, then what would happen?" If you accept that there is a larger consciousness to existence beyond people on this planet, then here is a possible explanation. If all of the elemental building blocks have a consciousness of their own, and the Earth is a consciousness made up of all the elemental building blocks, and the Moon is a consciousness made up of all its own building blocks, and each of the other planets is also another consciousness, and all the other solar systems are consciousnesses, you would need all of the consciousnesses to stop viewing the Earth and Moon for both of them to be able to revert back to wave form. And the longer the Earth and Moon remain solid, the harder it becomes to change to wave form again. Furthermore, the larger the accumulation of quantum building blocks, the harder it is to flow in and out of wave form.

It was a huge sacrifice for all things solid, liquid, and gas to help give us a smattering of life experiences. Maybe that is why so many tribes and cultures honor the elements of Earth, Wind, Fire, Water, and Ether. These elements made a huge sacrifice for us. Thank you to all the elements.

ANOTHER MIND-BENDING THEORY

I have been going over quantum possibilities mixed with other beliefs for the last few years. One of the thoughts I had recently that combined a possible holographic world with the quantum world is interesting, to say the least. At this time, I am not aware of any way to scientifically prove this theory. All I can do is present my thoughts and let you make a decision.

If electrons can be here, there, and everywhere at the same time, and if they have the ability to exist here and move to there instantaneously, is it possible that electrons can also appear instantaneously to create a different element from the periodic table to match the material needs for your fable? If consciousness does exist on all realms, then subatomic particles can also cooperate to create new and potential future realities.

Let's imagine you are in a holographic world and everything you need is created right before your eyes through thought, emotion, and intent. You want to fill up a bunch of balloons for the 25th wedding anniversary party. However, all you have are hydrogen tanks. Hydrogen has only one electron and is not what you want for the balloons. If you were able to focus your intent enough, show enough belief, and project all the right emotions that also project 100% unconditional belief, is it possible that another single electron could instantly appear in each hydrogen atom's shell to create a helium atom? This is another broad version of what some would call alchemy. If the electrons can be everywhere at once, and instantly collapse from wave form down to a solid when observed, can they also collapse from a strong intent in the mind to create any of the elements found in the periodic table? Can they become two, three, four, or more electrons instantaneously in an already existing elemental structure? Can they appear as needed to create an ever-changing reality? If we are in a holographic Universe as others suggest, and I see an electron in my mind appearing in a hydrogen atom to create a helium atom, and I observed this action enough in my mind to collapse the wave function—with no doubt in my mind whatsoever—then this seems like it should be possible. Just a few more thoughts that make you go, "Hmm..."

FROM MATTER TO PERCEPTION

This whole chapter combines scientific discovery with non-scientific theory. The possibilities are mind-boggling and intensely interesting. Before your mind turns to mush, it is just about time to change the dial and move on to techniques and stories that can help you make shifts in your perception, which in turn will help you achieve success and strengthen your natural abilities.

Whether you drank FABAL Juice or not, when you were born, you were given a conscious mind that was ready to learn, explore, and accept new thoughts and beliefs. It was almost a blank slate except for the knowledge to cry, burp, and create dirty diapers. Afterwards, every thought and belief you encountered from your parents, family, and teachers became the basic programming that you either accepted or decided to change later on in life. Most of what we encounter from infancy through adulthood is one person's perception of reality and how things work the way they do. In the next chapter, we will start with perception and work our way forward. Life seems to make adjustments in small shifts. Each story and technique presented here can help you shed some of the beliefs that no longer serve your life's purpose and help guide you to new programming to help you reach your dreams and desires.

CHAPTER FOUR

SIX SPECIAL BOYS

I T WAS A NEW DAY in the farm valley outside of New Delhi. Every bit of life, from the ants to the tigers, took its position in the play of life. Even the local farm animals and farmers were already stirring as the sounds from the rooster traveled through the morning mist. One farm in particular caught the attention of a friendly observer who liked to wander from place to place and take in the sights. He was a lifelong student and craved the lessons he would learn from people in the local villages.

The sun started to peek a little bit higher on the horizon as the observer took his position outside a farmhouse window next to the road. He heard a father calling out to his sons, "Boys, it is time to start your day and begin a new lesson. Finish your porridge and come meet me at the front door. I will have everything you need for your day when you get there."

The boys responded gleefully, "Yes, Father. We will be there in just a minute."

There were six boys in total, and all of them were well-mannered, behaved, and filled with a great zest for life. They never backed down from new experiences, work, or the lessons their father taught them. They also did not turn down any playtime, either, as you would expect from any child.

The boys' ages ranged from eight to sixteen. Their mother had passed away recently, so there was only the father left to raise the boys. There was something else special about these boys. None of them was able to see.

Now this did not stop the boys from enjoying life. From birth, they were taught that being blind was not a burden or problem. This was a special opportunity that should be seen as a blessing. As a matter of fact, they were taught that living life without sight would allow them to explore the world in a way that others could only imagine, and that the boys should cherish each and every experience with appreciation and excitement.

When the boys finished cleaning their bowls, they met their father at the front door. "Father, we are ready. What do we get to do today?"

The father spoke in a pleasing tone. "Boys, you will be most happy with today's activity. Each of you will get a large bucket filled with cool water and a sponge. I want you to walk in a line beside your eldest brother and go exactly forty paces from the front door. You will stand in line from oldest to youngest. When you get there, place your bucket on the ground, take the sponge out of the bucket, and wash whatever you feel in front of you."

He walked over to the boys and bent to whisper in each one's ear. "Raheem, my eldest, you are to wash everything you feel from your chest and over your head. My two twin boys, you are to wash everything you feel from your shoulders up. Guruttam, my fourth son, you are to wash everything from your waist and over your head. Tanveer, my fifth son, you are to kneel down and wash everything from your waist down to the ground. And Vivek, you are to reach over your head and wash anything that you can hold onto."

The boys reacted with smiles and curiosity. Their father purposely did not tell them exactly what they were going to wash, so they knew there was excitement at the end of the forty paces.

To help them on their way, the eldest brother, Raheem, decided to assist his youngest brother with his math lesson. "Vivek, would you do the counting for us as we walk our forty paces? We will all be here to help you with your counting if you need our help."

Vivek piped up, "Of course I won't mind counting, as long as I can pretend that I am counting pieces of sweet bread." Raheem laughed out loud.

All this time, the observer was astonished by the attitude of these children. He had run across others who had lost their sight, or were born without the ability to see, and some of them showed signs of self-pity, remorse, or anger. But these boys were different. They were amazingly cheerful and ready for any new adventure. They did not question once what they were going to meet at the end of their short walk. Instead, they showed incredible courage and appreciation for the new opportunity that their father had given them.

Raheem spoke to Vivek. "Vivek, it is time to pick up your sweet bread. Start counting, brother, and we will match our steps with your numbers. We will also repeat the numbers after you say them so we can stay in line together. We will reinforce your numbers as a family."

The observer smiled to himself. He was just as proud of these boys as their father was. He admired the self-empowerment they showed and could not wait to commend the family for working so well together.

Vivek started his count, and each brother did as Raheem promised. After each number, the other brothers echoed back, helping everyone stay close to each other while they made their way to the front of the farm. If Vivek counted a number out of turn, the other brothers called out the correct number with a friendly reinforcing tone. Again, this caused the observer to smile.

"Thirty-eight, thirty-nine, forty," called out Vivek.

"Well done, brother," spoke Raheem. "Let us follow the rest of the instructions and do as Father told us."

Each of the six boys put down his bucket, pulled out his wet sponge, and reached out to wash the strange new object in front of him. The observer watched the boys splashing and playing with the water as they touched, wiped, and washed with curiosity and excitement.

Guruttam, the fourth son, called out after a few minutes of washing and splashing, "Brothers, I love you very much, and I truly enjoy this time we get to spend together. I was wondering how you like washing this very large wall. It seems to go up forever. I try and try, but I can't reach the top. It also feels like there are little needles or bristles that stick out of the hard surface, which moves in and out. Tell me, brothers, are you having as much fun as I am? Can you reach the top of this wall?"

Tanveer answered back, "Guruttam, I love you very much, my brother. But I am not feeling the same thing that you feel, unless your wall is as big and as round as the tree Father showed us last week. Guruttam, this feels like one of the columns we felt when we visited the palace, and it is so large that I can't put my arms all the way around it. I tried to move it, but it won't budge an inch. It is firmly planted in the ground. We are standing so close together. I'm not sure why you think it is a wall that we are washing."

Guruttam was a little confused, and did not want to argue with Tanveer, so he called out to Raheem, the eldest. "Raheem, dear brother, please tell us what you are washing. Please tell me so I don't feel like I am going mad."

Raheem answered back, "Dear brothers, I, too, love you very much. But I am not washing a wall or a stone column. Your voices sound close as well, so I know we must be washing the same thing. You would truly love washing what my sponge is on. Every time I get my sponge wet, this large friendly snake wraps itself all around me and lets me squeeze water at its mouth and body. It hugs me gently without taking a bite and seems to be very friendly. I think that it likes this bath."

This confused Guruttam and Tanveer. They seemed so close to each other, but they weren't washing the same thing. "How could this be?" said Guruttam. "How could you be washing a snake, I a wall, and Tanveer a stone column? Something must not be right."

Being a good teacher and leader, Raheem called out to the twins. "Dear brothers, Sadiq and Saeed, tell us what you are washing. Tell us, please, if you are washing a snake, a wall, or a column."

In unison, both brothers responded, "Dear brothers, we love you very much, but we do not seem to be washing any of those things. We do not feel anything that moves like a slithering snake, a bristly wall, or a grand column from the palace. We feel two very sturdy branches. They have no leaves and they curve upward a little bit toward the sky. They almost feel like the bark has been stripped clean from these two branches. Why, brothers, why do you try to fool us? Surely we must be washing the same thing."

The five older brothers were beginning to feel a little disconnected from each other. In the past, they had always learned about the same thing at the same time. Their father had tried to introduce them to new objects in the same manner and at the same time so each brother could relate to one another. Now they were learning in a different way. It was still fun to them, but a little confusing.

Vivek piped up just in time. "Dear brothers, I love you very much. I am having so much fun trying to wash this dancing rope. Each time I get my sponge wet and raise it in the air, the rope swings away from me. It moves from left to right and back again. This is so much fun, brothers. I am glad we are together to share this experience."

Hearing Vivek's words caused the other brothers to break out in laughter. They could picture him in their minds chasing after a dancing rope.

The observer sat quietly off to one side watching the boys having fun and learning. He glanced to his left and saw their father approaching. Their eyes met, they both smiled, and the father continued onward to his boys.

"Hello, my dear sons," the father said. "How are you enjoying your morning so far?"

The air became filled with all six brothers asking questions of their father. "Father, Father, please tell us. Why have you confused us so much? Please tell us which one of us is right."

Raheem asked first, "Father, are we not washing a friendly snake?"

Sadiq and Saeed asked, "Father, are we not washing tree limbs?"

Guruttam added, "Father, we must be washing a tall wall."

Tanveer said, "No, Father, we must be washing stone columns."

And Vivek chuckled, "Father, I don't care what we are washing. This dancing rope is so much fun."

The father looked at the observer first. He could see that the observer was anxious to hear what he would tell his boys. Then he looked back at his sons. "My dear boys, I love you very much, and you have all done well with your lesson today. I could not be any prouder." Then he continued. "Now I wish to tell you that you are all correct in your perception. None of you is wrong. You are all correct in saying that you must be washing the same thing, and you can open your minds even more if you wish."

The boys were still confused, but they trusted their father completely. Raheem spoke first, saying, "Father, please tell us what we are washing. You are teaching us well."

The father said, "Boys, you are washing a living being with a soul and a personality. You are washing something that is alive and glad to be by your side. You are washing an animal called an elephant. Raheem, you are washing his trunk. His trunk is a long nose that can pick up food and other objects gently or with great force. And yes, it does feel like a friendly snake. Sadiq and Saeed, you are washing his ivory tusks. He uses these parts of his body to move things and to protect himself. Guruttam, you are washing the side of his body. He is a very tall animal, as tall as our farmhouse, and his skin has stiff hairs sticking out of it. His sides move in and out when he breathes. Tanveer, you were washing his legs. His legs are as round as a stone column and mimic tree trunks that are firmly planted in the ground. And Vivek, you were trying to wash his tail. His tail swishes and sways in the wind and dances just like a rope. You see, my boys, you were all correct in your perceptions, even though they were so very different from those of your other brothers."

All of the boys started smiling and laughing with their father. So did the observer. He was most entranced by the whole scene that had unfolded so pleasantly in front of him. And the father broke the laughter, telling his boys that he was going to help them switch positions. He wanted them all to experience what their brothers had experienced. He wanted them to know that a perception is personal and different for each one of them. He wanted them to learn that it is OK to have a different perception and still be correct.

The observer was beside himself. He was a smart and educated person, but this lesson struck him deeply. He was so proud of the boys and their father. He knew that some of the best lessons came from simple experiences of life. He knew that perception was a key to living in harmony with your fellow brothers. And the lesson that he observed was almost beyond words.

The observer finally spoke to the father and boys. "My dear subjects, you have taught me a lesson that is truly unforgettable. You have shown me a new way of looking at life, a new way of looking at challenges, and a new way of dealing with conflicts and strife. You are truly worthy of compliments and adoration." He turned to the father. "I noticed your family when you visited my palace. I was so intrigued by your family's friendly nature, in spite of the challenges that the boys have to face every day, that I had to come and see you at your farm. I knew there was much to be learned from you."

Just then, the prince reached into his pocket and pulled out a bag of rubies. He handed the bag to the farmer, and said, "Dear Sir, you have taught me well today. In return, every time that I share this story, I will give you another ruby. Is this acceptable to you?"

The father replied gleefully, "My dear Prince, it is with great honor that we accept your gift, and we openly invite you to stay and visit with our family for dinner. We humbly ask that you give the additional rubies to others who have special talents, as my boys do."

The prince responded, "And so it shall be. Come, let us have dinner together, and I will see to it that you have passage into my court anytime that you please. You are most welcome to dine with me and share in some sweet bread, too." And the boys let out a great cheer, especially Vivek.

This story is based on a traditional tale from India. The concept is the same, and no elephants were harmed in the making of this story.

CHAPTER FIVE

TRUTH AND PERCEPTION

PERCEPTION IS ONE OF THE GREATEST BIRTHRIGHTS we are granted in life. It is a freedom like no other. Cherish your ability to perceive. It is a freedom that builds self-empowerment and creates your unique character. One of the greatest abilities anyone can master is to see things from your own perspective and another person's viewpoint at the same time and still love others if they don't see things the same way.

A FEW MORE THOUGHTS ON PERCEPTION

I find it amazing that there can be so many different perceptions, and all of them can be correct. While I was snorkeling in the Atlantic Ocean off the Florida coast, I was reminded of the infinite and broad nature of perception. I was paddling my arms and flapping my fins, looking very much like I was not meant to be a fish, when I saw a number of beautiful coral reefs that clung to the ocean floor. Swimming in and out of the living reefs were barracudas, angel fish, parrotfish, clown fish, and numerous others that flashed their brilliant colors just a few feet below the glassy surface.

For a brief moment, I wondered what it would be like to be a fish living in these warm waters. I imagined that their perception of us must be completely unlike our own perception of the human race. I wondered what their thoughts were. Their perception of the sky must be very different from that of any land dwelling creature. Have you looked at the sky from underwater? We see the sky totally different than fish do, but it's still the same sky. We view air and dry land differently than the fish kingdom. The land and air are still the same, they're a constant for all species, but to the fish, constant exposure would kill them. We perceive birds, boats, and fish in a completely different way than the creatures under the sea. To people, fish can be a tasty snack, a colorful pet, or an important part of the ecosystem, but fish certainly don't see themselves that way. Boats are fun for people, but they can mean a slow painful death to a fish. And while we enjoy watching birds, with their graceful ability to fly, to the fish, they are predators to be feared. None of these perceptions is right or wrong, they are just different. But they affect our lives, and the lives of others, in such a tremendous way.

PERCEPTIONS THAT UNITE AND SEPARATE

One of our greatest gifts is also one of our greatest challenges. We experience, we perceive, and we feel emotion. Afterwards, we create more questions and thoughts based on these perceptions. If we like the outcome, we repeat the action until we grow tired of the result. Then the process starts all over again. Change and desire lead to a question. A question leads to a possibility. Possibilities can grow into probabilities. Probabilities can become realities. Realities create perceptions of the moment. Then we react to our perceptions in the form of an emotional response, with some of these reactions being neutral, and others going off the scale with happy or sad feelings.

I believe that all perceptions are unique and cannot be duplicated. We may share parts of a perception, but we will never know exactly what another person is truly experiencing. Let me explain. Every event in life is unique and builds upon the preceding event. Each perception of that event is also unique because it was also built upon all of the previous experiences, perceptions, and emotions. We also need to consider the freedom to change perceptions and thoughts after the initial perceptions were made. Since I will never know how it feels to live your life all the way up to the shared experience (at least in our current conscious awareness), our perceptions will always remain different. We may share similar base emotional responses and thoughts, but the details are always going to be infinitely unique.

Our greatest challenge comes from the growth of our perceptions. When a perception becomes anchored as a habit, a truth, or a belief system, it begins to act in two main ways. One way unites us with others who have similar perceptions. It brings us closer in the form of families, groups, teams, communities, countries, and religions. The other way separates us from those who experience life from a different viewpoint. If we do not see things the same way, if our ego gets in the way, or if our emotions overtake our senses and we become hurt, our perceptions can be the greatest divider known in existence. Perceptions can become the greatest barrier to a peaceful world.

I wrote this when I was in graduate school:

"For if there is a wall strong between thee,
A future is not for either to see.
While we live in our circles, safe for a thought;
A reality has been born, a reality which is not."

If we want to create more happiness in our lives, we can start by making small shifts in our perceptions. We are the ones who can bring down the walls and barriers that separate us from our brothers and sisters in our own homes and in distant lands. The wall can come down stone by stone or all at once. We get to decide how fast we tear down our walls of separation. We do this as we increase our tolerance, our patience, and our love for others. Appreciate the variety that is created by so much perception. It makes our world very flavorful indeed.

TRUTH

The only absolute truth in a dualistic existence is there is no absolute truth. Everything has its dual existence.
—MICHAEL J. RHODES

One morning, while deep in thought, I began to contemplate the meaning of truth. What is truth? It's a great question. I found my mind sifting through concepts and scenarios, trying to come up with a definitive answer. What would define something as being true in our dualistic world? It almost seems impossible. One person's right is another person's wrong.

One person's high is another person's low. So I sat there quietly for a good twenty or thirty minutes. I sifted through my thoughts and pieced together bits of a definition here and parts of a meaning there. I found myself changing my own definition more than once to make better sense of it. I was doing my best to fit these intricate fractions of information together like puzzle pieces, trying desperately to make them slide together until a picture of truth could be looked at by all.

I was very excited. I knew I was onto something big. Had I made a personal breakthrough? Was my definition destined for greatness? I wanted to compare my answer to the dictionary. Surely my answer must have been written down already by some scholar centuries before me. The same definition was surely engraved in black and white in a dictionary somewhere. Think about it, the dictionary is supposed to be an accurate depiction for defining truth. Remember back to when you were in school. If you didn't know the meaning of a word, and if you had a good teacher, she probably told you to look up the answer for yourself in a dictionary or an encyclopedia, then return and share the answer with her. She didn't just give you the answer because she wanted you to become self-reliant and to help anchor the information in your mind. So it seemed that the dictionary would be the ultimate last stop for truth.

I looked in a number of books, I went online, and I polled others for their definition of truth. From their responses, I saw and heard words like: factual, reality, sincere quality, something so real it must be true, faithfulness, following a law, and more.

I was disappointed at first. I trusted that the dictionary was a good source for truth and for the final definition. My definition, which I believe should be in there because it makes sense, was not written in black and white. I checked more sources, and again my definition was not mentioned. Then I became excited. Maybe I would be able to help others realize another possible meaning for truth.

To me, truth is (drum roll please) getting a majority of people to agree on a percentage or value of an individual's perception. I say individual perception again because no two people will ever have the same perception on any given experience or fact. That is not to say that they cannot have extremely similar perceptions, but an individual's perception cannot be duplicated. Perception will always be different as long as it is influenced by emotion, timing, light, history, a person's race, culture, religion, influence from family and friends, vibration, weather, and other numerous internal and external sources that influence how we perceive.

If enough people agree on similar perceptions, it becomes a new truth to those people. If enough people disagree, or they disagree on the values of the perception, then truth is no longer supported, and it will change from a truth to a falsehood.

Let's do a simple example. Take a piece of scrap paper and draw a five-pointed star. Then color in the star. Now look at this object and write down on paper, or in your mind, what you see.

Just to start with, you might have answered from the following possibilities: a star, a five-pointed star, a pentagram, a symbol for the planet Venus, a symbol for the Goddess Venus, a polygon, the connecting vertices of a pentagon, a holy symbol, a satanic symbol (if it is upside-down and you believe in Satan), a star polygon, a symbol used for ESP testing, a sacred geometric shape, a shape representing phi and phi squared—the golden ratio, an outline of Leonardo da Vinci's Vetruvian Man, a pentangle, a pentalpha, a magic symbol, a symbol representing Jesus' wounds, a Freemason symbol, a sign for Lucifer, a pentacle, a Pythagorean symbol, the symbol for Ub from ancient Sumaria, a symbol of the microcosm, a seal for the city Jerusalem, a Wiccan symbol, a symbol representing the five elements—earth, water, air, fire, and ether, a reward from your teacher for doing good work, the official symbol of the Bahá'í Faith, a symbol representing King Solomon, the outline of a concave decagon, and I'm sure there are many others out there that I have not listed.

Now somewhere, way back in history, there was no answer or definition for this five-pointed star. Not one! Not until one person in history saw it and gave it a meaning based on his perception. Then there was only one answer for this symbol, and there remained only one answer for this symbol as long as nobody else questioned the original label. It stayed that way until there was an agreement that the symbol could have another representation—in other words, another perception or truth. Furthermore, if enough people would not agree that this symbol could have more than one meaning, then disagreements, arguments, and wars could have been fought over the correct perception. Our religions of the world today make a great case in point for this.

CDF FAITH

Let's imagine that I saw the colored-in star as a concave decagon, and I had influence over others, or I gathered a number of people who shared the same feelings, so we started a new truth. We rallied around our thoughts and perceptions and decided that the five-pointed star, with a single point facing up, was a concave decagon, and couldn't be anything else. This symbol brought us good luck and prosperity. It became a religion to us. We started the Concave Decagon Faith, or CDF.

Everything was going along well in the city of believers. CDF was thriving well. Children believed that the concave decagon represented good luck and good morality because that was what their parents taught them, and their grandparents taught their parents, and so on. The children loved their parents, and they followed the direction of the town leaders out of respect. They also didn't want to disappoint their parents or become outcasts in the community. So, the children took their word as law, and the concave decagon remained the symbol for their faith. Everything was working perfectly because everyone shared the same truth that had become CDF. Crops were growing, animals were multiplying, and the weather was fantastic. CDF was the reason for all good things in life. Until... Enter the outsider.

A new person came to visit the village. He shared friendship and goodwill. He saw the concave decagon and asked why a symbol for Ub from Sumaria was hanging in all the homes and religious centers. He had never heard of the Concave Decagon Faith and was curious. He wanted to learn and share his perception about the symbol as well. He listened intently to the origin of their truth. The stories were fantastic. He could appreciate all they had to offer on the subject. Now it was his turn. He told them that where he came from, the star was turned upside-down and meant an angle, a corner, or a nook. It had nothing to do with faith, luck, or a happy lifestyle, but he appreciated their beliefs and honored them.

However, this rattled the faith of some in the CDF village. All they knew was the history of the concave decagon. How could it mean anything else? Their faith was being turned upside-down. Fear motivated them to make the stranger see things their way. Emotions boiled over and arguments ensued. "He is an outsider and doesn't see things our way. Nothing good will come of this. Look, one of our pigs has taken ill. It must be because of this Ub believer. We must convert him or send him away."

72

The visitor could tell he was causing a stir. He didn't want to make anyone unhappy or angry. He agreed to leave the town and return home. He appreciated their perception of truth and wished them well. All things returned to normal for a few days in the land of CDF.

A week after the visitor left, a few of the children began playing with all the concave decagons. Their imagination, curious nature, and willingness to try new things turned into a game that would rock the entire foundation of CDF. The children went to every star and turned it upside-down for fun. They didn't mean any harm. They were just playing a game. They were only reacting to what the visitor had shared with the community.

Then the bad events began happening one after the other. Crops started failing, more pigs became ill, and a person died while trying to return a star to its original position. The children were blamed for bringing a curse to the land. They had to forfeit all beliefs that Ub was the truth, and they also had to accept that everything to do with Ub was evil. Furthermore, the children were told that their generation, and all future generations, would be cursed and would have to live in penance for their sins. They were no longer permitted to turn the stars upside-down ever again, and they must deny themselves any pleasures or face the worst possible punishment: banishment from CDF and an eternity of suffering.

Fear grew more rampant in the land of CDF. "We must go and convert all Ub believers to our faith. We must return order to our village. It is the will of the concave decagon. The concave decagon has spoken. If we don't do this, our land and people will suffer and die."

Swords and shields were collected and an army was amassed. "If the believers of Ub do not convert to our faith of CDF willingly, we will do it by force. It's the only way peace will reign."

Battles raged on for decades. Both sides gained advantages and suffered terrible losses. In the process of trying to make each other's side see things from their own perspective, all they did was broaden the world of possibility within both villages. There were many people in CDF and Ub who were tolerant, loving, and willing to live with variety instead of fear, hatred, and anger. The war eventually ended with no one side changing the other's views. All that happened was a great deal of life was lost, and the financiers' pockets got richer.

I'm sure you realize this is not a factual event, but it does mirror many events in our world's history. (No intentions are meant in any way to disrepute the good nature of ancient Sumaria or any of its descendants. I used the upside-down star from Sumaria—a corner, nook, or angle—as it seemed to be the most benign of symbols.) You could replace the conflict between CDF and Ub, and easily insert the Crusades, the Indian Wars, WWII, and many others as examples of this story.

Truth, like beauty, will always be in the eye of the beholder. With so much truth and beauty, appreciation can be a new turning point in our lands. A simple shift in perception, allowing new ideas, and loving those who think differently, will create peace in our hearts and peace in the world.

HOW MANY APPLES DO YOU SEE?

It was Thursday after school, and Janice was sitting quietly in the office waiting for her parents to arrive. She was still very upset about something that had happened in math class about a week ago, but nobody could figure out what was bothering her. Janice's parents and math teacher were very concerned for her well-being, so they decided to have a conference to determine how they could help her.

Mrs. Carter, Janice's math teacher, was well-liked and a popular teacher. The faculty and parents respected her, and she was definitely one of the students' favorites. She was smart, funny, approachable, and always challenged her students to go beyond the norm. Mrs. Carter knew there was something wrong between Janice and herself, but she didn't know what had caused the problem. She had tried talking to Janice, but every time she approached her, it only seemed to upset her even more. All Mrs. Carter knew was that Janice had stopped participating in class, stopped completing assignments, and didn't seem to care anymore about her grades. This was definitely not like Janice, who before this had been at the top of her class in all her academics.

Janice was incredibly smart. Her IQ teetered somewhere around the genius level and she had always scored 100% on every assignment, test, and exam throughout her school career. As a matter of fact, her parents couldn't remember a time when she hadn't gotten a perfect score. Her parents were extremely proud of Janice and loved her dearly. They recalled just how quickly she had picked up reading, language, and basic math. Most of her friends were still in early development, but not Janice. By the age of thirteen, she could already speak five different languages and had written a children's novel. Her parents knew that she had a gift and did everything possible to encourage her abilities.

At 4:30 P.M., Janice's parents arrived in Mrs. Carter's room. They sat down with Janice, reassuring her that she had not done anything wrong and that they wanted to help her in every way possible. After a few tears, Janice finally began to open up. She felt she could now explain what had happened and be understood by everyone in the room.

Janice went back one week to the day when Mrs. Carter had given all her students a take-home math test. The exam consisted of twenty problems worth five points each. After passing out the exam, Mrs. Carter instructed her class to carefully go over each question and let her know if any of the problems needed explaining before they left her room. From the general reaction, Mrs. Carter knew that she had pushed her students well beyond their comfort zones. The moans and groans echoed loudly, and more than one student complained, "This is too hard, Mrs. Carter. We're never going to get these questions answered by tomorrow."

Mrs. Carter decided to give them a little a hint. She told the students about an unwritten bonus question (which she happened to have made up at that very moment). She instructed the class to look around the room and count how many apples they saw and then write the answer on the back of the test in one word. It would be worth five points if they got the answer right. Mrs. Carter's room was full of math posters that related to the exam questions, educational eye candy, the American flag, classroom rules, and a calendar. She thought this might at least get them to see that the answers were right in front of them on the posters.

Everything was good so far. Janice felt very confident about the exam. She understood the math concepts and knew that each question could be answered easily by applying the principles that Mrs. Carter had taught them. Math was a good subject for Janice. She especially liked that all of the math answers were finite and easy to calculate.

Janice turned in her paper the next day. She was beaming because she knew that she had produced yet another perfect paper. She was particularly proud of her answer on the bonus question. She turned in her assignment and didn't give it another thought.

The following day, Mrs. Carter passed back the graded assignments. She congratulated all the students on their efforts and for answering the bonus question correctly. Well, all but one student answered the bonus question correctly. The students thanked her for the clue she had given. It was smart of her to have them look at all the math posters while searching for the apple. To all the other students, it was an easy answer. There was only one apple, and it was on a poster near Mrs. Carter's desk. They were glad to get the additional pointer to help their exam scores. All were happy but one.

Janice received an A on her assignment. It showed 100%, but not 105%. "How can this be? How did I get the bonus question wrong?" she wondered. The other students had seen only one apple in the room, and it was on a holographic poster next to the teacher's desk that read, "Planting the Seeds of Education."

(Now before I continue with Janice's story, how many apples did you see in your mind? Back to Janice...)

Janice looked at the apple and saw a different picture. She saw one apple, but she knew that Mrs. Carter always pushed her students for more. She thought to herself, "Mrs. Carter never gave a simple question on an exam before, so why would she start now? How could she just give us something so simple? How could the answer be just one?" She thought for sure that she would be the only one to get the bonus question right. Her one-word answer was "infinity."

Mrs. Carter began to realize where Janice was heading with her story. You see, Mrs. Carter hadn't looked beyond the answer of "one" when she was grading the assignment; she just wanted the students to see that the answers could be found by reviewing the math posters. The students only needed that little nudge to help them out. So when it came to correcting the papers, anything that didn't have a "one" as the answer was not even considered.

By now, Mrs. Carter was smiling from ear to ear and told Janice to explain her answer. "Please tell your parents and me how you found another correct answer."

Janice stated that the clue was in the holographic poster. When she saw the apple, she didn't see just one apple, she saw the possibilities of the apple. She looked much deeper, way beyond the outline of the apple, the color, the skin tone, the stem, and the leaves. She looked beyond the depth of the apple in the hologram. She saw that the apple had more than one answer, and the answer was *infinity*. The apple itself was one, none, and an infinite number. She went on to explain more.

The apple's genetic code contained the knowledge and ability for survival. The apple contains the blueprints for reproduction, growth, change, and adaptability. Janice used her newly expanded thought process and looked up pomology, the science behind apple and fruit production and growth. She learned that apples can grow wild and they can be cultivated. She learned that the apples we normally eat are cross-pollinated and can produce numerous strands and varieties. Who knows what cross-pollination would produce, if anything. And the life of an apple tree is not calculated, even though they can live to be 100 years old or more. The statement "Planting the Seeds of Education" made Janice realize there was more than one apple on the poster.

Janice continued, "The picture of the apple was captured inside a holographic poster, and I know that if you cut any holographic image in half, you would have two identical pictures of the original. If you cut one of those in half again, you would then have three pictures of the original. You could cut a small piece off the corner and still have a complete picture of the whole hologram in that tiny little piece. So this led to me to believe that the answer was infinity as well."

Janice was also a student of quantum mechanics. On the quantum level, all the subatomic particles that make up the atom become a solid when they are observed. There is a possibility, albeit rather small, that the entire apple could revert to wave form. All of the subatomic particles of the apple could be in multiple places at the same time, it could be in infinite parallel dimensions, and the Universe could be part of one big apple. So, there was no way to determine how many apples could be produced from one apple itself. Without any more data given from Mrs. Carter, the only other possibility was infinity or none. Since the apple was only a picture of an apple, and not the real thing, she chose infinity as her answer because the wave of probability collapsed and she saw an apple.

With this pride, she turned in her paper fully expecting to receive the bonus credit. When her paper was returned with a red "X" over the answer, all her newfound excitement was dashed to pieces. She felt like she had taken a huge step forward, only to be yanked back to the Stone Age and back into the world of finite knowledge. This crushing experience hurt her more than could ever be imagined, and from her perspective, what was the use of continuing if constrained to a finite realm? She wanted to stretch beyond this constraint into the next exciting level. She wanted the new expanse of infinite possibilities. Never again would there ever be just one apple.

Janice explained that she didn't really care so much about the extra five points for the bonus question, and she apologized for acting the way she had. She just wanted to continue growing outside the box.

Of course, Mrs. Carter gave her the bonus credit along with the opportunity to make up any missing assignments. She and Janice's parents were very proud of Janice and her new approach to learning.

Now, let's take this story and apply it to our own world. I ask you now, how many apples do *you* see?

HOW MANY ZYGOTES DO YOU SEE?

When you view a human zygote through a microscope, how many cells do you see? If you don't remember your biology from high school, a human zygote is the combination of the male sperm and a female egg, the beginning of life. When you look at this zygote, do you see the early developments of a human being, made up of 1, 2, 4, or 8 cells? Or, do you see tens of trillions of cells that make up a human being? Are there two or more answers? Did life take the finite and turn it into the infinite? When you see the zygote again, do you see only one cell that makes up a human being, or do you see all the cells that continue to grow, divide, reproduce, and replace old dying cells? If an adult has tens of trillions of cells, and the body replaces its cells every five to seven years, and the adult lives on average for at least eight decades, that's an awful lot of cells.

Now apply this to every individual human being living on this planet. When you see another person, do you see only the shell of a human being, or do you see a soul living right there with you? Do you see the personality that came into your life's timeline for a few moments, or do you see the many lives of the soul? Go beyond the surface. Go beyond the skin color, nationality, religious belief, and social standing. Go beyond the outer realm into a much deeper, more exciting place. Look into the soul. Look into the lives of the soul. How many lives are present in this one person (not counting possessions or multiple personalities—ha, ha)? It could be one, two, a thousand, or infinity.

If you hold a religious or spiritual belief that supports the ability for a soul to progress and learn by reincarnation, then you might see what is labeled as a young soul or an old soul. Maybe you have come in contact with someone like this, or maybe your soul is experiencing its first time in human form. Or, perhaps you have been here a few times and are working on a progression of similar experiences over and over again for comparison.

If you come from the opposite spectrum, maybe your religion allows you only one soul and one chance at life. Maybe you have only one lifetime to grow, evolve, or stay the same. And when you return your body to the Earth again, your soul goes to heaven, hell, limbo, or purgatory, or disappears into nothingness.

Maybe your belief system does not involve a soul. Your life could exist to experience and contribute to society in your own manner. Your actions are living on in the history of your family tree, your social group, or whatever means your life contributed to another. Unless you lived on an isolated island, you interacted in one way or another with others of your species. I hope it was a good interaction.

LAST THOUGHTS ON PERCEPTION AND TRUTH

I have been getting better at appreciating all the varieties of perception, and I have come to know that my way is not the only way. If we can all make that one tiny shift, our lives can become richer than any vein of gold found on our planet.

I also look forward to the day when our nations and governments will start sharing truth with the people in their own land and with other governments. When governments hide the truth, they only instill fear in others. Our country can be the first to lead the pack. That would be a great sign of courage and a willingness to live in peace and love.

Based on what you have read so far, would you rather blindly live by someone else's perceptions, or would you rather continue empowering yourself and creating your own truth while still accepting others if they see things differently? Take a moment and answer that question before you read the last paragraph.

From the beginning of this book, we have discussed deep levels of perception and truth. With each new thought you create, you empower yourself more. You are creating a new you based on your own perceptions instead of following the beat of someone else's drum. If you are at peace with yourself, you increase the chances of bringing more peace into your life. If you are happier inside, and are projecting happiness because you are taking responsibility for your actions, then you increase the chances that happy events will increase in your life. It becomes a positive snowball effect. Small little shifts are all it takes. It's now time to meet a friendly dog named Duke.

CHAPTER SIX

JOE'S DOG DUKE

L ATE SUMMER FINALLY BROKE and released its hold on the warm
humid days and long sticky nights in the mountains of Virginia. It
felt like autumn moved in later than usual in 1872, but it still moved
in with an expected welcome from everyone living in the hill country. This
meant that the folks could sit outside again at night without having to battle the bugs and sweat, which played havoc on their evening social hour.

There were two times of the year that folks in these parts really enjoyed—spring and autumn. These were the times when you could sit on
your porch after all your work and chores were done, relax with a cool
drink, and spend time with friends, family, and neighbors until the moon
reached high in the clear Virginia skies. The biggest decision at that time
for most folks was to figure out if they were going to sit on their porch, or
go visit one of their neighbors and chat the night away. It was rather common to let the hours pass by while watching the lightning bugs fill the
nearby meadows and pastures. One of the local tales boasted that the lighting bugs were so thick and bright in these parts that you could read a book
at night without lighting a candle.

Jack and Betty Schumann were taking their stroll over to the Pattersons'
house to share a pitcher of iced tea. They lived only a short distance away
from Paul and Mary, probably no more than four houses over. Now four
houses over in those days meant that it could take up to twenty minutes or

so to walk because of the amount of land between each home. But that didn't bother people back then; they enjoyed the space and open environment.

On the way to the Pattersons', Jack and Betty passed by a good friend of theirs, Joe Woods. Joe was a gentle fellow. He was always well-mannered, tipped his hat to the ladies, and offered a cigar to any of the gents who came within earshot. He was in his late fifties, tall, around six-foot-three, and had a long, white beard that came down to his upper chest. His schooling gave him a special air of dignity. By no means was he snobby or snooty. Most people in those parts would describe him as a "learned fellow."

Joe's wife passed away before the war, and he had no surviving children. His only family at the time consisted of a very large bloodhound named Duke. Joe and Duke were inseparable and did everything together. If Joe got up, even if it was to stretch his body and yawn, Duke would stand up beside him. If Joe went to the trade store for supplies, Duke was glued to his side, keeping pace with Joe's every step. You might have thought that Duke was Joe's personal bodyguard, but there wasn't a mean bone in Duke's body to speak of. He just liked being with Joe. Joe was his best friend. Joe was always scratching behind his ear, petting his head, and scratching his back hindquarter for him. You knew Duke liked this because his large branch-like tail would swish from side to side, almost knocking Joe over at times. When they would sit on the porch in the evenings, you could always hear Duke's tail thumping loudly against the leg of the chair. Some folks would say it was so loud that you could hear Duke's tail thumping a mile away.

Betty and Jack looked forward to their walk in the neighborhood, and it was especially nice to see Joe and Duke at their station, relaxing the early night away. Betty called out, "Good evening, Mr. Woods. It's a fine evening again, isn't it? What good news do you have to share with us this night?"

"Ah, good evening, Mr. and Mrs. Schumann," said Joe, "and a fine evening it is," as he tipped his hat. "I just got word that my new rocking chair will be in tomorrow at the county store, so Duke and I will be taking a buggy ride down the hill to bring home this fine piece of workmanship. It will be a grand evening tomorrow night. I've been looking forward to this new rocker for months. Isn't that right, Duke?" Duke looked up with a doggy grin, thumping his tail loudly against the firm leg of his owner's trusty chair.

"Could I offer you a cigar, Jack?" asked Joe.

"Not tonight, my old friend, but thanks for your kindness. Maybe I will stop by in a few days to admire your new rocker and share an evening smoke with you." With that said, Betty and Jack continued on to the Pattersons' house, making their way up the well-worn path to enjoy their pitcher of tea.

Once at Mary and Paul's home, both couples quickly settled in and engaged in the local gossip that one would expect from these good folks. Stories about hunting rabbits, wild turkey, and deer were traded back and forth between the men, while the women went on about how good the latest batches of canned beets and corn had turned out. Surely they were in contention to win a blue ribbon at the county fair this year for their tasty efforts.

Not forgetting to share the latest news, Betty told Mary that Joe would be getting a new rocking chair for his porch. Betty also mentioned how excited he seemed. Joe even got Duke's seal of approval and a few good thumps of his tail.

Everyone in the neighborhood loved Duke. Duke was one of those great dogs that never made much noise. He was always friendly, loved to be petted, and had a great spirit to him. On occasion, you would hear him barking while chasing a squirrel up a tree, but nothing much else. Duke was just a good old, sweet, loveable dog.

There was more gossip to share that evening, but it was getting late, so the Pattersons and the Schumanns decided to take a rain check on the remaining local news until tomorrow. They bid their farewells and started to part ways for the rest of the night. Before Jack and Betty made it off the porch, Mary invited them over for dinner the next day so they could share a wild turkey that Paul had brought home from his last hunting trip.

It was around 3 P.M. the following day when Betty called out for Jack. "Jack, it's time to head over to the Pattersons'. I want to get there in time to help Mary bake the biscuits and put my apple pie in their oven. Are you 'bout ready, dear?"

Jack answered back, "Of course, honey. I'll be right there. I just want to get that box of nails that I promised Paul. I'll meet you on the porch in a few minutes."

Jack and Betty made their way over to the Pattersons', passing by Joe's house as usual. "Joe must not be back from the county store yet. His old chair is still on the porch," said Jack. "We should make it a point to bring him a couple jars of those great beets and corn when we come to visit him. What do you think, Betty?"

"And maybe a slice of my tasty apple pie?" chuckled Betty. "That is, if there is any left when you and Paul get through with it."

After dinner, Jack and Paul went out to the shed to nail in a few loose boards with the extra nails Jack had brought over. They interrupted the nightly symphony of crickets with their loud banging and hammering. They worked hard and long, way into dusk. "Ah, now that this job is complete and off my honey-do list, it's time to relax with the ladies on the porch. You 'bout ready to drink some tea, Jack?"

"I'm always up for some tea and relaxing," laughed Jack.

As usual, the birds' songs continued to fade away as the nightly insects took over with their new chorus of evening melodies. It was another pleasant night, which meant more people would be on their porches again to enjoy the cool evening air. Paul, Jack, Betty, and Mary were sitting outside, already engrossed in another round of funny stories, when a most unusual blood-curdling scream broke their heavy laughter. It was a long, loud, and very scary sound. They had never heard anything like it before, and they couldn't tell which direction it was coming from. You could tell that they were all a little startled as they looked at each other with puzzlement in their eyes.

"What in tar-nation was that, Jack?" asked Paul. "Sounds like some poor critter got swallowed up by a black bear."

"It sure sounded like it, Paul. Maybe it was one of Farmer Tom's pigs on his way to the butcher house," answered Jack. "I don't hear it anymore, so it must be over. Let's get back to your funny story about your trip to the big city."

Time went on at the Pattersons'. Amusing stories and jokes were still the topic of choice as they chatted the night away. Once again, during another one of Mary's enticing stories, the most horrendous, blood-curdling howl filled the night air. Betty looked more concerned this time as she looked at Jack, and Mary was definitely more frightened as she held onto Paul's hand, giving it a tight squeeze for comfort. "What in tar-nation? What's the chance that two critters were swallowed up by the same bear?" blurted Paul.

"Maybe you and Paul should take a look, Jack. Take your gun with you and see what's out there," Betty said with a shaky voice.

Wanting to comfort their wives, both men got up and looked around the yard. They searched high and low, from one end to the other, but they found no sign of any animal that could have made that terrible noise. They looked at each other, shrugged their shoulders, and headed back to the porch.

"It's all right, ladies, there's nothing out there but lightning bugs. And unless they learned how to howl very loud, it seems you are safe," chuckled Paul. "All that walking around made me famished. How 'bout another piece of your delicious apple pie, Betty?"

As the night began to wind down, both couples mentioned that they had to get up early the next day to take care of a huge list of chores. They bid their farewells and wished each other a safe and happy night.

On the way back home, Jack glanced over at Joe's house. "Hey, looks like Joe's rocking chair made it from the county store onto his porch just fine. My, that's a fine piece of workmanship."

"I wonder where Joe and ole' Duke are?" asked Betty.

"All that terrible noise must have chased them inside," boasted Jack. "We should visit with him in a few days, and maybe he'll let me try out that new rocker."

It was relatively quiet for the rest of the night. Jack and Betty made it home safely and everyone in the neighborhood got a good night's sleep. No one heard the noise again that evening.

The next day rolled out a fair amount of sunshine with a few puffy clouds that hung lazily in the light blue sky. Jack and Betty were busy taking care of their list of chores and completely forgot about last night's excitement. Jack was hard at work adding new shelving in the cellar, which was badly needed for Betty and Mary's canning. Betty was in her sewing room finishing her mending so she could start on a new winter quilt. The Farmer's Almanac called for a colder winter that year.

Time slipped by quickly that autumn day. Lunchtime came and left without any takers and dinner snuck up on both of them without warning. "Betty, how 'bout we take a break for a bit? Do you think you could rustle up some of your biscuits and stew? I'm famished."

"That sounds great, dear. I'll start the stove and meet you at the picnic table for dinner as soon as it's hot."

Jack cleaned up from being in the cellar all day and went out to the picnic table to cool off. His wife joined him shortly with two bowls full of her tasty beef stew. "Here you go, dear. It's a good idea to eat outside at the picnic table. It's gorgeous outside again."

Just as they were finishing their last spoonfuls of stew, a nail-gripping scream filled the air. You could hear its echo rippling through the hillsides. It was the same blood-curdling howl that they heard the night before while sitting with the Pattersons. "Jack, I'm scared. What is that noise?"

"I don't know, Betty. It sounds like it's coming from over at Joe's place this time. Maybe I should go take a look. Let me get my gun and I'll check it out."

"I'm going with you, Jack. There's no way that I'm staying here alone."

Jack ran into the house, grabbed his gun and ammo bag, and rushed back down the stairs to meet Betty. "Betty, let's get going and fast. I hope Joe is all right." While on the path to Joe's house, the howl came back, and this time it was even louder and more frightening.

"Jack, I'm really scared. Maybe we should go back."

"No, Betty, we have to make sure Joe is OK. I'll protect you."

It only took another minute or two to reach Joe's house. They expected to see him outside with his gun since the terrible noise was louder for the third time as they approached his home. Much to their surprise, though, when they got close enough to Joe's house, all they saw was Joe sitting on his new rocking chair as peaceful as could be, with Duke lying at his side. He wasn't holding his gun, either. Nothing was out of the norm.

"Joe! Joe! Mr. Woods! Are you all right?" yelled Jack. "We heard the most terrible sounds coming from this area. It sounded like some poor animal was being attacked or mauled. We feared the worst. Did you hear those howls of terror?"

With an unusual grin, Joe smiled back and answered, "For sure, I did, Jack. I heard those noises. What's all the fuss about? Why did you bring your gun?"

Jack and Betty were completely puzzled by Joe's response. They didn't know how to react. They saw Joe sitting comfortably still in his new rocker, with Duke lying right at his side. Joe wasn't even the slightest bit concerned. He just sat there and smiled. He reached down to pet Duke and started rocking. Nothing was amiss. Joe was enjoying his new rocker, Duke was getting attention from his best friend, and there were no horrible sounds to be heard anywhere.

Suddenly, without warning, Duke's head jolted up from the floor and gave a blood-curdling howl. He howled and howled, then put his head back down on the porch floor. Poor Betty was scared half to death by Duke's blood-curdling scream. She didn't expect that kind of noise from Duke at all. When she heard it, she jumped right into her husband's arms, burying her head in his shoulder.

Jack was stunned. "Joe! What in the world has gotten into Duke? He's never acted like this before."

"Well, Jack, you see, ole' Duke here, well, he just likes sitting beside me no matter what. And if you watch as I rock back and forth, Duke's tail is in perfect rhythm with my rocker. When I move forward, his tail wags behind my chair and doesn't get caught by the rung. He's happier than can be. But just like life, every once in a while things get out of sync. And as you know, this brings a little excitement and sometimes a little turmoil."

"That's just ridiculous, Joe. Why doesn't Duke get up and move? Why in the world does he stay there? After getting his tail caught under the rocker once, you'd think he would high-tail it out of there."

"Well, I reckon that Duke doesn't take kindly to change, and the small amount of discomfort that he goes through when his tail gets caught under the rocker isn't enough to make him leave. He's becoming more human every minute. Go figure," chuckled Joe. "You see, I even tried to help him a few times last night and this afternoon. I moved my chair away from him a bit so his tail wouldn't get crushed, but he moved right next to me again. People do the same thing. They place themselves right back in situations that cause them minor pain, but they endure the pain because it's not bad enough to cause them to make a drastic change. He really does mimic us well. Have you seen people do that, Jack?"

"Wow, he must be the most human dog I've ever seen. I know plenty of people who are like that, including myself," said Jack. "We gravitate right back to what was comfortable, even if we get caught under the rocker once in a while."

"Do you mind if we try a little experiment, Joe? I think I can help Duke."

"Really?" asked Joe. He was intrigued by Jack's proposal. "What do you have in mind?"

Jack went over to Duke, stepped behind him, and lifted his heavy back end up and placed it on an angle away from the chair. Duke gave a big dog woof, but he didn't stop Jack from sliding him around. "There, let's see how Duke likes this. I didn't try to change the situation, and I didn't make a huge change in his life, either. All I did was angle his hind end away from the chair. That way, his head can still be right by your hand to get petted, and his tail is just out of reach from the back of the rocker. You see, Joe, sometimes all we need to do is make a little shift in life, a little shift in perception, and not make a complete change. Sometimes our perception is all we need to tweak."

"Well, I'll be, Jack. You *are* smarter than the average bear. Ole' Duke took right to this new place beside the rocker. He isn't moving back to the old spot, and his tail is swinging again just like a branch in a summer twister. Maybe he'll do this on his own next time we come out to the porch."

"Let's hope so, Mr. Woods. I think Betty would like her quiet evenings back again."

Tune in next chapter when you get to hear Duke say, "Woof, woof-woof, woof!"

CHAPTER SEVEN

ALLOWING CHANGE

CHANGE IS A WONDERFUL EVENT that takes place in everybody's life. Change keeps us alive, keeps us motivated, sometimes scares us, often excites us, and provides new opportunities for learning, growth, and personal experience. No matter how hard people try to stay the same or stop change from happening, change always wins. It's inevitable. This is a good thing, too. Change is one of those constants that people can rely on, just like the sun rising in the east. Well, until the poles shift and the sun rises in the south, north, or west. That's another change we can count on. In the meantime, we can still be confident that the sun will continue to rise for a long time, no matter which direction. There may even be a day when our sun will no longer be there as we know it. That's also a change we can rely on. No need to worry, though. This event is not expected to happen for about four to five billion years from now.

Here is something to think about. We experience change and enjoy something brand new every second of the day, and we never have to pay a dime for it. How do I know this? Well, as the Earth spins on its own axis, and as it rotates around the Sun, and as our solar system rotates, and as the solar system continues to expand outward in our Milky Way galaxy, and as our galaxy expands through the Universe, we are experiencing a brand new piece of space every single second of our lives. Unless you suffer from cainotophobia, which is the fear of change, this is a remarkable event.

We don't even need a travel agent for this. We get to enjoy a new piece of space from the time we are born until the day we leave our bodies. No one else in the galaxy can experience the same place in space that you and I get to experience. How awesome is that?

I know this; change can be very simple and takes no conscious effort on our part. Our bodies change constantly, sometimes for the better, and sometimes for the worse. Our cells divide, repair, grow old, and die. It's been said that we get a new body and outlook every seven years. Some cells die off faster than other cells, and some cells do not continue to rejuvenate. Once you lose your baby teeth, you only get one more shot at each tooth. If you lose your replacement tooth, that's it—no more tooth. Whether it's a one-year or a seven-year replacement package, I have noticed a marked change in my outlook and body structure as time has gone by.

It's fascinating to watch how people react to change. As you would guess, some people truly welcome all types of change in their lives. These people love hearing fresh new ideas. They seek out new variations in food, clothing, and trends. They welcome the unexpected. These people thrive on daily transformations, even if they encounter a few bumps and bruises along the way. They take the good with the bad and embrace each and every new event. While others cringe at the very thought of change. These people choose to live their lives without a single alteration or adjustment. They shudder at the idea of something different happening to them or around them. Their goal is to keep the same structured routine working like clockwork day in and day out. Security in the known is what they live for. I have heard that people don't like change, but I don't believe this is true for all people. It is a phrase that is taught. Unfortunately, some people believe it and base their life on this statement, and others have found a way to use it as an excuse or a weapon.

Now if you are reading this book, I imagine that you are looking for some type of change. Even if you don't agree with all of the content, you are still changing. You are reaffirming your current beliefs and making them stronger. A strengthened belief system is a change. Or, you are shifting your ideas to allow room for transformation and variety. Don't look now, but either way, you are changing. See, it doesn't hurt. Good for you.

So, let's assume there is something you would like to change in your life, something that would improve your life or make you happier. And if there is nothing you would like to alter in your life, then you can use this information to pass along to others and help them with their growth and pursuits. Here are some thoughts to consider.

Getting something to change in your life is really very easy. It may seem hard at times, but it really is easy. Here is one of the major deciding factors. Are you allowing change to happen? I am not talking about change that occurs naturally, like your body growing, or the weather changing daily. Those are changes that you can't stop even if you wanted them to. I am talking about a new goal, a new desire, or a new outlook. These are the changes we are going to focus on. Now in order to start the process, you have to establish your desire. Then you have to allow the change to take place.

Take a moment right now to define a new goal, or use one of the goals you chose back in Chapter 1. Think of something new that you really want in your life. Don't read another word until you define this again. Fix a picture of a person, a place, a thought, or an event that you would like to change, alter, transform, or improve in one way or another. Start the process right now. It's easier than you think, and it's fun. Give it a whirl.

Congratulations! You have taken another step towards success. See this event in your mind again. Make this picture last as long as possible.

After you have made your choice, say these words out loud to yourself and see the change happening in your mind: "I allow change to take place in my life. I welcome any change that will improve my life and improve the world around me. I welcome change."

Good for you. That was step number two. That wasn't so hard, was it? I have found that saying your thoughts out loud has a much stronger effect on your belief system than saying words in your mind. Adding visualization to the process will aid in collapsing the wave of potential and will help make your desire become a reality. We will cover a few more steps that will help you with personal change in this chapter.

For good measure, say these words out loud again and see the change happening in your mind. "I allow change to take place in my life. I welcome any change that will improve my life and improve the world around me. I welcome change." I'll bet that felt good. Feel free to modify any of these words to match your individual needs.

BATHTUBS AND RUBBER DUCKS

Image yourself sitting in an empty bathtub. You are calm, relaxed, and ready to embark on a timeless adventure. You create the perfect ambiance in the room by dimming the lights and controlling the sound to meet your eclectic tastes. Your hunger to fill the tub with warm, soothing water begins to grow. You anticipate the feeling when the water rushes onto your skin, creating a rhythmic massage of free-flowing ecstasy. You turn on the faucet and torrents of fresh clear liquid begin to surge all around you. The rushing pulse from the stream feels electric against your skin. As time goes by, you feel more of the glassy beads forming on your sensitive flesh. Your outside perception is now changing. You accept the insatiable feelings of water as it wraps around every inch of your body. Your body temperature changes to match the warm embrace. You know what this feels like. You begin to remember. You adjust to your environment. Slowly, more water surges onto your skin until you are completely covered in liquid silk.

The tub has completely filled with a watery bliss. You feel safe, comforted, and secure. Your body has completely adjusted to the change in your surrounding environment. You accept and welcome this transformation. The water has reached the rim of the basin, and any major motion or disturbance will cause the water to breach the barrier and overflow. You decide to remain as calm and as motionless as possible. You choose calm over chaos. You choose stagnation over motion. It feels good to relax and enjoy.

Time begins to fade. Your perceptions of reality come to a slow crawl. Everything feels wonderful. For a few sensational moments, all of life is well. Life is predictable and enjoyable again. But change doesn't stop here; even the delightful world of this watery heaven changes how it feels against your body. The water begins to cool and your skin begins to shrivel. New thoughts and desires are set in motion. You say in your mind, "Do I stay in the tub, even though the water is getting colder? Do I add more water and risk changing the atmosphere of stillness and bliss? Do I try to make an escape and leave the tub?" All of these options will cause chaos. Any action that you take will cause a surge of water to run over the side.

All is not lost, though. Change is a natural part of evolution. There are ways to allow change without causing chaos. There is a way to allow change in this situation as well. So let's recap. The tub is full to the rim, and any movement you make will cause instant ripples and commotion that will result in an overflow of water. Adding more water is not an option, yet, as this will also cause a torrent of water to run over the side. So what is the next crucial step?

Before I reveal this simple answer, notice how much this imagery could easily mirror the life of someone we know or even ourselves. We have filled our daily lives with safe, motionless, predictable routines. In time, our friends, family, co-workers, and neighbors will also move silently into predictable patterns that are repeated daily, weekly, and even yearly. We want change, but how do we go about beginning the process without making waves? Of course, there is no way to guarantee that waves will never happen, so accept the overflow if it does occur. Water evaporates in time, and so do all events. Ripples in a pond fade in intensity as they travel farther from the source. Emotional vibrations from an event will also fade from the initial timeline if you allow them to.

So here is the simple answer. Allow change to start in your life by releasing part, or all, of the old patterns that no longer serve your present or future self. I am going to say this again because it is very important. Change works best when you allow part or all of your old belief patterns, actions, or reactions to be released or set aside. While in the bathtub, it's easiest to open the drain for a short while and empty out some of the cold water. This simple action will free up room in the tub and allow for additional warm water. The free space you've created by releasing the old could also give you enough room to get out of the tub without causing a major overflow. By releasing the old, you allow new opportunities to come in. If you choose not to release the old, you could end up seeing your rubber ducky floating down the hallway from your abrupt actions. Goodbye, rubber ducky. Sniff.

I want you to know that I am not telling you to abandon your current belief system. I am not telling you to quit your job before you find a new one. I am not telling you to leave your current relationship in hopes of a better one. I am giving you suggestions that can help with the process of change. You have to decide how much to release. There is no magic answer, and every situation will be different. You must trust yourself and follow your instincts. Feel free to seek counsel if you are not up to making the decision on your own, but make the decision based on your knowledge and perception, not because someone says you must do it.

This bit of information is a great motivator to clean out your room, house, or apartment. If you want fresh new energy to come into your home, give it some room so there is no major commotion when the energy finds its way into your living space. If you've ever done a major spring cleaning, you know how good it feels to let go of the old. What a great feeling it is to be able to park your car in your garage again, walk into your closet without the fear of being able to get back out, or see a clean empty space that used to be filled with clutter. And don't just throw away all your old stuff. If there is a way to allow others to benefit from your temporary possessions, give them away. Other people are also looking for new energy to come into their lives as well. As you give, you receive. Please, if you let old stuff go, don't wish for the same stuff back again. That wouldn't be very productive, now, would it? Unless what you receive back into your life is love or chocolate.

LESSONS FROM A SHOE RACK

My wife gave me a great example. She reminded me that change is similar to a woman's shoe rack. You know, similar to the ones you might find hanging on the back of a closet door. Picture this in your mind. There is a woman with all of her most prized shoes hanging on her shoe rack. Each pair of her shoes has a special space reserved for it, almost like a place of status. In time, all of the shoe spaces became filled with pair after pair of her favorite shoes. This woman wouldn't dream of getting rid of any of them, either. Each pair goes perfectly with her favorite outfits and can't be replaced. Eventually, this woman's shoe rack becomes so packed that it can't support another pair of shoes. Some of the slots already have two or three pairs of shoes stuffed inside them. There is no more room for change. Can any of you relate to this?

A few weeks later, this woman goes out shopping, and lo and behold, she sees the most incredible pair of new shoes. She must have them to match the new outfit she recently bought. She comes home, looks at the shoe rack, and has to make a decision. She knows she wants her new shoes on the rack, but she doesn't know where to put them. If she tries to shove them into one of the overstuffed holes, the shoes will fall out and get scuffed or damaged. If she pushes too hard, the entire shoe rack could fall. Something must give. This woman will not dream of throwing out any of her shoes.

So the obvious comes to mind. (No, it was not to build a bigger shoe rack.) Instead, this woman decides which pair of shoes she is willing to take off the rack to make room for the new ones. She doesn't throw away her shoes, either; she just finds a different place for them. You don't always have to let go completely of what you have in order to make a smooth change. But there must be room if you want to avoid chaos.

DUKE'S NEXT ADVENTURE

Joe and Duke were over at the Pattersons' getting a piece of Betty's tasty apple pie. They finished the short walk back to their home and decided to enjoy another evening on their porch. Before Duke settled down, he looked out into the yard and saw a squirrel running away from him with the greatest of haste. Duke wasn't in the mood to chase the squirrel around the yard, so he gave him his signature, "Woof, woof-woof, woof!"

Joe patted his head and said, "That's a good boy. You're doing a great job protecting me from those squirrels." Joe sat down in his rocker, and Duke took his faithful position by his side. Duke made sure he was on a slight angle so his tail wouldn't get smashed by the back of the rocker. (See, you can teach old dogs new tricks.)

After Joe finished his pie, Duke abruptly raised his head and let out a deafening, blood-curdling scream, reacting just as he did the other day. This startled Joe, and he dropped the plate and fork on the porch. Duke yelled for a moment, then put his head back down on the wooden surface.

"Duke, what's the problem, boy? Your tail wasn't struck by the rocker this time. What's the matter?"

Joe looked around Duke to see if he was in any pain. He couldn't see anything physically wrong. "Maybe it was a bad dream about the other day, huh, boy?" Joe rubbed the top of his head. "You let me know if something is the matter, all right?"

Joe cleaned up the plate, took it inside, and Duke followed him in the house and back out to the porch again. Then they both took their same positions as before.

About ten minutes later, Duke raised his head one more time. He wailed and howled as if in terrible pain, and then put his head back down on the wooden surface.

"Duke, what is the matter? Your tail is nowhere near the rocker. Are you hurting? Maybe we need to take you to the vet tomorrow. Here, get up for a minute and let me take a look at you."

Duke stood up and Joe looked him over for any cuts, bruises, or tick bites. Just when Duke was ready to lie back down, Joe noticed that one of the boards had begun to splinter and part of a jagged edge and a nail tip were sticking up where Duke was lying down.

"That must be what's causing the problem. I'll take care of that for you tomorrow, Duke. I lent my hammer and saw to Jack. Do you think you could find a new place to sit for tonight?"

Duke had already changed once. He wasn't ready for another shift so quickly, so he plopped right back down on the pointy edges.

Along came Jack with the saw and hammer. (Synchronicity was in the air that night.) As Jack approached the porch, Duke let out one more howl.

"Joe, why is Duke hollering again? He's nowhere near the rocker."

"Well, Jack, Duke likes his new place, but something else came up. Part of the board is splintering and exposing the edge of a nail. It must be causing him some pain, but not enough to make him move. I was going to come over and get my things from you tomorrow so I could take care of this board for Duke."

"No time like the present, Joe. I can empathize with Duke, though. There are plenty of times in my life when I had something that bothered me, but it didn't hurt badly enough to change the situation. I screamed, hollered, and complained at times, but I never changed my situation. Actually, sometimes I didn't want to change. The benefits were so great at times that a little pain wouldn't cause me to look for something better. I already had the best situation ever in my life."

"Once again, Jack, you are a smart feller. Do you want to help me fix the porch?"

"Sure, I'd love to. It's the only way we can get a good night's sleep," laughed Jack.

They fixed the porch in less than a minute, and Duke flopped down beside Joe, happier than can be.

Joe and Duke lived happily ever after, and Duke no longer howled while lying next to Joe. I hope this story helps your life in many ways.

KEEPING YOUR WOODEN BOAT AFLOAT

Remember, every wooden boat needs nails to keep the frame together, to keep boards firmly held in place, and to create a solid structure for transporting people and cargo. Some nails squeak and groan during a long voyage, but they help the boat stay afloat. It is possible to remove nails and keep your boat intact to eliminate the squeaks, but if you remove too many nails, you'd better have a bunch of life preservers on board.

You can easily relate some of life's experiences to this boat analogy and Duke's time spent on the porch. We hold our lives together with perceptions, relationships, jobs, hobbies, thoughts, ideas, and belief systems. Any one of these can cause discomfort at times. The question to ask is this: Does the situation, thought, idea, or perception cause so much pain in your life that you would rather remove the nail, or is it worth the pain to keep the situation the same? Is it possible to shift the nail to a new place, or shift the situation somehow so it no longer causes as much pain as before? It's OK to howl sometimes. What do you want to do after the howling is over?

As you're reading these concepts, use your own judgment for making change. This is another of your greatest gifts. Use your self-empowerment to create the best situation for everyone to enjoy. You could always ask me to build your boat and sail it for you, but then it would be my boat. I would be the captain. It's time for you to be the captain and enjoy the freedom of the seas. Where do you want to sail your boat? Plot your course, and let down the sails. Ahoy, Mateys!

THE MAJOR SHIFT

Our last stop on change is the biggest one of all. If you had only one thing in your life that you could shift or change, what if that one thing was *fear*? Imagine how your life would change if you could transform fear into courage, love, and confidence. Think of how the entire world could change. And if you've decided you don't need to change, I say, "Good for you!" What if all the people who wanted to keep fear in their lives helped all those who no longer wanted to live in fear? What a wonderful place this would be!

Think about it. People would no longer be afraid to share their true feelings for fear of being rejected, ridiculed, or shunned. People would no longer fear dying and could live fuller lives. People would no longer be afraid to take a chance for fear of failure or judgment. They could live their lives to their fullest potential. And most rewardingly, people could live in a peaceful world, no longer afraid of not having enough land, possessions, or wealth.

Like many of you, I believe in a balance of fear. Without fear, we could not know courage. We need fear for a reference point. Without fear, we could not know unconditional love. Without fear, we would not have heroes. But too much fear can cause harm to one's self and to others. Living in complete fear is as tasty as a nose nugget sundae with extra mucus sauce, body hair, and scalp flakes sprinkled on top. Yuck! I hope that all of you can find your balance of fear so you can enjoy every second on this beautiful planet that is filled with so many beautiful people and so many beautiful things.

LEARNING FEAR

I believe that the majority of fear in life is learned. It is learned from our parents, teachers, friends, and ourselves when we get old enough to make decisions on our own. "Don't climb too high; you could get hurt." That could become a fear of heights or flying. "Don't wear those clothes; they aren't flattering and don't look good on your figure." This could develop into a fear of other people's perceptions and could cause low self-esteem, low self-love, and even weight management problems. "Don't run through the house; you could break a leg." This could prevent someone from going into sports. "Why do you procrastinate? You never finish your projects." This could result from a fear of being judged. Statements as simple as these could lead to a lifetime of being controlled by fear.

When a child is born, there isn't much fear in that baby's eyes. Yes, I believe that cellular memory and genetics do play a part in the development of fear, but I also believe that the majority of fear is taught. A baby is not afraid to put things in its mouth until it is taught otherwise. A baby can crawl up to a muddy worm and put it in its mouth without thinking twice about this being a good or bad event. All you see is a baby with a huge smile on its face and a worm wiggling around in its lips. It's other people who make this event a bad thing, and now the baby could be afraid of snakes, worms, or anything that wiggles.

I am sure you realize that some fears are good. I tell my clients to always keep the fears that keep them alive for as long as they want. You can release a fear, but be aware of the consequence if you try to go beyond balance. You may release your fear of flying, but don't jump out of a plane without a parachute just to prove you are no longer afraid of heights. You can release your fear of being under water, but don't shoot out of a torpedo tube from a submarine at 100 fathoms without a pressure suit and a good air supply. You can release your fear of spiders, but don't pick up a black widow and put it on your tongue. You can release a fear without placing yourself, or your life, in harm's way.

KNOWING YOUR FEARS

You knew this question was coming. What are your fears? If you don't want to be afraid anymore, and you don't know what makes you afraid, it could make the transformation take much longer than necessary. Do you know what your fears are? Can you define all the fears in your life right now? We have all heard that many people are afraid of speaking in public. Are you afraid to get up in front of millions of people with only one chance to make an impression? Are you afraid of dying because you don't know what will happen in the afterlife? Are you afraid of needles? Are you afraid of snakes, spiders, dogs, cats, or anything that can nip at your skin? Are you afraid that this list will never end? Knowing your fears is the first step. Now you have the choice to change or stay the same.

One of the best pieces of advice I've received in life was given to me when I was a child. I don't remember the event, but I know it was said to me by many different people. (Thank you to all the people who said this to me.) I remember that I didn't want to do something because I was afraid. The other person noticed my fear and asked, "What is the worst thing that could happen if you tried?" I thought about the question and made up my mind that the worst thing that could happen was not trying at all. I may not have succeeded the first time around, but I kept going until I accomplished my goal. And I am very glad I tried. You have probably heard that question in your life at one time or another. I know I have heard it many times from my parents, grandparents, teachers, and loved ones. It's always good to hear it again to help you move beyond fear and embrace life's greatest opportunities. "What is the worst thing that could happen if you tried?"

Almost every goal that my hypnosis clients have is related to a fear in one way or another. The only thing that I do with hypnosis that doesn't relate completely to fear is past life regression. (I call this a soul record, and not past life regression, as that person's next lifetime might actually take place in the past. But that is another topic for another book.) I work with clients to help them transform their fear into courage and to release the subconscious links to the initial events that anchored the fear in the first place.

HOW CAN YOU RELEASE FEARS?

We've already covered a few ways to transform fear. Here are a few more techniques that I've come up with, including what was mentioned earlier.

1. Consult with a counselor, therapist, empowerment coach, or spiritual leader. Meet with more than one if you wish, and discuss your fears. Sometimes, getting your fears out into the open takes care of the fear all by itself.
2. See a certified hypnotist. Hypnosis helps people release blocks and start new habits that they are not able to do on a conscious level.
3. Just let go of the fear. It can be done. I have seen others do it, and you never know if this might be the easiest way or not until you try.
4. Face your fear without placing yourself, or anyone else, in harm's way. Seek council again.
5. If you are spiritual, use your faith and prayer.
6. Meditate on the fear and see what comes to mind.
7. Shift your focus from the negative to the positive. So, instead of seeing yourself in situations of fear, see how you can transform the situation into courage. Always see yourself becoming more courageous than before.
8. Write out your fears and write down the worst thing that could happen. Sometimes, when we write down our deepest emotional blocks—like fear, anger, and hatred—we find a solution to our own problem, or we just let it go.

SOUL REBIRTHING

Soul Rebirthing is a technique that I developed a few years ago to help people bring forward their ability to experience life from a new perspective of openness and a freedom from past perceptions. It is an easy technique and involves directing your subconscious to accept a new program that will benefit your life. (We will talk about the subconscious in much more detail in Chapter 10.) Soul Rebirthing only takes one minute to perform.

Our first memory of openness and our ability to explore without preconceived perceptions occurred when we were first born. I have heard that all a baby knows is love when it is born. Wouldn't it be great to see everything through the eyes of love again? This technique will rebirth our ability to perceive life with love and utilizes something that we all do quite naturally—breathing. The last thing we do in life is to exhale. The first thing we do in life is to inhale. So if you want to anchor loving emotions from your birth state, breathe with openness as you did when you were a baby.

This technique is not a magic pill. The shift in perceptions will occur, but the change will happen in small perceptible shifts. You may not notice anything right away, but the more you do this, the more you increase the chance that your desired effect will become a new reality. Here is how it works. (Read all the steps before you perform the technique.)

STEP 1. Find a peaceful place. Peace promotes peace. Love promotes love. A place where most people have a moment to themselves is in the bathroom. I hear that a lot of people meditate in the bathroom because that's the only place they have a moment of peace to themselves. You don't have to do it there. It's only a suggestion. Another tip is to do Soul Rebirthing in the morning before you start your day and in the evening before you go to bed.

STEP 2. Have a thought in mind that you want to increase your ability to see life with love and complete openness to your perception. It could go something like this: "I see life through the eyes of unconditional love, and I perceive every event with a clean and clear perception."

STEP 3. Breathe in for 4, 6, or 8 counts and hold your breath for just a moment.

STEP 4. Exhale all of your air, and do this for at least the same number of counts that you inhaled. If you inhaled for 4 counts, exhale for 4 or 5 counts. If you inhaled for 6 counts, exhale for 7 or 8 counts.

When you exhale, allow your shoulders to drop and relax. (A lot of people hold tension or stress in their shoulders. If you know of a specific place on your body where you hold stress, relax that part of your body when you exhale.)

STEP 5. Hold your breath out for a moment, but don't do it too long where it's uncomfortable or not safe—2 or 3 counts will do. This will be the subconscious anchor for Soul Rebirthing that you will reinforce when you inhale again.

STEP 6. Say your intention while you are holding your breath out and when you inhale again. For example: "I see life through the eyes of unconditional love, and I perceive every event with a clean and clear perception. I ask my subconscious to anchor this for me every time I inhale."

STEP 7. Repeat steps 3 through 6 two more times, or as many as you wish. I like to do things in threes.

STEP 8. Believe, and love. You increase your chances of success if belief and love are the core emotions behind every action.

Feel free to perform this technique for as long as you like. If you really want to increase your chances for success, every time you experience something new in your life with love and an open perception, thank your subconscious for helping you. Your subconscious is there to help in all ways and wants to please you. The more you use positive reinforcement with your subconscious, the more your subconscious will try to keep pleasing you. Give to yourself and receive from yourself. By creating a happier you, you are creating a happier world, one thought at a time. Cool, huh?

The next story is one of my favorites. It will help inspire you to never give up, create a desire to reach your goal, and to support others along the way. We now meet Michael and Lucie.

CHAPTER EIGHT

WHEN LIFE GIVES YOU MILK CANS

I N THE GREAT PACIFIC NORTHWEST, a special flock of Canadian geese finished their long flight home to settle down for the spring and summer months. As most people know, these remarkable creatures can fly amazing distances in a short period of time. They travel hundreds of miles in their familiar V formation to migrate for safer habitat and better surroundings. With every powerful flap of its wings, each goose cuts through the wind and helps create an updraft for the goose that follows close behind. This lift makes it easier for all the geese to conserve their energy and fly longer distances. In addition, one by one, each goose takes its turn up front, sacrificing itself against the elements and using even more energy as the leader.

Admirably, the geese at the back of the formation always support the leader with positive honking sounds. Because they help each other, they are able to fly much farther and longer than if they were on their own. Every goose who spends time at the front receives huge amounts of praise, encouragement, and thanks for helping the flock reach its final destination.

All of the migratory birds seem to have their own migration song. They honk, sing, or chirp away, giving their personal chorus of praise. I can just imagine what they might be saying. "Stay the course. You can do it!

You are a strong goose and can fly miles and miles. We are very proud of you. Your flying skills are incredible. You have great stamina and strength. Your sacrifice is greatly appreciated!"

This one special flock of geese especially loved coming home to the budding trees and flowers that paint the scenic landscape of Seattle. This was a great place for a flock of geese to raise their young. Water habitat could be found all around in local streams, ponds, and tiny rivers. Food was plentiful, with an abundance of tasty green grasses and multitudes of insects to satisfy their diets. And of course, there was great shelter provided by the countryside and local farms for raising their babies.

Tabitha, a young female goose, had just turned two years old. She knew this was a special time in a goose's life when one finds a mate and starts a family. Canadian geese usually remain monogamous and stay together for life, so finding a loving partner is not something a goose takes for granted.

There was more flirting and courting going on during mating season than you would find at a middle school dance. Just like a teenage boy might push a girl into a locker as a sign of affection, the young ganders boyishly bumped into the young females so they could stand out from the crowd. To increase their chances, the young males jerked their necks up and down and flapped their wings wildly. They puffed up their broad chests, ruffled their feathers, and gave manly boasting honks.

It didn't take long before an excellent suitor presented himself to Tabitha. A young gander named Sam approached with confidence and poise. His straight black neck and characteristic white under chin gave him an extra regal presence. He didn't need to flash his wing span or prance around chasing girls. Sam had already proven himself and earned a great reputation in the flock for his bravery on their flight home to Seattle.

Tabitha recognized him right away. He was the first two-year old to lead the formation when they were migrating home. As a young male, Sam spent more time at the front than anyone could remember. He took the brunt of the worst weather and never looked back or fell out of position. His strength and leadership was an inspiration to the entire flock, especially the elders and young females.

When Sam looked into Tabitha's eyes, she knew they would be together forever. He would make a great mate and father for her babies. Tabitha's parents were also supportive. They both saw how strong Sam was in flight.

He was a great match for Tabitha. Both of them could easily protect a new batch of goslings until they were old enough to care for themselves.

Sam and Tabitha walked right up to each other. They caressed necks, ruffled their feathers for a moment, and took position by each other's side. Time seemed to disappear, and they became oblivious to everything else. After a short stroll away from the group, they nestled down at the edge of the field and enjoyed getting to know each other. As they began their life together, still continuing the courtship with glances and neck rubs, they watched as the rest of the two-year-olds paired off. The activities finally wound down as each of the pairs found a peaceful spot in the meadow to call their own.

A month or two passed, and the flock was already buzzing with good news. Eggs were appearing in all the nests, and this made the new couples extremely happy. Everyone was excited and shared their egg counts. Tabitha and Sam were also blessed. They had six healthy eggs. All told, there were over fifty eggs counted in the flock.

Tabitha kept faithful watch over her nest. With her flight feathers gone, she and her eggs were more vulnerable than ever. Sam made sure to keep a faithful watch for predators and anyone else who could harm Tabitha and their unborn babies. He made sure that everyone stayed a safe distance away and chased anyone that came too close to the nest.

The first three weeks passed by as quickly as a brisk summer shower. The eggs were incubating perfectly as Sam and Tabitha took turns keeping them warm and protected. Baby geese usually start hatching within a lunar cycle, so it wouldn't be long before the goslings cracked their shells.

Sure enough, just like Mother Nature intended, the eggs started to hatch on the new moon. One after the other, Sam and Tabitha's goslings broke free from their shells and emerged into a brand new world of wonderment and excitement.

As you would expect, proud parents were flapping their wings wildly and proclaiming the arrival of their babies. Heads were held high as they honked into the wind. Sam and Tabitha had already picked out the names for their children. The first out of the shell was Lucie, followed seconds behind by Michael. The other babies were named Gabe, Ralph, Uri, and Zack.

Lucie and Michael had a special brother and sister bond right from the start. Their eggs had always been side by side in the nest, and when they broke out of their shells, the first move they made was toward each other.

Michael and Lucie were inseparable from that moment on. Where one went, the other was sure to follow. As Michael made his first gosling sounds, Lucie answered right back. (Lucie and Michael might have created the game of Marco Polo.) In a few days, Lucie was the first to stumble out of the nest and feel the grass under her feet, only to be run into by Michael. And while Lucie was the first of the newborns to stretch her wings, she immediately found herself being fanned by Michael a few seconds later. It was as if they had hatched from the same egg.

Not much time passed before all the goslings were lined up between Sam and Tabitha for their daily walks. Exploring the countryside had always been the high point of their day. Everywhere Sam and Tabitha's family went, their stroll became a new adventure movie with Michael and Lucie as the main characters. The two of them showed incredible courage, boldness, and innocence at all times, and they investigated everything without fear or worry. Sam just about had a heart attack when Michael poked his beak at a slithering snake and asked, "Dad, what was that?" In similar fashion, Lucie strayed into the open field just as a bald eagle soared overhead. Lucie told her mother, "I just wanted to get a better look, Mom. The eagle looked so pretty soaring high above in the sky."

More than once, Michael and Lucie ventured away from the flock to play their favorite game of honk-and-follow. They took turns chasing each other and honking to see how many times they could walk around the pasture without passing out from exhaustion. None of the other goslings could even come close to the number of times they circled around the grassy field.

After mastering this game on land, Michael and Lucie took their fun to the water. They loved making circles around their family during their daily swim. Tabitha and Sam couldn't have been more proud. Sometimes they would let Michael and Lucie lead the group as they gave their loving honks of support from behind.

The goslings' wings were getting stronger by the day. They weren't ready to fly yet, but you could see them stretching and flapping their wings to build up their flying muscles. It was at this time, as tradition dictated, that all the new goslings met with the leader of the flock before they took to the skies. Tron was a strong male goose. He had led his group safely back and forth for more than ten migrations. Everyone respected his knowledge and guidance.

Tron enjoyed this special gathering. His words of wisdom and stories always captured the young geese's attention. He shared important survival tips, and he was the first one to give them flying lessons. At the end of his speech, Tron would gather the young geese in pairs under his wings. He would give the newborns a special message that was meant just for them. Then he would repeat this process until all the geese heard their message and felt the strength of Tron's love for each and every one of them.

When it was Michael and Lucie's turn, Tron pulled them in extra close. He looked deeply into both of their eyes and said, "Together, you two can do anything." He looked at them again and said, "Together, you two can accomplish great feats." And one more time, he said, "When you two work together, there is nothing you can't do." He gave them a final big squeeze with his powerful wings and scooted them on their way.

As part of the passage into the flock, all the young geese were taken to the highest point of land near the meadow. This is where Tron and all of the parents taught the goslings how to take off and land safely. From the top of this hill, you could see the snowy cap of Mount Rainier through the trees. At the bottom of the hill was an extremely soft patch of high grass. It was a perfect landing site for new flyers who sometimes needed a cushion for an emergency crash landing.

Michael and Lucie were especially curious about this white-capped mountaintop. "Mom! Mom! What's all that white stuff on the tall hill?" asked Michael. "It looks like someone covered the ground with a big white blanket."

"Well, Michael, that white covering all over the mountain is called snow. You will get to see it in a month or so when you are able to fly," said his mother.

"Snow? What's snow? Can we go see it now? Please, Mom and Dad, please, please?" begged Michael.

Sam replied, "To answer your question, Michael, snow is very cold water that has turned white. Sometimes it can be hard, and sometimes it can be soft. It all depends on how much snow you touch at one time, my boy. There will be plenty of time for us to see snow later."

Lucy piped in, "Mom, Dad, we have to go to the snowy mountain now. White water sounds so cool. We have to go. Please? Please?"

"Snow, snow, snow!" was the new chant from Michael and Lucie.

"Patience, little ones. Once your wings are strong enough, we will all take a trip to the mountain so you can feel snow. But for now, we must head back to the meadow before it gets dark.

All the way down the hill, Michael and Lucie talked excitedly about how great it would be to feel white water under their feet. "I wonder if you can swim through snow?" chuckled Lucie.

"I don't know, but I'm sure going to try," said Michael. "I'm going to fly head first into the powdery stuff and pretend it's a huge pond of cold water."

The next day, Sam and Tabitha decided to take their family to the farm that lay just beyond the training hill. There was a large pond on the property where their close cousins, the ducks and swans, made their home. It was important to introduce their babies to the ducks and swans because, like geese, they also migrate south for the winter, and there was a lot to learn from other species who shared similar lifestyles and passions.

"OK, kids. Down to the lake so you can swim with the ducks and swans," said Sam. And off they went. Tabitha was in front, the young ones in the middle, and Sam took up the rear.

The young ducklings, swans, and goslings began playing together immediately. They stretched their wings to see who had the widest wing span, they held their breath under water to see who could do it the longest, and they played follow-the-leader until the sun slipped below the top of the hills. Their parents looked on happily and talked about their next big trip down south.

Michael and Lucie spent a lot of time chatting with their new friends. They wanted to know if any of them had seen or felt white water like the snow on top of Mount Rainier. One of the ducklings said, "I've seen white water. The farmer keeps it in large metal containers in the barn. I don't know where it comes from, but he always has buckets full of it. He brings out at least one large bucket a day. We were told to stay away, so I don't know how snow is made in the barn. We heard a story about a duck that went into the barn once and was never seen again."

Michael and Lucie looked at each other with great excitement. They weren't fazed in the least by the duckling's warning. This was their chance to see snow up close without having to wait a month or two to fly to the mountain.

Lucie paddled beside Michael and whispered, "Michael, let's sneak away from the flock tonight and come back to the barn. I saw an opening between the boards that's just big enough for us to squeeze through. We can find the snow buckets, dive in, and be back before anyone knows we were gone."

"That's a great idea, Lucie. I was thinking the same thing. We'll come back just after the sun goes down and everyone is asleep."

As the sun fell below the edge of the horizon, Lucie and Michael positioned themselves at the far end of the nest. This would help make their silent escape easier and lessen the risk of waking up their parents and brothers. They waited patiently for about an hour after sunset before making a move or talking to each other.

"Psst. Michael, are you asleep?"

"No, Lucie, I think everyone else is asleep, though. I'll go first, and you follow right behind me."

"OK, but don't get too far ahead of me. I don't want to get separated on the way."

"I won't lose you, Lucie. This is going to be so cool. I can't wait to feel the snow on my feet."

"Shhh, Michael, you don't want to wake everyone before we get to the barn, do you?"

Off they went. Lucie stayed right on top of Michael's tail feathers as they waddled their way through the woods and underbrush. Everything was illuminated by the bright full moon that hung high over head. "Michael, if we stay off the path, will we be able to find the barn before morning?"

"Lucie, I can smell the snow. I know where we are going. Besides, we have to stay off the path to avoid any predators."

"You can't smell the snow, you silly goose. You've never even seen snow up close to know what it smells like."

"I know, Lucie, but I know where we are going. Trust me."

"I do, Michael. I do. I wonder what snow really smells like?"

Once they reached the barnyard, Lucie looked over at Michael with a smirk on her beak. "Race ya'! Last one to the barn has to eat snow." With a good head start, followed by a laughing Michael, Lucie reached the tiny hole at the wall. She peeked in and noticed it was pretty dark except for a light over the row of milk cans. "I see it, Michael, I see it! Snow cans, lots of them, all lined up in a row. Are you ready?"

"What are you waiting for, Lucie? Let's go in."

Michael gave her a little nudge and helped push her through the opening. It was a tight squeeze and just large enough for them to fit through.

"Michael, look, there are a bunch of hay bales next to the snow cans, and there is a short board leaning up next to the bales. I'll bet we can knock it over and use it as a ramp to climb up to the top."

"I can push that over by myself, Lucie. But if you want to help me, I'll let you push on the board, too," snickered Michael.

Grunting and puffing, both little geese got the board rocking. "Push harder, Michael. Flap your wings with me and give us some more umph." With a few muscular flaps of their wings, they easily managed to tip over the board and slid it to the edge of the hay bale.

"We did it, Lucie! Our wings are getting stronger and stronger."

"Yeah! Remember what Tron told us? We can do anything if we do it together."

"He's one smart goose, Lucie. Who knew?" laughed Michael.

They raced up to the top of the bales and looked over the edge. "Look Michael, look. It's beautiful. Just look at all that white water. Buckets full of it. I'm going to swan dive right into the middle of the fluffy white stuff."

"Lucie, the snow doesn't look that deep. If we get in, do you think we can get back out?"

"Well, we didn't come all this way just to look at it, you silly goose. Besides, the snow is almost all the way to the top of the rim. We can easily hop out from there, don't you think?"

"Well, if we get in, we can always get out, as long as we work together. On 3—1, 2, 3!"

With a huge splash, both Michael and Lucie went head first into the milk can. "Woohoo! I'm touching sno-ow. I'm touching sno-ow," sang Michael. And the two young goslings splashed and swam in the metal container. They dove down deep into the bucket, completely immersing themselves from head to toe in the thick white liquid. For ten minutes they laughed, giggled, and flicked white water at each other with their wings.

"Hey, Lucie, this doesn't feel very cold at all. It feels just like pond water. It's as warm as pond water, too. I expected it to be as hard as the ground. Dad said the more snow there was, the harder it was. I was sure we would be able to stand on it."

"I know, Michael. I'm a little confused, too. Maybe this is what snow is supposed to feel like."

Michael put his bill into the thick liquid. "Hey, this doesn't taste like any water I've had before. It's not bad, but I can't place my feathers on what it tastes like. But look at all the bubbles I made from blowing in it. You try it, Lucie."

Lucie also took a sip and made bubbles. "Hmm. Not bad, and you are right, Michael. It's not like any water I've ever tasted. It doesn't smell like pond water, either. It has a unique smell."

"Yeah, it smells like… It smells like… Lucie, I don't know what it smells like. Is this really snow?"

"Well, whether it's snow or not, we are the only ones in the flock who've touched this type of white water."

"We'd better be getting back home, Lucie. I think the sun will be coming up soon."

"All right, what a great story this will be to tell everyone at home. They'll all be so jealous that we touched snow without going to the mountain." With that said, both Michael and Lucie swam over to the edge of the bucket.

"Hey, Michael, I can't get out of the bucket. The edge is two or three inches too high and the walls are too slippery. Give me a push so I can try to get over the lip of the bucket." Pushing with all his might, Michael couldn't get his sister out of the milk can.

"Lucie, maybe I can swim under you and lift you up."

"Good idea. Once I'm out, I'll reach down and pull you out, too." Michael tried his best to gain enough momentum to push his sister out of the bucket, but the bucket was too small to maneuver in.

"Lucie, I can't get enough speed in this small space. See if you can push me out."

"All right, I'll put my wings under you and lift hard." Without any leverage, Lucie couldn't get her brother out of the bucket, either.

"Michael, I can't push you up. When I try, I sink down into the snow. It looks like we're stuck here. Maybe this is what happened to the duck that never returned to the pond. Do you think he died in this can? Maybe he couldn't get out and drowned. Maybe he is lying at the bottom of this can right now."

"Don't be silly, Lucie. We aren't going to die here. I'll bet there is a way out. We just haven't found it yet. Let's try again. If only we could stand on top of the snow, I know we could hop right out. It's just an inch or two out of reach."

They tried over and over valiantly to get past the edge of the milk can and reach freedom. "Michael, I think we are stuck here. I can't get over the edge. Maybe we should have waited until we could fly. If we had, we would be able to fly out of here in a second."

"Don't worry, Lucie. I know we will get out. Maybe Mom and Dad will come find us and help us get free."

"I hope so. I don't want to live here forever. Or worse, die in here."

"Hey, Lucie, let's play honk-and-follow. Maybe if we get the white water going around fast enough with our webbed feet, it will lift us high enough to get over the edge."

"Hey, that's a great idea, Michael. We'll have to go around pretty fast, though, to make the water spin around fast enough. And you'd better honk extra loud to keep me moving and help me build up speed. I'll be the leader first and flap my wings to help move the air in the bucket. You flap, too, and pretend we are going south for the winter."

Off they went, round and around the bucket. Michael and Lucie's webbed feet were paddling in the milk, and they were flapping their young wings. Michael followed close behind, honking, "Lucie is the best flyer ever. My sister can swim and fly for days and days. My sister is the best leader. I'm so proud of my sister. Lucie is great! Lucie is great! Yea, Lucie!"

While Lucie and Michael were swimming around in the milk, morning crept over the pasture and made its presence known to the flock. With the sun's bright rays peeking over the tree tops, Sam, Tabitha, and all the brothers opened their eyes to two empty patches in the nest.

"Mom, Dad, where are Lucie and Michael?" asked Gabe. "They aren't in their sleeping spots."

Tabitha said, "Sam, would you go out to the field and look for them? I'll check with my parents and see if they went over there for an early morning swim. I'm sure they are around here somewhere."

The whole family joined in the search. Gabe, Ralph, Uri, and Zack helped look for Michael and Lucie by turning it into a game. It was a combination of hide-and-seek mixed with Marco Polo and peek-a-boo. They went from one nest to the next, calling out their names, lifting up other parents' wings to see if they were hiding under them, and looking in their favorite play spots. By the time the sun came into full view, every adult goose and gosling knew that Michael and Lucie were missing.

"Sam, I've looked everywhere. I went to the river, to my parents, and to the edge of the field. I can't find them. I'm so worried, Sam. What if the eagles or foxes got them?"

"Tabitha, I'm sure they are fine. Those two have more courage, strength, and curiosity than any geese I know. I'll bet they found a new place to play and explore. We'll find them soon."

Tron walked over to Sam and Tabitha. "I see that your two young ones have decided to grow a little more today. I have a feeling they are safe and will rejoin the flock by the day's end. Come, we will all help you look for them. Tron announced to the entire flock, "We will split into small groups and check the nearby fields, river, and lakes. Then we will all meet back here at mid-morning. We never leave one of ours behind, and we always see our own returned to the flock."

Back at the barn...

"Michael, the sun is up, and we have been swimming for hours. I'll bet Mom and Dad are worried."

"I know, Lucie. My legs are getting a little tired, too. Either the water is getting thicker, or I can't fly and swim as far as I thought I could. Let's trade up. I'll swim in the front for a while and flap my wings. It will be great practice for when I am leading the flock on the next migration."

"I can see you leading the flock, Michael. You are a good swimmer. If you fly half as well as you swim, we'll make it home in record time," laughed Lucie.

Lucie started to cheer. "Michael is great! Michael is strong! Michael can fly so far and long!"

Michael laughed so hard it made his neck move up and down and he got milk up his nose. "Hey, Lucie, that's a great rhyme. It has a good honk to it. What else can you come up with?"

"I'll come up with something. You just keep paddling your feet and flapping your wings. I believed what you said before. Maybe we can get out if we get this snow moving fast enough."

"Look out, Lucie. I'm going to create a whirlpool right here in this bucket. Make sure you stay in my draft."

"You got it, Michael. I can already feel the breeze. Maybe the updraft from your flapping will lift me right out of the bucket," chuckled Lucie. "Just keep listening to my honking, and you will believe how great you are. Maybe that's why we honk on long trips. The more we support each other with good thoughts and positive words, the greater we becomes inside. Everyone starts believing in themselves, and they accomplish great things by flying longer and farther than they believed they could on their own."

"Hey, Tron said the same thing to us, Lucie. Together we can accomplish anything. Now I know we'll get out of this bucket." Michael started shouting, "I'm not giving up! I'm not giving up!"

Back at the geese's home...

All the families met back at the field by mid-morning. "I'm sorry, Sam and Tabitha, no one has found your children yet. I'm sure they'll show up, though. Don't give up hope," said Tron.

Zack went up to his father. "Dad, Dad, I remember that one of the ducklings talked about snow buckets and white water. The duck said there were snow buckets in the barn. Do you think Michael and Lucie went back to the farm to touch snow?"

"That's good thinking, Zack. Tabitha, you stay here with the children, and I'll go look for them."

"There is no way I am staying here, Sam. The worst storms and broken wings couldn't keep me away from my babies. I'm going!"

Tabitha looked toward the leader of the flock. "Tron, would you look after our children while we go to the barn? We must leave immediately."

Tron just smiled. "My dear friends, we are all going to the barn together. There is something for all of us to see." With Tron at the lead, the entire flock made their way swiftly toward the farm.

In the bucket...

"Michael, I need to rest for a minute. My feet and wings are aching something fierce. This snow is getting too hard to swim through, and I can barely move my feet anymore. I'm afraid we are going to die in here. Why don't you climb on top of my body and get free? Just leave me here."

"Lucie, I would never leave you. A goose stays with a fallen or hurt goose until she is well enough to fly again. I'm staying. We will both get free, even if I have to push you through the snow. We'll take a break for a minute, but we won't give up."

While catching their breath, Michael looked around the barn. "Hey, Lucie, guess what? Before we started swimming, I could barely see over the edge of the can. But now my neck is up high enough that I can see the doorway. Maybe our swimming is fluffing up the snow. I'll bet if we keep swimming through it as fast as we can, we will be able to get out."

"Hey, you're right, Michael. My neck is also up to the edge. I'm so tired, though, I don't know if I can swim anymore."

"We'll keep switching every ten laps or so, Lucie. That way, we can keep encouraging each other in shorter intervals. I'll go first." Michael shouted again, "I'm not giving up! I'm not giving up!"

Lucie followed right behind her brother, honking away, "We won't stop, we won't quit, Michael will turn this snow into whip. Then we will stand, then we'll get out, because my brother is strong and stout. Gooooo, Michael, go!"

After switching places a few more times, Michael stopped to check their progress. "Lucie, look, the snow is getting harder. It's really slushy under my feet. I can almost get a foothold to jump out. We are doing it, Lucie. We'll be free before you know it. There's no giving up now. I can smell freedom."

"Does it smell anything like snow?" laughed Lucie.

"We aren't giving up. We can do this."

"Michael, let's pretend that we are leading the entire flock. Maybe if we make believe that we hear the whole group behind us, we'll be able to swim and fly long enough to hop out of this snow bucket."

"Sounds good to me, Lucie. I'll change my voice to mimic other members in our family."

Down at the pond...

From outside of the barn, the sounds of little geese honking reached the ears of a young duckling at the pond. "Mom, do you hear that? It sounds like the geese are coming back. I liked them. They were fun to swim and play games with. Can you hear them, too?"

"I do hear them, but they don't sound like they are getting closer. It sounds like they're in the barn. We should go take a look."

"Mom, the barn is scary. I don't like the barn."

"Have courage, my dear. They may need our help. Stick by my side, and you'll be fine. I won't make you go in the barn, I promise."

Both Mom and her son made their way up the hill. "Mom, the door is closed and latched shut, but there is a small hole in the window over here to look in."

The mother duck stretched her long neck to the window, but the hole was too small for her bill to fit through. "I can barely see two little goslings' heads inside the milk can. It looks like they are stuck and can't get out. I'd better go find their parents and let them know."

The mother duck took her son back down to the pond and told him to stay with the others. She flew off immediately in search of the geese who had visited yesterday. Just as she reached the outskirts of the farm, the entire flock came into sight.

"Sam, Tabitha, I think two of your children are trapped in a milk can in the barn," said the mother duck. "They appear to be fine, and I could hear them honking and encouraging each other to keep flying and swimming. Oh, you would be so proud of them. They were not scared in the least. They must be trying to get themselves free."

Tron stopped the group for a moment. "Sam, Tabitha, when we get to the barn, I must ask you not to run in and rescue them. There is something special about these two, and I have a feeling we will be able to help them get free from outside. Trust me, and you will see the next leaders of our group grow up right before your very eyes."

"Tron, we have always trusted your wisdom. We will follow your request," replied Sam and Tabitha.

With the entire flock of geese approaching the barn, all the ducks and swans couldn't help but come and watch out of curiosity. It was an incredible sight to see that many geese, swans, and ducks all gathered in one place to help one another.

Tron looked through the small hole in the window. He could see the two young ones swimming around in the can. He could also hear the faint honking. "Listen, everyone. You can hear them helping each other get free. Listen to their words of praise and encouragement. They are true leaders."

Michael kept honking, "Lucie is so strong, her wings are powerful and long. She flies with great ease, and helps the flock with her breeze. I'm so proud of my sister because she's not afraid of a blister. Go Lucie, go! Go, go, go!"

"Michael, you are doing a great job of mimicking our family. I can almost hear Mom and Dad as if they were right behind us."

"Thanks, Lucie. We are almost high enough to get out, too. My feet are getting higher and higher in the snow. It's getting really hard to move them anymore, though. It's like swimming in thick mud."

Outside, Ralph wanted to help somehow. "Mom, can we go inside and rescue Michael and Lucie?"

"Yeah, Mom, we want to help," said Uri and Zack.

"Of course we can help," she replied, "but we must do it from out here. Tron asked us not to go in yet."

"Mom, how about we honk with them? We can cheer them on from right here," said Gabe.

"That's an excellent idea. Everybody who wants to help can join in with our migration song."

Almost immediately, the entire group of geese, ducks, and swans started singing their migration songs. It was a beautiful chorus of praise and encouragement. Never before had all three groups worked together like this to help one another. This was a new first, and a special event to be remembered for a very long time.

"Lucie, how are you doing that? I swear I hear our flock right behind me. It's really loud, too. I just got a huge surge of energy, and now I can go faster."

"I hear the same thing, Michael. Maybe we are dead and we hear ghosts."

"I don't think so, Lucie. It sounds wonderful. I can hear geese, ducks, and swans. Maybe I'm hallucinating. Whatever it is, hang on, 'cause I'm going to turn on the after burners and get us out of here. I'm not giving up! I'm not giving up!"

Michael swam and flapped his wings faster and faster. The milk was churning through its final stages and began turning into butter.

"Michael, whatever you are doing, keep doing it. The snow is getting really hard."

"Help me out, Lucie. We are almost high enough to hop over the edge."

Lucie started honking even louder, and so did the group outside. The migration song could be heard for miles and miles.

"Michael, you did it! You did it! I can stand. Stop paddling your feet and pull them out of the snow."

"Wow, you are right, Lucie. I can stand now. Woohoo! Let's get out of here fast before the snow melts."

It took a few hops to get over the edge of the can and land on the hay bale. "Lucie, we did it. We survived being trapped in the snow bucket. I couldn't have done it without you." He ran over to his sister and gave her a big hug.

"You said it, Michael. I couldn't have done it without you, either."

"Hey," chimed Lucie, "I can still hear our migration song."

"Yeah, it's coming from outside the barn. What's going on?"

Michael and Lucie's legs were exhausted from their ordeal. They stumbled down the board and reached the small opening in the barn door.

When they stepped outside, they were met by all the geese, swans, and ducks singing their praise.

Sam and Tabitha flew over to Lucie and Michael right away. They scooped both of them up in their wings and held them high up into the air. "We are so proud of both of you. And we're so glad you are safe. Listen to all the flocks of birds that you helped bring together."

Michael said, "Mom, Dad, we knew you would find us. And we're so glad to be out of that snow bucket. We touched white water, Mom. I don't think it was snow, but we touched it anyway."

Tron flew over to the young geese. "My young courageous ones, look what you were able to provide for our group. We have never sung together like this before. You two are destined for greatness."

"We couldn't have done it without you. When Michael and I heard the combined groups singing together, it gave us an incredible boost of energy. We could feel your love and support," said Lucie.

While the birds still sang, Michael spoke, "Tron, you were right. When we work together, we can accomplish anything. And with all of you helping us at the end, even when we thought we couldn't go any farther, we were able to make it out of the bucket. Thank you so much. I'm pooped!"

Tron looked at the two of them. "We heard you encouraging each other, and nothing could make us more proud. Because you never gave up swimming in the milk, you were able to churn it into butter and help yourselves get free. What a great feat that was. We will all be talking about this for years to come. We will talk about your strength, your courage, and your keen sense to keep working together. You never stopped helping each other, and you didn't let a small challenge break your spirits. It will be an honor to have you lead our flock during the next migration."

The three groups finished their migration songs and hugged each other as they flapped their wings in joy. Sam and Tabitha thanked everyone, and the geese thanked the ducks and swans for lending their support. They, too, were moved by the gathering and the courage of the young pair of geese. They flapped their wings goodbye and enjoyed a happy ending.

CHAPTER NINE

PURPOSE AND IDENTITY

"WHO AM I?" and "What is my purpose in life?" are two of the greatest questions we may ask ourselves. The third most common question we often ask ourselves is "What does my future hold in store for me?" By the time you finish this book, I hope that you will be able to answer one, if not all, of these questions. You may find yourself reading this book more than once to come up with your answers. I wrote this for that very purpose.

I feel fortunate to know my main purpose in life. I know what I am to do while I am here on this fantastic blue ball we call Mother Earth. I am a teacher. I serve by teaching. I love to share knowledge and help others define their own truth, understanding, and happiness. I continue to improve my craft and expand my knowledge so others can benefit from my skills. I share my skills because that is what I do best. Part of my mission statement is to help people move from the finite to the infinite in possibility and perception. I help people find freedom by transforming their fear into courage. The other part of my mission statement is to help as many people as possible become self-empowered and to help them find personal happiness.

I do not believe that any one person's purpose in life is more important than another's. To me, a caring and supportive mother is just as important as a president or queen. An air-conditioning repairman is just as important as the CEO of a multibillion-dollar corporation. A student is just as important as a teacher. It's pretty hard to be a teacher without a group of students, right? We all play our parts in this incredible mix of personalities and abilities that make up our world. I believe that we are all equal as human beings. Our major difference, however, is that we are taught to be different.

On the next two pages are a few questions to help you discover what your purpose in life is right now, or what it may be in the future. There are no right or wrong answers. When you read a question, start with a yes, no, or maybe, and you will start to identify your purpose. You may find yourself answering *yes* to more than one of these statements. You surely are allowed to have more than one purpose in life, and your purpose can change or evolve as time goes on.

QUESTIONS TO HELP IDENTIFY YOUR PURPOSE

Does your current occupation or role in life define who you are? (Occupation in this sense does not necessarily mean a paying job. Your occupation or role could be anything from a mother, a father, a child, a student, an employer, or an employee. You get the idea. Read the question again.)

Are you proud of your occupation or role in life? How does this benefit your life and the lives of others? If you are not proud of your occupation or role, why aren't you? Can you change this?

If you could change your current occupation or role to be anything you want, what would it be? Why? Will you make the change?

Does your current role in this world serve a higher purpose? If yes, what purpose does it serve? If not, what can you do to help serve a higher purpose?

Are you a teacher? If yes, what do you teach?

Are you a caretaker? If yes, whom do you take care of besides yourself?

Are you a role model? If yes, what positive characteristics do you hope others will duplicate?

Do you inspire other people? If yes, what have you helped other people accomplish?

Are you a leader? If yes, how do you help others achieve or produce success and happiness?

Are you a healer? If yes, whom or what are you able to heal?

Are you a servant to society? If yes, how do you help society grow and coexist?

Is your occupation indispensable? If yes, why is it indispensable?

Do you create anything that is beneficial for the world? If yes, what do you create? If no, what can you create?

Does your occupation hurt other people in any way? If yes, why do you continue?

Does your occupation hurt the planet in any way? If yes, why do you continue?

Does your occupation abuse or hurt any animal or plant life on our planet? If yes, why do you continue?

If your occupation does hurt people, the planet, or its other inhabitants, what can you do to change this right now? Will you change this right now?

Of course, this is obviously not a complete list, and I did not intend for this list to outline or define your entire purpose. That would not be very teacher-like of me, would it? I know you have it in you to be self-aware and deduce your own questions and conclusions. I know you are becoming increasingly self-empowered every day. What other descriptive questions can you come up with that help you define your purpose?

I also imagine a lot of you probably answered yes to more than one of these questions. I hope you answered yes to the upper portion and not so much the last four questions. If you did answer yes to more than one of these questions, what purpose seems to hold more weight for you at this time?

If you don't have a purpose yet, that's OK, too. There is nothing written in stone that says you must have a purpose. If you desire a purpose, though, you can always use the questions from above to help guide you to your role in humanity.

FINDING IDENTITY AND EMPOWERMENT

You have probably heard this famous quote of Socrates: "Know Thyself." Those same words were also said to be printed on a plaque that hung outside the Oracle of Delphi temple in Greece. The other message at the temple was *meden agan*, which translates into "Nothing in Excess." Not a bad bit of advice from those who lived a few thousand years ago. We are taught to live in the moment, but there is something to be said about the simplicity and knowledge that our past provides us.

Knowing one's self empowers an individual to better act and live within his environment. This self-knowledge enables a person to interact with other people with greater confidence and understanding. By knowing yourself, you are able to relate to others on higher levels of consciousness. This leads to better cooperation, understanding, and coexistence. Take every advantage to know yourself by your own perceptions, and not by the perceptions imposed by advertising, political correctness, or social prejudice. Social acceptance and trends always change, but the sincere quality of character does not. People may be attracted to a candy bar wrapper at first, but it is the candy bar inside they enjoy most.

MY IDENTITY

How did I come to know my own identity? I know my purpose, but how did I come to know myself? I have read countless books on empowerment, self-analysis, personality traits, and social character. I have expanded my understanding by reading everything from metaphysics to quantum physics. I have studied various belief systems, religions, and philosophies. I have also taken numerous personality tests, but none of them really defined who I am inside. Sure, there were some outside qualities that were confirmed. However, most of these characteristics I already knew, and I felt that the outcomes of these tests were rather generic. I also know that a person's outside characteristics can change in a moment's notice depending on his external environment. So how did I really learn about my inner self?

In an effort to discover who I really am inside, I made it a point to seek out the finite characteristics that would define the inner me. I wanted to know each little intricacy. The more I kept looking for these deciding factors, the more I learned who I am not. It came down to the point that I could say, "I am not this characteristic, I am not that personality, or I am not that motive." The more I scratched off the list, the more I learned who I really am. I was able to discard many identities that no longer served my current role. By doing this self-search, I was able to free up more room for change. I learned I am more like everyone else when I stripped away all that I am not.

Ask yourself these questions: Are you defined by your body? Are you your name? Are you your skin color or nationality? Are you your educational degrees or social status? Are you your résumé? Are you a representative of your country? Are you your car, house, or clothing brands? Are you your financial status? Are you the stuff in your house? Are you what the commercials and advertising say you should be? Are you what the politicians, judges, and lawmakers say you should be? Are you what those in fear say you should be?

What are you, then? What am I? I am me. I am you in another skin color. I am you in another belief system. I am you on another walk of life. I am myself and you at the same time. Like you, I am the material of the Earth, the sky, the wind, and the solar system. You and I are the Universe in walking form. I, we, are a part of the all. I am connected to all of you, and all of you are connected to me. I am a part of the whole, inseparable, and as One. You are part of the whole, inseparable; you and I are the One.

It is time to start putting this together. In the next section, you will learn more about personality and identity builders. You will also learn what parts of your identity you are able to lessen, release, or put aside in order to facilitate future change. You can also choose to stay exactly as you are. I am certainly not going to tell you that you have to change, and no one else should tell you to change, either. If you decide to make a conscious change in your personality or belief system, this change must come from inside. Is there something in your life that you would like to alter, improve, or change all together?

COMMON IDENTIFIERS

From the moment you were born, from the moment you took your first breath of life, you were programmed and taught to accept an identity. You were given a name, which probably implied your gender, and possibly your nationality. Your new name was spoken over and over, repeated again and again, until you became programmed to accept and respond to it. This name became your first badge of identity—the first of many to come. Having your own name gave you a sense of individualism, belonging, and security. It was the first sign that you were a human being. All humans are given something to identify themselves with, something that will help separate them and classify one from another. From a grunt, to a number, to a call sign, we were all given something by which to identify ourselves.

My identifier was Michael, from the early Hebrew Mikha'el, which means "who is like God." I am not sure why my parents chose that name, but I get a kick out of seeing the translation. My last name, Rhodes, translates into "he who dwells by the clearing" or "field of roses." Does this mean that "the entity who acts like God dwells by the clearing, or by a field of roses?" Is my name my identity? Well, temporarily it is. In another time, I may decide to take on another identity, or no identity at all. Only time will tell. The next time I am near a clearing or a field of roses, I will let you know if I am feeling Godlike and if my name fits.

Next, you were given a position in your family. You were taught that you were first born, second born, middle child, youngest child, and so on. You were taught an identity in comparison to your grandmother and grandfather, uncles and aunts, nieces and nephews, cousins, and close family friends. This became another identifier in your life. Your place in your family taught you how to interact with your closest relatives, what respect should be given to each family member based on their position and title, and how to learn, teach, and share with them.

In time, you were taught a social status from the language and actions of those around you. You were defined as white collar, blue collar, rich, poor, or middle class. Even as a child, you started to learn about your family's position in the economic and social ladder. Spending habits, rules of money, and social class became other identifiers in your life. These identifiers gave you a sense of belonging, but in many other ways, they also kept you separated from the whole of human civilization.

Just about everyone is taught a religious or spiritual belief system of one type or another. You might have been raised to be Catholic, Muslim, practice Judaism, been an Agnostic, Atheist, Wiccan, Baptist, Methodist, Taoist, and so forth. There are way too many religious and spiritual systems to list here. I know that some of you do not practice any religion or spirituality.

Having no belief system can also be looked at as a belief system. Based on human history and war, religion seems to be one of the biggest identifiers that separates one human being from another.

As time goes on, more and more identities accumulate in our lives. We become doctors, teachers, workers, nurses, executives, mothers, fathers, worshipers, spenders, takers, givers, sports enthusiasts, and political activists. Our collection of identities mixes in with our personalities and controls our actions toward others. We have fun with our identities, and we suffer from them just as easily. Let's use sports for an example.

BLEEDING BLACK AND GOLD

Let's imagine that you grew up in Pittsburgh, PA, in the 1970s, like I did. The Steelers were dominating the game of professional football and won four Super Bowls from 1975 to 1980. A lot of people became devoted Steelers fans and added a new identity to their list. It was a great time for fans to wave their towels and "bleed black and gold." When the Steelers won, the fans felt great; they were on the top of the world. However, when the team suffered a loss, the fans felt sad, hurt, and let down. Those who strongly identified with the team suffered a blow when their team lost a game or lost the season. (You may not be a Steelers fan, but can you relate to this? Or do you know of someone who reacts the same way?)

There is a great give-and-take for this type of strong identity. And not just with sports. This happens within any group, religion, or belief system. Part of the fun of belonging to a group is celebrating the victory, rooting for your team, and supporting the coaches, players, and leaders of the organization. But when things get bad, and the identity is out of balance, you feel hurt and dejected. You are now relying on others to make you feel good. You can't control how everyone on the team or group performs. And because of this attachment to your identity, you are now at the mercy of their actions. Your happiness now rests on their shoulder pads. This is a sign of an identity out of balance.

If your team continues to do poorly, you continue to feel down in the dumps. You are angry, hurt, and upset at the team. You start to blame the team because you have fewer good feelings in your life. If you aren't projecting good feelings, it's hard to attract good feelings. It becomes a negative spiral.

The normal reaction that I have observed is to begin blaming the head coach, the players, the draft system, the referees, and anyone else related to the football organization. It all becomes their fault. People's egos become hurt because of pride and the need to win. This strong identity creates a demand for the team to win all the time so the fans can feel good.

The other downside to this strong identity is the separation it creates between people, communities, and countries. If someone says something about one of your identities and you take it the wrong way, even if it isn't meant in a negative way, that person automatically becomes less of a friend. They can even turn into your enemy. I have seen this happen at children's soccer games, baseball games, basketball games, and so on. It happens at schools, colleges, universities, job locations, in government, and within political parties. It happens a lot in religion. I have witnessed this first-hand with colleagues and friends. I remember when I said something that went against their belief system or identity, and they automatically separated themselves from me and became less of a friend. Have you witnessed something similar in your life?

Identities are meant to be fun. Enjoy your identity. That's what it's there for. Enjoy it until you are tired of it. Then release it and appreciate the experience. Use it for a reference point. If you don't want to release an identity, balancing that identity is the key to creating more peace and happiness in your life. And let me tell you, there is nothing wrong with team pride and spirit. Just accept the responsibility for giving away your freedom to create happiness to the control of others for a while. You can always gain your freedom back by lessening or removing that identity. The choice is always yours.

BOXES AND BADGES

I mentioned before that perception and truth are one of our greatest gifts as well as one of our greatest challenges. Another one of our greatest gifts is the freedom to choose an identity in life. Like truth and perception, it is also a great challenge and divider.

We wear our identities like prized badges on our jackets. I call it our *Identity Cloak*. We are proud to say, "I belong to this group; I am a proud member of this society; I show pride for my nation; I support this cause; I root for this team; and I am proud of my religion." With each new badge we attach to our *Identity Cloak,* we create a small sense of unity, but we also increase the chance of separation between ourselves and humanity.

Imagine each badge as a ten-pound weight. Eventually, with so many badges and weights holding us down, we are unable to move forward, backward, sideways, or in any direction at all. We become stagnant. We become bound to our beliefs and identities and are unable to move freely amongst our brothers and sisters.

Is it all right to be stagnant? Sure. Who is to say whether or not you need to change? But as we pointed out earlier, change will happen. So why not support the change and allow it to move as smoothly as possible? Think of it this way. What happens to water when it becomes stagnant and doesn't move? Of course, you know the answer. Water becomes stale, smelly, and eventually starts growing things on top of it. Since your body is primarily made up of water, is this what you want for your own present and future experiences? Water stays freshest, oxygenated, and alive when it moves. Shouldn't we take a cue from nature and do the same thing with our identities? Shouldn't we consider letting go of the old identities that no longer serve our present self so we can move forward in peace and happiness?

This leads us to the next important question: Why would anyone want to let go of an identity? My theory is that we receive what we project. We are influenced by the thoughts, the intentions, and the good and bad vibrations that are projected from our personal identities. If we want to live a happier life, we can stack the odds in our favor by releasing the identities that no longer serve our purpose, or release those identities that are creating more negative outcomes than positive feelings and results.

Identities are also like nails that stick out of a board. We love the good part of the identity when it's working in our favor. If the identity harms us somehow, maybe by creating feelings of hurt, anger, or sadness, we put up with the identity until it becomes so painful and negative that we decide to remove it from our lives. The more identities we have, the more we increase the chance for chaos. The fewer identities we have, the less we will be harmed if someone makes a comment about an identity tied to a group or belief system.

Is it possible to live with everyone in peace and keep your identities? Of course it is. Keeping a good balance with identity is the best way to accomplish this worthy goal. I also know that a person can find a completely different type of peace by releasing identities and living as part of the whole without separation. I am living proof of this.

Like anything else in life, there is an upside and a downside to identities. The upside is the happiness you gain from being a member of a group. The group empowers you and gives you a sense of pride. You feel good when your group does well, wins, or dominates. You become connected to others and create small families that can grow into even larger populations. You feel like you belong to something.

The downside to identities includes: separation from a larger group; separation from oneness; negative emotions that arise if your identity is attacked in any way, even if it's unintentional; increased negative emotions if your identifier loses a competition; and increased negative emotions if your group or family identifier is harmed in any way.

Find your balance, and you will improve your chance for harmony and peace.

IDENTIFIER EXERCISE: WHAT TO KEEP AND WHAT TO RELEASE

I used this exercise at one of my self-empowerment workshops and it received great reviews. I heard from everyone in the class that they learned a great deal about their own identities and that they also found that they could willingly let go of some of their identities.

INSTRUCTIONS:

1. Copy these pages so you don't have to write in the book. That way, you can do this quiz later and not be influenced by your previous answers.
2. Answer the first question. Rate your answer on a scale of 1 to 10, with 10 being the strongest.
3. Decide if you are willing to lessen the intensity of this identity or if you are willing to release it completely.

The blanks are only for a reference. You may surely have many more answers for each category than is provided.

For further knowledge about your identity, you can also use the questions on page 133–34 for each of your answers. This will give you a deeper understanding about yourself, your loyalty to your identities, your loyalty to your groups, and how much this can bring you closer to or separate you from others.

HOW MUCH DOES THIS REPRESENT YOUR IDENTITY?
Scale 1–10 (10 is strongest)

What is your first and last name?

_____ 1 2 3 4 5 6 7 8 9 10

Are you willing to lessen or release this? YES____ NO____

What is your nationality, your heritage?

_____ 1 2 3 4 5 6 7 8 9 10

Are you willing to lessen or release this? YES____ NO____

What is your current religion, spirituality, or belief system?
(e.g. Baptist, Christian, Muslim, Agnostic, etc.)

_____ 1 2 3 4 5 6 7 8 9 10

Are you willing to lessen or release this? YES____ NO____

What is your age group? (e.g. middle-age, senior citizen, etc.)

_____ 1 2 3 4 5 6 7 8 9 10

Are you willing to lessen or release this? YES____ NO____

What is your gender?

_____ 1 2 3 4 5 6 7 8 9 10

Are you willing to lessen or release this? YES____ NO____

What country do you live in?

_____ 1 2 3 4 5 6 7 8 9 10

Are you willing to lessen or release this? YES____ NO____

What state or province do you live in?

_____ 1 2 3 4 5 6 7 8 9 10

Are you willing to lessen or release this? YES____ NO____

What city do you live in?

_____ 1 2 3 4 5 6 7 8 9 10

Are you willing to lessen or release this?   YES____ NO____

What housing community or apartment complex do you live in?

_____ 1 2 3 4 5 6 7 8 9 10

Are you willing to lessen or release this?   YES____ NO____

What is your occupation?

_____ 1 2 3 4 5 6 7 8 9 10

_____ 1 2 3 4 5 6 7 8 9 10

_____ 1 2 3 4 5 6 7 8 9 10

Are you willing to lessen or release this?   YES____ NO____

List any schools or colleges that you or your family members
have attended.

_____ 1 2 3 4 5 6 7 8 9 10

_____ 1 2 3 4 5 6 7 8 9 10

_____ 1 2 3 4 5 6 7 8 9 10

Are you willing to lessen or release this?   YES____ NO____

List your closest family members.

_____ 1 2 3 4 5 6 7 8 9 10

_____ 1 2 3 4 5 6 7 8 9 10

_____ 1 2 3 4 5 6 7 8 9 10

_____ 1 2 3 4 5 6 7 8 9 10

_____ 1 2 3 4 5 6 7 8 9 10

Are you willing to lessen or release this?   YES____ NO____

List your closest friends' names.

_____ 1 2 3 4 5 6 7 8 9 10

_____ 1 2 3 4 5 6 7 8 9 10

_____ 1 2 3 4 5 6 7 8 9 10

_____ 1 2 3 4 5 6 7 8 9 10

Are you willing to lessen or release this? YES____ NO____

List your most important recreational activities or hobbies.

_____ 1 2 3 4 5 6 7 8 9 10

_____ 1 2 3 4 5 6 7 8 9 10

_____ 1 2 3 4 5 6 7 8 9 10

_____ 1 2 3 4 5 6 7 8 9 10

_____ 1 2 3 4 5 6 7 8 9 10

Are you willing to lessen or release this? YES____ NO____

List your five most important personal possessions.

_____ 1 2 3 4 5 6 7 8 9 10

_____ 1 2 3 4 5 6 7 8 9 10

_____ 1 2 3 4 5 6 7 8 9 10

_____ 1 2 3 4 5 6 7 8 9 10

_____ 1 2 3 4 5 6 7 8 9 10

Are you willing to lessen or release this? YES____ NO____

What political party, if any, do you support?

_____ 1 2 3 4 5 6 7 8 9 10

Are you willing to lessen or release this? YES____ NO____

Do you have any pets? If so, list them.

_____ 1 2 3 4 5 6 7 8 9 10

_____ 1 2 3 4 5 6 7 8 9 10

Are you willing to lessen or release this?   YES____ NO____

What economic/social status do you belong to? (e.g. middle class, upper class, etc.)

_____ 1 2 3 4 5 6 7 8 9 10

Are you willing to lessen or release this?   YES____ NO____

List any sports teams that you like or root for.

_____ 1 2 3 4 5 6 7 8 9 10

_____ 1 2 3 4 5 6 7 8 9 10

_____ 1 2 3 4 5 6 7 8 9 10

Are you willing to lessen or release this?   YES____ NO____

What clubs, social movements, or social groups do you support or belong to? (e.g. environmental awareness, save the whales, SPCA, NAACP, etc.)

_____ 1 2 3 4 5 6 7 8 9 10

_____ 1 2 3 4 5 6 7 8 9 10

_____ 1 2 3 4 5 6 7 8 9 10

Are you willing to lessen or release this?   YES____ NO____

What professional groups do you belong to?

_____ 1 2 3 4 5 6 7 8 9 10

_____ 1 2 3 4 5 6 7 8 9 10

_____ 1 2 3 4 5 6 7 8 9 10

_____ 1 2 3 4 5 6 7 8 9 10

Are you willing to lessen or release this?   YES____ NO____

What is your body type? (e.g. tall, short, large, petite, medium)

_____ 1 2 3 4 5 6 7 8 9 10

Are you willing to lessen or release this? YES____ NO____

ADDITIONAL IDENTIFIERS:

How long has this identity been a part of your life?

_____ 1 2 3 4 5 6 7 8 9 10

How much happiness does this identity bring into your life?

_____ 1 2 3 4 5 6 7 8 9 10

How much does this identity bring bad feelings into your life?

_____ 1 2 3 4 5 6 7 8 9 10

If someone made a negative or judgmental comment about this particular identity, would you become upset or defensive in any way?

_____ 1 2 3 4 5 6 7 8 9 10

Do you like this identity for yourself?

_____ 1 2 3 4 5 6 7 8 9 10

Does this identity serve your life's purpose?

_____ 1 2 3 4 5 6 7 8 9 10

Can you lessen or release this identity if it no longer serves others?

_____ 1 2 3 4 5 6 7 8 9 10

Does this identity hurt other people in any way?

_____ 1 2 3 4 5 6 7 8 9 10

Does this identity separate you from anyone else?

_____ 1 2 3 4 5 6 7 8 9 10

Does this identity hurt the planet in any way?

_____ 1 2 3 4 5 6 7 8 9 10

Can you survive without this identity?

_____ 1 2 3 4 5 6 7 8 9 10

Is there a new identity that would better serve your life's purpose?

_____ 1 2 3 4 5 6 7 8 9 10

Is there a new identity that would better serve others in any way?

_____ 1 2 3 4 5 6 7 8 9 10

Is there a new identity that would better serve the planet in any way?

_____ 1 2 3 4 5 6 7 8 9 10

CHAPTER TEN

THE GENIE WITHIN

W HETHER YOU HAVE BEEN to a casino or not, you probably know that casinos place rules and restrictions on their games so they favor the house to win more often than the gambler. They've figured out a way to gain an edge by stacking the odds in their own favor. They even watch for those who try to gain an advantage over the casino and remove card counters, cheaters, and cool those on a very hot streak. Basically, the casinos have removed almost all chance and skill and replaced them with calculated odds tilted in their favor. That is how casinos get to stay in business. They're happy casinos.

Does this mean that the casino always wins? No, otherwise nobody would go there to gamble. If you had no chance of winning, you might as well walk in the door, hand them your $200, say, "Thanks for the experience," and walk right back outside again. Casinos are a break from the norm and provide people with an opportunity for winning big in the blink of an eye, even if the odds are very slim. It's a form of entertainment mixed with intense moments of exhilaration and gut-wrenching defeat—much like life, don't you think?

We don't have a casino in our mind, but we do have something even better. This gift in our mind and body requires no pills, no prescriptions, no oil, no electricity, no flashing lights, and no money to make it work. Everyone has one, and it was free from birth. You are free to use it as often as you wish to stack the odds in your favor. If you learn the basics, you can remove blocks from your past and increase your odds of living with happiness and freedom. You can use your natural-born gift to hurdle obstacles and reach your goals faster. It is time to reintroduce you to the magic genie within. Your subconscious awaits your first command. It is time to rub the lamp.

INCREASING YOUR ODDS

I share with my clients that there are no guarantees with any technique or belief system. I have yet to see the magic pill that creates instant health, wealth, and happiness. There just aren't any guarantees in medicine, law, or life. The best we can do is increase the odds in our favor by increasing our belief that something will work. Here is my philosophy.

I feel the more you believe in a specific technique or system, the more you increase the chance this system will work for you. Now, this isn't a guarantee that it will work, but it can improve your chances and place the odds in your favor. Likewise, if you believe that a system or technique will not work, you increase the chances that it won't. Again, it does not guarantee it, it only improves the odds. Here is another point that I share with my clients: If you aren't sure about your belief, or if you don't think that something will give you the desired outcome, it can still create your wish. That's what makes life unexpected and exciting. You never know what will work, whether you believe in it or not. Miracles can still happen.

Here is a good example: Imagine that you just made a batch of your favorite cookies. (Mine are warm chocolate chip cookies that leave tasty chocolate smears all around the lips.) You want your little child (subconscious) not to touch the cookies until you get home so you can eat them together. If you don't tell this to your little child and leave for the day, what are the chances that all the cookies will be there when you get home? Pretty slim, right? You know some, or all, of the cookies will be eaten. If you are lucky, there might be a few crumbs left for you to lick off the plate.

Let's try a different approach. You talk to your little genie (subconscious). You tell your genie that you want to eat the cookies together when you come home. It's really important to you that your genie waits until you can eat them together. You tell your genie that you will even warm up the cookies again so the two of you can enjoy the melting chips with a tall glass of cold milk. You leave for a while and then come home. Now tell me, have you at least increased your chances that the cookies will be there when you get to the cookie plate? Of course you have. There are no guarantees, but you have increased the chance that all, or most, of the cookies will be there. If you tell your subconscious what you want, you increase the chance that your subconscious will form a new habit and produce your desired result. Start now and tell your subconscious what you want.

MEET YOUR GENIE

Your subconscious, your genie, is like a little child that wants to please you more than you know. It can create a new habit instantly based on your daily actions. It can read your thoughts and emotions and start you on a whole new journey without any conscious knowledge on your part. Your subconscious can also be the channel between yourself and your higher soul or belief system. If the higher self is the grandparent, our conscious self is the parent, and our subconscious is the child. To reach balance and enlightenment, we train our subconscious by our actions to grow into an upstanding young adult with high morals and positive deeds. As our subconscious grows in aptitude, we move up the ladder of knowledge and ability. Now that you've read this, you are probably wondering how to activate your genie.

All children need guidance and support, and so does your subconscious. You can talk to your subconscious like you would a young adult. Give your subconscious direction. Tell your subconscious what would make you happy. It's better to give your subconscious direction than to let it guess on its own. You have a genie inside that wants your direction to make you happy. If you don't tell your subconscious what you want it to do, it can only guess by your current behavior. Sometimes that behavior is not always in your best interest, but your subconscious doesn't know that on its own. That's one of the reasons why people can fall into addictions. Your subconscious does not have the same degree of reasoning as your conscious mind. You have to train it to work with you in order to reach your goals. Treat your subconscious well. It is a part of you. Your subconscious has feelings, too. It is a part of your very being and will help you enrich your life if given the right motivation and positive guidance. (I wish they'd taught this in school.)

How do you talk to your subconscious? First, your subconscious is listening all the time. If you go on vacation, your subconscious goes with you. If you go to work, your subconscious goes there, too. I am not aware of any time that you and your subconscious split from each other. All you have to do is tell your subconscious that these messages you are about to send are for him or her.

Think back to our casino example, and place the odds in your favor. The language of the subconscious is visual. During sleep, we enter into a state of deep sleep known as REM (rapid eye movement) in which we dream. Dreams are the subconscious' way of exploring, experimenting, and working out solutions for your personal blocks and problems. The majority of us dream in pictures or in mini-movies, not in words. So it makes sense that the language of the subconscious is geared toward pictures and visualization. That's not to say that words will not work, but pictures are the mode of choice. To increase your odds of communicating effectively with your subconscious, use words, mini-movies, and pictures. If you want to increase your chances beyond this, add positive emotions to your visualizations.

It is true that you can guide your subconscious to create new and desirable habits. You can also get your subconscious to release unwanted habits and release emotional links to past experiences. However, it may take longer if you do it by yourself. I ask my clients, "Is it easier to tickle yourself, or is it easier to be tickled by another?" They always answer, "It is more effective to be tickled by someone else." Hypnosis is very similar to this example. You can increase your odds and save time when you have a certified hypnotist guide your session. It is easier because you can let your conscious mind relax and allow your subconscious to get right to the blockages and instill your new goal.

If you do hypnosis without a guide, you still need part of your conscious mind to direct the session. Your conscious thoughts can get in the way or block you from reaching your goal because of your own ego and fears. A guided session is more effective because your conscious mind can easily wander off task, so it's possible that you may never get to the productive part of your own session. That is why some people find it hard to meditate and attain *no thought.* Many people have shared with me that they find it challenging to go sixty seconds without forming a thought in their minds. However, when you are guided by another, it is much easier to focus your attention and reach altered states of awareness.

If you are guiding your subconscious every day, you will see results in the long run. If you don't see the results you wish, there may be a block from your past that is keeping you from achieving your goal. That is when you step back, assess your situation, and decide if you want to seek professional counsel or see a certified hypnotist.

This leads me to the next question: What is hypnosis, and how can it help?

HYPNOSIS AND MEDITATION: FACT VS. FICTION

People experience different levels of awareness all day long. These states can fluctuate between our beta, alpha, and theta levels of brain function. We also go into different levels of awareness at night, primarily our delta level. Hypnosis and meditation are nothing more than altered states of awareness where the conscious and subconscious minds shift roles to achieve a desired result. When you are fully awake and alert, your conscious mind is most active and your subconscious helps you along the way. When you are asleep, your subconscious is most active while your conscious mind rests. Your conscious and subconscious remain ready to assist you in times of need, but neither ever completely shuts down, unless you're dead.

Hypnotists also call hypnosis a focused state of awareness. When you are in hypnosis, you are not asleep. Your subconscious is more active and can communicate, remember, and accept new programming.

This is a big sigh of relief for a lot of people: No one can place you in hypnosis without your consent. All hypnosis is self-hypnosis.

What is the difference between hypnosis and meditation? Clinical hypnosis is primarily used for helping people release old habits and create new desired perceptions and lifestyles. Meditation is used most frequently for enlightenment, spiritual evolution, relaxation, and is said to be the vehicle to know one's self. Like hypnosis, meditation can also help a person to release old habits and create new ones, if that is the desired intent. Both mediums share many of the same characteristics. They both utilize altered states of awareness; they can be done individually or in a group setting; and they can be guided or done by the self. I tell people that the main difference between the two is intent. I could easily call my hypnosis sessions guided meditations.

I am often asked, "What does hypnosis feel like?" After a session, most clients tell me they are very relaxed, centered, and enjoyed the session immensely. They were aware of their surroundings at all times, they could hear all my words, and they were amazed at how good they felt when they moved back into full consciousness. All of them agree that time is different in the subconscious state.

How do people go into an altered state of awareness, hypnosis, or a meditative state? It's easy. Going into altered states happens naturally and occurs often throughout the day and night. To increase your ability, the easiest way is to find a place where you feel safe and comfortable. You can increase your chances by closing your eyes. I tell my clients, "As soon as you close your eyes, your mind no longer has to process all the photons that are bombarding your cognitive system to organize the light into pictures and define a meaning for those images. Your mind starts to relax as soon as you close your eyes."

Of course, you can still enter meditative states with your eyes open. It is called open-eye meditation. Here is a good example. Have you ever driven through a light with your eyes open, but after you got to the other side of the intersection, you wondered if the light was red or green? After you were done looking for the police to pull you over, you regained full consciousness and continued on your way. That is an example of being in an altered state of awareness, even with your eyes open. People can also enter altered states of awareness with prayer, rhythmic music, and repetitive phrases such as mantras. *Om mani padme hum* is a good example of a mantra.

I love it when people ask if they can be hypnotized. I ask them if they can close their eyes. They always say, "Yes." Then I ask them if they can go to sleep at night. They also respond with, "Yes." As I stated earlier, closing one's eyes starts the process of entering altered states of awareness. As people allow themselves to relax, or refocus their thoughts with guided words and imagery, the more they can explore even deeper levels of awareness. The individual is primarily in charge of how far he or she enters into different states of awareness. The person guiding the session also has a small influence, and so does the environment and ambiance, but not nearly as much control as the subject. We are a perceptive race. All factors play a part in our ability to reach new levels of awareness.

Hypnosis is not the same as being anesthetized. You are not blacked-out during a session. You don't lose control, and you keep your secrets safe. You control what you say and what you do. Don't let the TV and movies fool you. TV and movies are like politicians. Sometimes they are truthful, and sometimes they are not. It is up to you to decide.

Below are other benefits for hypnosis, meditation, and working with your subconscious.

- Hypnosis helps release blocks or habits that the conscious mind cannot release by itself, or cannot release in the desired timeline
- Release stress
- Release emotional links to previous life experiences that have formed blocks for desired habits and lifestyles
- Helps focus visualization directly to the subconscious
- Program new wants, thoughts, and ideas
- Move awareness from left brain function to right brain function to enhance creativity
- Relaxes the body. This allows the body to focus on rejuvenating cells, metabolizing food, or healing itself without having to battle stress first. A relaxed body also helps create a relaxed state of mind. Information flows more freely, it is stored more easily, and helps create direct pathways for instant access to the desired memories and facts.
- Improves recall of blocked or forgotten information, including past lives
- Improves sports performance
- Improves memory
- Improves awareness beyond consciousness
- Helps release and transform fear, such as fear of speaking in public, flying, test taking, fear of insects, snakes, and things that go bump in the night

Hypnosis does not:
- Force someone to perform an act without consent
- Force someone to perform anything that goes against a person's moral standards
- Place someone in a harmful situation
- Function like a magic pill. Results can be instantaneous, but it should

not be looked at as a miracle cure. Everyone responds differently to hypnosis, meditation, and altered states of awareness.

- Force someone to do something. For example, hypnosis will not force you to stop eating sweets.

You can release habits consciously. I believe this. I have met people who quit smoking and didn't need hypnosis to do it. They didn't need this tool to reach their goal. I think that is awesome. If you need a tool or don't need a tool, it doesn't make anyone better than the other. The end result is what is important. Some people can dig a hole without a shovel. I say, "Good for them." It's great that they have this ability. There are also people who would rather use a tool. And, there are people who need to use a tool. Hypnosis is only a means to help people who want to reach their goal faster.

This leads me to my next question: Why should people awaken the genie within?

THE CORE OF REPETITION

I believe one of the reasons people place themselves in similar situations over and over again is because they have not become tired enough of the resulting emotional response. As we covered before, people do the same thing with identities and perception. When people have had their fill of an identity or viewpoint, or if they learned their soul lesson, they move on to a new type of experience, emotional response, or identity. Have you ever witnessed someone who gets out of an abusive relationship, only to put himself right back into another abusive relationship with a different person? Do you know someone who's kicked one bad habit or addiction, only to replace it with another addiction or habit? This can be from a lack of self-love, a lack of self-worth, low self-esteem, or they might not be tired of that emotional response yet. They could also be satisfying another emotional need by receiving sympathy and support from others. There are many reasons why people may repeat an action or are unable to release a habit.

This mirrors the *Identity Cloak* that I mentioned in the last chapter. People can also develop an *Emotional Identity Cloak,* which they can wear every day. People can change their emotional identities as easily as they change a shirt. We have many emotional characteristics that identify ourselves, so knowing your emotional identity signature is as important as knowing your identity and purpose. People can easily become addicted to their emotional responses and will continue to create situations consciously and subconsciously to fulfill their emotional need, even if they don't want to. Emotions create vibrations, and they also produce numerous chemical reactions in the body. It is possible to become addicted to these vibrations and hormonal responses. In time, and if repeated often enough, the need for these chemical reactions can become a subconscious habit anchored in your neural net. Your subconscious wants to please you, so it will also help create lifetime scenarios to fulfill your emotional highs and lows.

If it is true that we attract life situations by what we think or feel, this would also explain why certain situations continue to come into our lives. If the morning starts off with you stubbing your toe, the rest of the day can spiral downward and continue to bring other negative events into your path. We project our inner feelings like emotional badges of honor. I believe the potentiality of the wave function can also collapse by our emotions and not just our ability to visualize. If this is true, what type of emotional badges do you want the quantum particles to sense and feel? What do you want the Universal process to duplicate for you?

You've probably guessed my next question. You knew it was coming. Do you know your emotional identity signature? What does your *Emotional Identity Cloak* look like? The easiest way to decipher this code is by looking at your emotional responses and writing them down. List your lowest emotional states, such as sorrow, sadness, fear, rejection, feelings of low self-worth, and so on, and include the events that caused them. (Please seek professional counsel to assist you with this process.) Then list all of your highest emotional responses and the events that caused those emotions. List what makes you laugh, sing, jump for joy, and love. When you have completed these lists, look for the repetitious patterns for each high and low emotional response. How many times did you place yourself in similar situations where you were hurt? How many times did you place yourself in similar situations that made you happy? What caused this reaction to occur? Find the pattern and know your emotional signature. Once you find the patterns, you have won half the battle. Releasing becomes much easier, and sometimes instantaneous, when you realize the patterns on a conscious level.

Another way to know your emotional identity and perception characteristics is by reading this book. If you read something that feels great to you and you resonate with the content, you've probably discovered, or verified, one of your identity badges. Likewise, if you read something that makes your skin boil and makes you angry, you've likely found another strong identity of yours. Remember, I didn't write this book to make you see it my way. Life would be boring if we were all the same and had the same likes and dislikes. I wrote this book to help you learn more about yourself and to give you techniques to find happiness, inner peace, world peace, and to get your three wishes.

THE OTHER CHEEK

I believe we are all vibrational beings, and as we send emotions and thoughts out into the world, we receive similar emotions and lifetime scenarios to match how we feel. Sometimes what we send out comes back in equal intensity, but usually it comes back with less intensity and does not occur immediately. This response could be delayed by days or even weeks. This makes sense, because all waves dissipate over distance and time and may not immediately return to the original source. It's a good thing, too. If you look at all the bad things that have happened over the course of our history, I am glad that our original intentions lessened over time and space.

Have you heard the parable about turning the other cheek? If you are struck on one cheek, you are supposed to turn the other. I believe this means you should not retaliate with the same negative energy that was sent to you. If you want to receive love, happiness, and abundance, send out as much love, happiness, and abundance as possible, even in the worst of times. You may not love the person hitting you at the moment, but you can still send out love to the world, your God, or whomever you choose. You can even defend yourself. (Remember to send out love as the core emotion while defending yourself.) Defense is not an aggressive act; it is an act of conscious protection. Your vibration, or intent, is one of protection.

This is a challenging task. You probably aren't feeling love for the person hitting you, but you can still train yourself to think of something that you do love. Instead of hitting them back, try thinking of all the people you love in your life and send them love. If you retaliate and send out negative energy to your attacker, you are increasing the chance of another negative event occurring in your future.

ANOTHER WAY
TO IMPROVE YOUR ODDS

I believe in the power of words, the power of visualization, and the power of thought. I also believe in the power of numbers. I believe that when a number of people focus on a single intent, they increase the possibility of that intent becoming a reality. If enough people visualize a world of peace, we increase the chance that a world of peace will come to be. Likewise, if enough people visualize the end of the world is coming, as some do for the Dec. 21, 2012 prophecy, or Armageddon is knocking on our door, then we increase the chance that the quantum wave of potential will collapse to create situations that mirror those prophecies. Which future would you rather visualize and create? I vote for a happy place—no more thinking of doom and gloom. Instead, think of your little slice of heaven.

If words, visualization, and emotions can cause a quantum wave of potential to collapse and create our future realities, then why not also utilize another natural gift, namely your family, friends, loved ones, and others with similar interests. Group meditation, mass prayer, and shared hopes and dreams can also improve the odds in your favor. If you want a happier life, why not meditate with others and see everyone involved living happy lives. Pray, chant, sing, or do whatever feels natural to you and gives you a good feeling while you are doing it. Get together with as many people as possible who have similar interests. Share the emotions and vibrations that will strengthen the effect. It works!

You can start with a simple—but very powerful—phrase coined by Émile Coué, "Every day, in every way, my life is getting better and better." This can be changed in a variety of ways to meet your needs. Start today, use the words, use the visualizations, and add emotions to your thoughts to increase all the odds and chances in your favor. Wake your genie and ask for your three wishes. Start the process today.

FRIENDLY REMINDER

OK, you have finished the chapter. Have you told your subconscious what you want yet? Don't forget to reinforce your new habits and outlook on life by thanking your subconscious. Think back to what Tron told Michael and Lucie: "Together, you can do anything. Together, you can accomplish great feats. When you work together, there is nothing you can't do." Flap your wings and honk your song of support. It's time to take flight and enjoy your new journey.

CHAPTER ELEVEN

TOOL CHEST FOR HAPPINESS

I AM GOING TO SHARE WITH YOU a few more tools to help you create your palace of peace and happiness. These are natural gifts that everybody possesses and there is no charge to use them. Welcome to the wonderful world of visualization, internalization, and vocalization. Each of these techniques can improve your odds of success and get you one step closer to paradise.

TWO STEPS TO SUCCESS

I am inspired by people who pick up self-help books, seek counsel, or take classes to enrich their lives. This tells me they are still willing to reach for their dreams. These people haven't given up yet, and that is fantastic. These people are expressing their bravery by seeking help and searching for a new tool or method to achieve victory.

These people continue to seek because they want to change a part of their life to be a little happier, become more successful, become a little richer, become a little healthier, or find a better relationship. They become the new inspiration for others as they achieve their goals. You are also an inspiration to others by reading this book. You deserve a standing ovation. Bravo! You are stretching your mind, taking in new information, reaffirming your thoughts and ideas, and you are open to making new ones. You are taking another step forward and becoming a new leader. You are reading this information to make a change in your life. And for this, I applaud you!

I look at people who are growing and searching with admiration and encouragement. Any action or thought a person makes toward achieving a personal goal is a step in the right direction. The only way to stop progress is to stop trying. Success may come quickly, or success may come slowly, but success will always be there as long as you keep trying. All you have to do is keep moving your life in that direction and it will happen. It's already in your future timeline. It may be today, or it may be years away, but it is there for you to experience. Believe this, and it will be so. Say this to yourself out loud: "With every new goal I set, I know that success has already happened. Time is just the vehicle to get me there. Every action I take is a step forward. I am successful."

Imagine that every goal you are working on is like walking up a flight of stairs. There is only one direction to go, and the only thing you desire is to reach the top. When you do this, there is no right or wrong way to get there. There is no failure. There is only going up the stairs until you reach that last step.

Of course, there are a number of ways you can move up the stairs. Sometimes you can make it to the top by leaping two or three steps at a time with superhuman strength. Your superhero cape instantly appears and you fly up the stairs with ease. Nothing can stop you or get in your way. Success is yours for the taking, and you do. It is as if there was only one step to climb.

At other times in your life, you take your time going up the stairs. You enjoy the slow walk. You know you will reach the top and it's not a race. Every step is a new learning experience for you, something to cherish and share. The trip is smooth, but takes time, feeling much like a slow-moving escalator. You accept this and keep your focus on the top of the stairs. You go along for the ride until you reach your goal.

And at other times, you may stumble. You might miss a step and fall down, but you keep going. Exhaustion may set in, and you may need a little break every once in a while, but you never stop. The only way to get to the top is to keep going. The small stumbles and pain you experience along the way are minor deterrents. You know they are part of the journey, but they don't keep you from moving up, up, up. You may grumble, scream, yell, swear, or shake your fists, but you are determined. You wish you didn't have to experience the pains and bumps in the road, but they happened, and you know you can overcome them. You survive. You finally make it, bruised and tattered, but you are there, and the success outweighs the journey.

Sometimes these little bumps in the road make it seem like you are taking one step forward and two steps back, but you aren't. When climbing the stairs to reach your dream, the stairs only go in one direction. When you feel as if you're not making any progress, just think of yourself walking up the stairs backwards. Thomas Alva Edison realized this while inventing the incandescent light bulb. "I have not failed 1,000 times," he said, "I have successfully found 1,000 ways not to make a light bulb." Stairs can also be climbed going backwards.

RE-EVALUATING STEPS

Here is another way to look at reaching your goal and establishing progress. Think of each goal as having only two major steps. Once you make the first move, you are already 51% there. The rest of the journey can be taken in little chunks or big chunks. Again, time and experience are only the journey. By taking the first step, more than half the goal is already achieved.

Now here is the best part. Even after you've made the first move, you can always choose to stop pursuing your goal if it's not in your best interest. If you do this, you only have to go down one step to return to where you began. You can then re-evaluate what to do next. There is no right or wrong answer, only choice. Make this choice based upon what is best for you and best for the world, and you will never go wrong.

Of course, a lot of people would like to avoid the failures along the way. It would be much more time-effective if life worked that way. But I don't look at any failure as a failure. I see failures as just another experience toward reaching a goal. Failure is only a perception. One person's failure is another person's success. If you are able to make a small shift in this perception, life can change immensely for you.

One more thing to consider: Whether you are trying to help others reach their goals or others are helping you, every action is a step in the process. People must still decide for themselves what the next step should be in their lives. There is no right or wrong, only opinion, and people's opinions are what matter most for them. (I am not talking about moral right and wrong. That is a completely different book.) No matter what happens, progress is still being made, and I am always glad to help others by being a step in their process.

LANDING THE BIG ONE

My friends know that I like to fish. While fishing, I learned a very valuable lesson from those who cast their bait into the unknown waters. All fishermen believe that success is swimming around somewhere under the glassy surface. Even if they haven't seen any fish in the pond, they will throw in a line. Fishermen have faith and hope that a fish will find their bait enticing and come take a nibble. Better yet, if they don't catch anything the first time, they try again, and again, and again. They reel in their line and recast their bait over and over, knowing that success is swimming around out there in the watery underworld; they just don't know when, where, or how a fish will strike. Fishermen trust the system; they dream, visualize, vocalize, internalize, and keep fishing. They keep using their different tools until they become successful. Fishermen will bring an entire tackle box of potential to help them reach their dreams for landing a prized fish. Sometimes they bring two tackle boxes and still borrow more lures from their fishing buddies. Rarely will a fisherman venture out with only one type of bait, rod, or reel. They have learned to stack the odds in their favor and have as many different tools in their tackle box as possible.

Here is another thing I learned. When I first started fishing, I didn't care what kind of fish I caught. I was ecstatic that I had something on my hook. (Actually, I was so excited that I yelled across the lake and probably scared away all the other fish for miles.) I appreciated whatever the Universal process gave me. But eventually, I developed more specific goals. And unless I was in danger of getting in trouble with my wife for staying out too late, I would cast my line back into the water an *infinite* number of times for another chance to land the big one.

Even the quantum world has developed a theory and phrase for the possibility of the unknown or the impossible happening with *infinite* attempts. If a wave travels at a barrier wall for an infinite number of times, by statistics of probability, at least one of those times the wave will pass through the barrier and reach the other side. This is called quantum tunneling. In theory, if you walk up to a solid door that is closed, and you do this over and over again for infinity, one of those times you will find yourself on the outside looking in. That's awesome.

Become a fisherman for your dreams. Your success is waiting for you just below the surface to reel it in. Use all your tools to get you there. Never stop trying. You can do it. Now, go pick up your rod and reel and bring in a whopper!

SELF-TALK AND VISUALIZATION

"Change your thoughts and you change the world."
—MY FORTUNE COOKIE

I believe it's safe to assume that a lot of people have conversations in their mind on a daily basis. We may or may not be aware of all the words spoken, or even know the number of thoughts we process at any given moment, but there is a lot of inner vocalization taking place within our grey matter.

Of course, not all people will fall under this category. There are those who love to talk out loud instead of bantering back and forth in their own silent debate. But I still believe that most people are inclined to keep their self-conversations rather private.

These daily conversations, which sometimes seem to go on for hours or even keep us up late at night, are usually generated as a question-and-answer session. "Why did he do that?" "How do I fix this?" "Here is what I will do next." "What are the winning lotto numbers?" Other times, these verbal exchanges might be a quick reaction to an outside stimulus, such as a response to a beautiful sunrise, or a foul odor that one might smell while stuck in a subway car in late August. Our thought processes can easily be triggered to solve personal problems, or find an ingenious way to present a business solution. Some people will initiate self-talk to assess their current situation. "Should I buy the red one or the green one?" While others will use self-talk to find a good resolution to an argument. Either way, people seem to love—and have become accustomed to—the endless mind chatter that fills the airwaves between our ears. (Does anyone know where the OFF button is?)

These self-conversations take place on the conscious and subconscious levels of the mind. It has been said that an average person will think 9,000 to 12,000 thoughts a day. Someone who spends more time in their thought process might think 50,000 thoughts a day. It used to be a running joke that people who talked to themselves were mentally unstable. I think these statistics might put this to the test. If people are considered to be mentally unstable for thinking out loud or talking in their mind, it would be a good time for everyone to invest in a straight jacket company. We would surely need to pad the entire Earth if this were true.

We actually benefit from talking with ourselves. For one thing, it prevents loneliness. You are your own best friend. After all, who knows your favorite smells, tastes, sounds, and touches better than you do? Brain usage is another good reason to continue self-talk. There are approximately 100 billion nerve cells, called neurons, that primarily make up your brain. It has been shown that neural connections of the brain continue to last longer if they are used. Neurons that aren't used often, or not continuously used, can stop their electrical signals, and the connection can cease to exist. However, our brain has an incredible ability, and new neural pathways can be created and reinforced with usage and training. If you want to keep your neural connections, or start new ones, keep thinking, analyzing, creating, and assessing your life and your surroundings.

GOOD WORDS = GOOD LIFE

Now that we have talked about the thought process, what kind of thoughts do you have running around in your head? Are your thoughts helping you become the person you desire to be? Are your thoughts more positive than negative? How much of your internal conversation is focused on fear and other people's perceptions?

Before you picked up this book, what were the last ten thoughts you had? If you are not able to recall all ten, what was the last thought you can recall? Was it a good thought or a negative thought? Out of the last ten thoughts, how many were positive and helpful for yourself or others?

Now think back to the last few conversations you had with someone else. Did you have more nice things to say or more negative things to say? Did you encourage someone else, or did you put him down? Did you talk about someone else who was not with you? If so, was it in a good way or in a negative way? There are people who say, "What you give is what you receive." What do you believe? Even if you don't agree with that statement, is it more rewarding to build someone up or tear them down? I'll bet you would all prefer for nice things to be said about you. There is always the potential to change a vibration, word, or idea to a positive one. Make it a point to say more good statements than negative statements and watch the world change before your eyes.

As a reinforcement technique, I have seen some people use a money jar for accountability. When a person uses a negative word or statement, he or she has to put a certain amount of money in the jar. Or it can be turned around. Every time someone says something nice or positive, she adds to a vacation fund, education fund, or to a nice date. Which one fits your lifestyle best? You could always start with one and shift to the other.

If you believe that what you think and say also manifests in your body, this is a great motivator to speak kind words and do good deeds. I have seen many people change their way of life, their health, and their success by changing their thoughts and words alone.

MIND PAINTING

Visualization is as easy as painting a picture or doodling on your notepad. The only difference is that it is done in the mind. If you can imagine it, you are visualizing it. I'll bet if I asked you to see a color, your favorite color, most of you would be able to picture it in your mind's eye right now. Let's play a quick game. See a red apple in your mind. Now see some green grass. View a blue sky with the ocean surf pounding at the shoreline. You may have even been able to hear the sounds of the surf rolling onto the sandy beaches with seagulls singing in the wind.

See? You *can* visualize. It is a natural ability that we all have. Even if you say you cannot visualize, you can. You might need a little practice, and it may take some time, but I believe you can. If you close your eyes and see nothing, or see black, you are still visualizing nothingness and blackness. Congratulations. You did it. I told you that you could do it.

The next step is to change nothing into something, and this can be done by taking little steps or big steps. You decide. Start slow and simple if you wish; there is no prize for finishing first with visualization. If you see nothing but black, add a small dot of light anywhere in the picture. If you see nothing, pretend you see something. Pretending is a good way to begin any new skill. When children are at play, they create the most incredible castles, spaceships, and fairytales all by pretending. The more they pretend, the more real it becomes to them, and the more fun they have. Isn't it amazing what a simple cardboard box can become to a child? Start pretending and you will increase your ability to visualize. Be a kid again. It's fun!

STRENGTH WITHOUT A GYM PASS

Vinoth K. Ranganathan, Vlodek Siemionowa, Jing Z. Liu, Vinod Sahgal, and Guang J. Yue performed an experiment at the Cleveland Clinic Foundation in Ohio to determine if muscle strength could be gained with mental training alone. The results were pretty amazing. Subjects were able to increase muscle strength without lifting a finger, bending an arm, lifting a dumbbell, or going to the gym.

Participants in the experiment were able to increase their pinky strength by 35% with visualization alone. Those who worked on increasing elbow flexing strength with visualization showed a 13.5% increase. That is astounding.

The conclusion to this experiment showed that neural output and visualization can stimulate muscle growth and increase muscle strength. In my own observations, I know this experiment does not suggest we replace traditional exercise methods with visualization. (I am not promoting a couch potato exercise DVD. Get up and take a walk.) This study provides information to support the benefits of mental imagery and could help people in numerous ways, like those who need physical rehabilitation. If you want muscles, you should first see your doctor for an approved physical fitness plan. Then, in addition, use mental imagery to assist with your program and possibly improve the results.

COLLAPSING POTENTIAL

If visualization can increase the potential for muscle growth, just think of all the great things the power of the mind can do. Many professional and amateur athletes use visualization to perfect their abilities and help with muscle strength. It would probably be safe to say that most Olympians are also masters at visualization.

Musicians and actors also increase their abilities by playing their parts in their minds. I have done this myself many times when I took part in music competitions during my college days. I believe that my mental preparations were just as important as my physical preparation, and it showed in my success. When I wrote my percussion compositions, I played them in my mind long before I ever wrote them on staff paper. I remember hearing three songs in my head almost completely before I went to the keyboard to match the pitches to specific notes. Those compositions became a playful bell and vibraphone duet called *Trilogy of the Sea.*

Jumping way back to the earlier part of this book, I spoke about the great developments our scientific minds have theorized and discovered. There is a world of potential that has opened up before our very eyes with the possibilities presented in quantum mechanics. If our minds can create ability, strength, and success, what else can our minds create?

Scientists have shown that light and other quantum particles can be in wave form and in solid form at the same time. When observed, particles take on a solid form. When they are not observed, they are in a state of potential. If you visualize enough, believe enough, and if it fits into your pre-life list of experiences while not interfering with others' perceptions of Universal Laws, a vision can become a stronger possibility. A strong vision can become a stronger probability. A strong probability can become a new reality with the help of a collapsing wave function. And a new reality creates new building blocks for future potential. Even predicted future events can change with enough people believing and focusing their intent.

ANOTHER VISUAL AID

When you paint your dreams in your mind, you increase the chance of your desire becoming your new reality. Even as a child, I remember cutting out pictures of toys and things that I wanted in my life. Many years later, I learned this technique was called a dream board. It doesn't matter what the name is, it is the concept that helps stack the odds in your favor. You can make this an individual project or even a family project. You don't have to do it at all if it doesn't feel right. It is only a different type of hammer to drive in the nail.

Here is what you do. Get a piece of cardboard that you can hang or place somewhere where you will see your dreams every day. Then gather as many pictures of all your most cherished dreams and desires as you can and place them on the board. Think big here. Go for all you want. Your inner genie is watching every time you look at this board and can help create subconscious habits of success that will lead you to your prize. If you want to go to England, find brochures of England. If you want a new car, find a picture of your new car. If you want to form a family, cut out pictures of a family you would like to emulate. The sky is the limit here. Infinite choice is the preferred choice. If you see yourself traveling in space, reach for the stars.

MY VERSION OF AFFIRMATIONS

I like affirmations, and I also like the positive intent behind using affirmations. Affirmations are usually short phrases that help someone strengthen or rewrite a belief so that it can become a new reality, such as "I love myself and others unconditionally," or "I am healthy in mind and body." I also believe that affirmations work best when they align with the life experiences that you chose before you came to this beautiful planet. If these new thoughts are in your best interest, they will work. They increase the odds in your favor.

As before, there are no guarantees. If all affirmations worked, everyone would be instant millionaires, be incredibly healthy, and would have their idea of nirvana just by saying a few positive phrases. Affirmations are another tool in your tool box to help you build a new palace. Remember, most palaces take a little time to build. Don't be surprised, though, if you witness a miracle. There is always room for the unexpected.

I have said many affirmations in my life. Some of them never felt quite comfortable because of the words I was using. You need to find something that you believe in to stack the odds in your favor. As an example, it was not believable for me to say, "I am a multi-millionaire," because I knew I wasn't a multi-millionaire. It felt like a lie because I knew in my subconscious that I didn't have millions of dollars at that moment in time. I needed something that sounded more believable to me. This isn't to say that those words won't work for someone else. They just didn't work for me.

The other things that were missing from my affirmations were visualization and emotions. Visualization is the language of your subconscious genie, and emotions sweeten the cake. Here is how I shifted my affirmations. Maybe this will help you as well.

I took out the words "I am" and replaced them with "I see." (This is in line with collapsing the wave of potential into my reality and using the language of the subconscious.) I did this to create the visual for my desired need, want, or intent. Then I added three scenarios that helped my subconscious genie see my goal in action. I created a little mini-movie for each. I included in my mini-movies the emotions I would feel for this reality.

The following is an example for one of my vacation affirmations. I've underlined my answers for the blanks you will be filling in shortly. After my personal example, I will give you six others for finance, health, achieving goals, relationship, passion, and occupation. You can use this first one as a template for all your future affirmations.

I see myself in <u>Hawaii</u>. While in <u>Hawaii</u>, I see myself <u>fishing off the coast of The Big Island</u> and I feel <u>excited because I caught a huge marlin</u>. I see myself <u>attending a luau and enjoying Kalua pua'a, or roast pork, prepared in a Hawaiian imu</u>. I feel <u>wonderful and satisfied as the pork melts in my mouth like butter</u>. I also see myself <u>learning the forgotten arts from the Kahunas</u>. I feel <u>honored and proud to spend time with them and to partake in their knowledge</u>.

Here is the same affirmation without the blanks filled in. Pick a place you would like to go for vacation and have three activities in mind with corresponding emotions to match. See how this feels when you say it. You can always modify the action words or any part of this template to meet your needs.

I see myself in _____.

While in _____, I see myself_____,

    and I feel _____ while doing _____.

While in _____, I see myself_____,

    and I feel _____ while doing _____.

While in _____, I see myself_____,

    and I feel _____ while doing _____.

Great! You just set this in motion. If this is what you really want, keep doing this until you reach your vacation spot and you are soaking up all the good rays of sunshine.

Here is another example of an affirmation that I use for goal achievement. Use it as a template if you wish.

I see <u>my book in millions of people's hands, giving them words of encouragement and techniques to help them reach happiness and peace.</u> This makes me feel <u>fulfilled to help my brothers and sisters all over the world.</u> I see myself <u>on all the wonderful talk shows, radio shows, and in the magazines and newspapers, spreading words of peace and hope for all humankind.</u> This makes me feel <u>fantastic inside to be a servant to society.</u> I see myself <u>living in a community with peace as the core value, where everyone is living their passions without the need for money, fear, and control.</u> <u>There are no governments or military rulers trying to take control for their own personal greed.</u> This makes me feel <u>overjoyed because everyone else is happy and content.</u>

TEMPLATE FOR FINANCE:

I see myself with $ _____ in my bank account.

With this money, I see myself able to _____,

　　and this makes me feel _____.

(Or, having this money) brings me feelings of _____ .

With this money, I see myself able to _____,

　　and this makes me feel _____.

With this money, I see myself able to _____,

　　and this makes me feel_____.

TEMPLATE FOR HEALTH:

I see myself with a perfect body. I see my (body part you want improved or healed) rejuvenated and in perfect health, and this makes me feel　_____.

With my healthy body, I am able to _____,

　　and this makes me feel _____.

With my healthy body, I am able to _____,

and this makes me feel _____.

With my healthy body, I am able to _____,

    and this makes me feel _____.

TEMPLATE FOR RELATIONSHIPS:

I see myself spending time with my (future or current boyfriend, girlfriend, or spouse, with or without children),

    and this makes me feel _____.

While we are together, we get to _____,

    and this makes me feel _____.

While we are together, we get to _____,

    and this makes me feel _____.

While we are together, we get to _____,

    and this makes me feel _____.

TEMPLATE FOR OCCUPATION:

I see myself as a _____

    getting paid $ _____ and working _____ hours.

    This makes me feel _____.

As a _____,

    I get to (produce/create/manage/build) _____,

    and this makes me feel _____.

As a _____,

    I get to (produce/create/manage/build) _____,

    and this makes me feel _____.

As a _____,

    I get to (produce/create/manage/build) _____,

    and this makes me feel _____.

TEMPLATE FOR YOUR PASSION IN LIFE:

I see myself living my passion, which is to _____.

   This makes me feel _____.

While living my passion, I am able to _____,

   and this makes me feel _____.

While living my passion, I am able to _____,

   and this makes me feel _____.

While living my passion, I am able to _____,

   and this makes me feel _____.

PUTTING THINGS IN MOTION

If you are going to build a new palace of your life, don't forget to clear away the old foundation. You can wish for all the things you want, but if you still have feelings of guilt, low self-worth, or low self-esteem, you can hold up your own process or not get anything at all. This is where you can use any of the suggestions from previous chapters, seek professional counsel, or find your own way of releasing your manifestation blocks.

In the next chapter, I will give you another process that you can use to reinforce all the good things you would like to strengthen and anchor in your life. I recorded this for my clients and called it *You Are Worth It!* It is a compilation of over 100 positive phrases and suggestions that you can use to enhance your inner belief system, help you become the best you can be, and receive all that you are worth.

CHAPTER TWELVE

---◆--◆---

YOU ARE WORTH IT!
CLEARING MANIFESTATION BLOCKS

T HE EXERCISE YOU ARE ABOUT TO READ is a very effective tool to help you anchor new thought patterns into your daily life. You can use this system in many different ways. I will give you three suggestions to help you get started, but I'm sure your creative mind can come up with many more.

You could see instant results from any of the techniques I've already shared with you, but expect this one to take time. If someone goes to a gym to lose twenty pounds, she will have to go to the gym more than once to reach that goal. If you want to change some of your beliefs about yourself that you've carried with you for most of your life, this will also take some repetition. You will get out of it what you put into it.

SECTION 1

Instructions for clearing manifestation blocks:

1. Copy the next six pages before you start so you won't have to make permanent marks in the book.

2. Read each affirmation OUT LOUD. (Reading them in your mind does not have the same effect.)

3. Place a mark beside any statement that you would like to reinforce or positively change about yourself.

As you read each phrase, notice how it makes you feel. Does the statement correctly portray how you view yourself? Do you resonate with the phrase? Does it make you feel good? If you believe the statement to be true, go on to the next statement and notice how it makes you feel. If the statement doesn't feel good because it's not how you view yourself, put a special mark by that phrase. Also, place a mark beside any statement that you would like to reinforce in your subconscious mind. You'll use these marked phrases in Section 3.

There are no right or wrong answers, and it doesn't matter how many marks you have. Just go with how you feel when you read each statement.

AFFIRMATIONS

Success is my birthright.
To be loved is my birthright.
Self-acceptance is my birthright.
Being happy and fulfilled is my birthright.
Sharing love and abundance is my birthright.
Freedom is my birthright.
I am free to live my life the way I want.
I love myself more and more.
I appreciate myself more and more.
Good things happen to me on a daily basis.
I attract success into my life.
I am successful.
I am accepting of others.
I am accepting of myself.
I forgive others easily.
I forgive myself easily.
I attract wealth.
Money comes to me easily.
Money comes to me frequently.

I attract abundance.

Money is neutral to me, neither good nor bad.

Abundance is OK.

I expect wealth and abundance to come to me.

Wealth and abundance are my birthright.

I give myself permission to release old programming about money.

I am releasing all old programming about money.

I am happy all the time.

I vibrate toward happiness.

I attract happy people into my life.

I attract the right people to help me in my life's process.

My identity is controlled by me.

I give myself permission to release all old identities that no longer serve my present self.

I release all my old identities that no longer serve my present self.

My old identities fade away to make way for my true self.

I gravitate toward positive people.

I enjoy feeling good.

I allow all of my emotions to flow through me.

I feel good about myself.

I feel great about myself.

I find that I am more giving than before.

I enjoy receiving gifts.

I am grateful when I receive gifts.

I am grateful no matter what I receive.

I enjoy being cared for.

I enjoy caring for others.

I enjoy sharing as well as receiving.

I give myself permission to release negative programming about self-love and self-acceptance that no longer fits my life's purpose.

I release all negative programming about self-love and self-acceptance that no longer fits my life's purpose.

I give myself permission to release any social identities that no longer fit my life's purpose.

I release any social identities that no longer fit my life's purpose.

My identity and self-acceptance are not bound to social acceptance.

I decide what is good for me.

I decide what is in my best interest.

I decide what is not in my best interest.

I am influenced less and less by media.

I am influenced less and less by those outside myself.

I accept all truth as a perception.

I decide what perception to follow.

My past is a tool for my future.

I do not focus on past emotions and memories.

I focus on my desires with positive emotions.

I give myself permission to release emotions from my past that no longer serve my life's purpose.

I release emotions from my past memories that no longer serve my life's purpose.

I decide what my identity shall be.

I take responsibility for my actions.

I am responsible for my actions.

I blame others less for my outcome.

I blame others less for my perception.

I am responsible for my perceptions.

I trust my instincts more and more.

Failure is a perception, so I am not afraid to try over and over to succeed.

I set my focus clearly on the goal and not on the problem.

I finish all my projects.

I am committed to success.

I expect to succeed in all areas of my life.

I trust the Universe will provide what is needed for my life's purpose.

I allow the Universe to provide my desires to me in its own way.

I allow the flow of abundance into my life.

I accept what the Universe provides.

I am grateful for what the Universe provides.

As I receive, I also share.

I like the way I look.

I love the way I look.

I like the way I generally feel.

I love the way I generally feel.

I like other people.

I love other people.
I like my present situation.
I love my present situation.
I like my occupation.
I love my occupation.
I am living my passion in life.
I like the path I am currently on.
I love the path that I am currently on.
I accept my family.
I accept the person who is closest to me.
I love the person who is closest to me.
I forgive others for any wrongdoing toward me.
I accept criticism as an outside perception.
I love other people even if they see things differently than I do.
I act positively toward other people.
I am more loving toward other people.
I am more loving toward the environment.
I am more loving toward Mother Earth.
I am not afraid to live.
I am not afraid to try new things.
I am not afraid to meet other people.
I am not afraid to try a new occupation.
I am not afraid to die.
I am not afraid of the unknown.
I am not afraid of the future.
I create the future, so I am not afraid of it.
I cannot change my past, so I am not afraid of it.
I accept the present moment and enjoy it.
I have the power to change my thoughts.
I have the power to change my perception.
I have the right to accept or not accept others' perceptions.
I have the right to decide what is true or not true.
I am free.
I create my freedom.
I decide when to follow others.
I help others when they ask for my help.
I can help others without expecting praise.

I help others without expecting anything in return.
I accept that what I give is what I receive.
I accept that others are not out to get me.
I accept that others are not out to hurt me.
I accept that I create my future.
I am worthy of a great relationship.
I am worthy of good things.
I am worthy of love.
I am worthy of a great job.
I am worthy of money, and lots of it.
I am worth more than all my possessions.
I do not have to accumulate money because of fear that there is not
  enough.
I do not have to accumulate wealth to impress others.
I do not have to accumulate cars, houses, clothes, and jewelry to im-
  press others.
I do not have to accumulate weight because of fear that there is not
  enough love.
I do not have to suppress my emotions to fit in.
I believe there is an abundance of money, food, and shelter.
I believe there are people who love me in this world.
I believe that a better life is my birthright.
I make things happen.
I believe in my abilities.
I am creative.
I can speak my true thoughts without feeling afraid.
I can speak in public without fear.
I am intelligent.
I am smart.
I am confident in my skills to learn.
I am confident in my skills to teach others who wish to learn.
I am sexy.
I am good looking.
I am attractive to myself.
I look good in the mirror.
I look great in the mirror.
I am friendly to others.

I am friendly to myself.
I am kind to myself, even when things don't go my way.
I am kind to others, even when things don't go my way.
I am kind to animals.
I am kind to all living things.
I am confident about my ability to live and to love.
I love myself unconditionally.
I love others unconditionally.

How many statements would you like to reinforce in your life? If you find that you only have a few, you can immediately start using them as your daily affirmations. Plug your desired statements into one of the templates from the last chapter and add visualization and emotions to your mini-movies to increase your odds for success. You can also write out your affirmations to help instill these thoughts in your subconscious. In fact, make these phrases into a short song, if you like. I have heard that other realms of existence like it when we sing. Who knows where your help may come from?

If you have more than ten statements to reinforce, take the top three and use them as your daily affirmations. I would then suggest making an audio recording of all your desired affirmations to help with the process. There are plenty of free voice-recording programs online, and you can use a digital recorder or CD player for playback.

The most effective way to use this exercise is to offer these suggestions directly to your subconscious. The best way I know to do this is in an altered state of awareness, also known as a meditative state. You will increase your odds by clearing away all your past beliefs of guilt, low self-worth, low self-acceptance, and low self-esteem before you begin to anchor your newly intended beliefs. Also, make sure you are in a safe and comfortable environment before you begin listening to your affirmations.

As I mentioned earlier, the process of entering an alternate state of awareness begins as soon as you close your eyes. To help you further, there is a progressive muscle relaxation script in the next section that can help your body relax. If your body is relaxed, your mind easily follows. You can record the relaxation script first and then follow up with your intended phrases. However, if you plan to listen to this recording while driving, DO NOT USE THE SELF RELAXATION SCRIPT IN YOUR RECORDING.

You need to keep your attention on the road. What good is having a healthy mind and body if you are in a car wreck? For legal reasons, I cannot recommend listening to your affirmations while driving in your car, at work, or while operating a nuclear-powered chainsaw. Use your best judgment and consult your local authorities before engaging in these activities.

To increase the effectiveness of your personality phrases, use an action word before each statement in order to direct your subconscious mind to accept and reinforce the personality phrase. As an example, if you say "I am wealthy," your subconscious can instantly disagree with you, and you can find yourself making little or no progress in reaching your goals. Your conscious mind can also disagree with you if you are not currently wealthy. However, if you place the action word "YES" before each phrase, you are telling your subconscious mind what you want it to do and how you want it programmed. "Yes, I am wealthy" is a command to your subconscious mind; you are telling it to accept this new belief. You can also use "I see..." in addition to the command phrase: "Yes, I am wealthy. I see myself wealthy." This will help enhance the visualization process. After all, pictures and movies are the language of the subconscious.

Feel free to change the personality phrase any way you wish in order to meet your needs. My way is not the only way. Good luck!

SPECIAL NOTES...

- Do not listen to your recording while driving, operating machinery, or when personal or family responsibilities are required.
- Find a quiet place where you will be safe and undisturbed to listen to your recording. It is best if you do not cross your legs, your feet, or your arms, unless this makes you very comfortable.
- As with any meditation, you can always bring yourself to full awareness at any time by counting backwards from 5 to 1. Say to yourself, "5, 4, 3, 2, 1, eyes wide open and I am fully aware." Remember, you are always in control.
- If you are on any medication or receiving medical care, seek advice from your medical provider to see if it is safe for you to use this recording in conjunction with your prescribed medication and care plan.

SECTION 2

This section contains a short progressive muscle relaxation script that works really well. Feel free to use this as a template to help you enter an altered state of awareness, or use any other means that you are familiar with and bypass this part. You can also find many progressive muscle relaxation scripts online or in other books to suit your individual tastes.

Read the script first before you record it. This will ensure that you are comfortable with the wording and will help you to establish a pace. Speak slowly and clearly while recording. If you speak too fast, or your voice becomes too hard to hear, your subconscious can lose focus, be less cooperative, or shut down during the help session. If you speak too fast or unclearly to a child, they will give you that "huh?" look.

Let me reiterate: **DO NOT** use this self relaxation script if you plan to listen to the recording while driving, operating machinery, if your doctor does not recommend it, if you have family obligations to attend to, while playing with guns, knives, or explosives, or if it will place you or anyone else in harm's way. I mean it. Don't make me turn this book around and go back home!

SELF RELAXATION SCRIPT

I have closed my eyes, and I am ready to enhance my life and begin my positive change. I am ready to relax my mind and body completely. I will be able to relax very quickly and easily, and because my mind and body will be relaxed, I will enter an altered state of awareness without any effort at all. This is very natural and does not require any special skills. I go in and out of altered states of awareness throughout the day and night, and I can go into a meditative state whenever I choose. When I enter into this planned meditative state, I will be able to help myself achieve my personal goals and manifestation skills.

I give myself permission to enjoy this relaxing session and all the sounds and sensations that I will encounter. In order to help myself relax completely, I breathe in slowly and fully. I begin by taking in a long, deep, very slow breath. I hold my breath in for just a moment, and then I simply concentrate on the exhale. I take my time and enjoy the wonderful feeling of the air as it escapes my body. I exhale completely until I have no breath left in my lungs. Again, I breathe in very slowly, deeply, and fully, smelling the fresh clean air as it fills my lungs. I pause for just a moment, and I appreciate the relaxation as I focus on my exhale; I exhale slowly, deeply, and completely. I allow my shoulders to drop, drop, drop. And for a third time, when I am ready, I slowly inhale, filling my lungs with life-giving air. After a short pause, I exhale and allow my shoulders to drop even more. I feel them relaxing; I like this relaxed feeling throughout my entire body.

In a moment, I will be moving into my own personal space deep within my mind. In this special place, I will feel completely safe, comfortable, and secure. This special place in my mind gives me growing feelings of love, confidence, and everlasting support. My special place will help me relax my mind and my body even more than they are right now, and I will experience incredibly wonderful, peaceful feelings in every muscle and bone in my body. In this special place, I can move into an altered state of awareness, much like a meditative state. I will still be aware of what is going on around me, and I can easily regain complete awareness or open my eyes any time I choose. But for now, I will enjoy keeping my eyes closed and soak up the relaxing feelings that are beginning to flow over my entire body.

I am moving into the special place right now. In my mind's eye, I can see myself sitting, standing, or lying down in this inviting space. I can instantly create the perfect environment in my own creative mind. It makes no difference whether I am inside or outside. What matters most is that I enjoy where I am. I am deciding right now where that place will be for the rest of this meditative session, and I am taking myself there now. (Pause for a moment.)

When I have finished listening to this help session and come back to full awareness, I will remember things better than before, and I will have full consciousness of my thoughts. But for now, I enjoy keeping my eyes closed, and I enjoy this feeling of complete relaxation, knowing that I am bringing myself closer to my dreams and goals.

I know that my mind and body will cooperate completely, and this allows the process to begin immediately. I already feel the relaxation spreading over my body. All of my body parts will relax without any conscious effort at all.

As I comfortably breathe in, I am aware of how my toes, arches, and heels of my feet feel. When I exhale, I release all tension and stress in those parts of my body and allow relaxation to flow into every muscle, tendon, and bone in both of my feet. If those individual parts of my body are already relaxed, then I allow them to relax even more.

I enjoy how this feels, and I want my body to relax even more, so I allow the relaxing feelings to flow up into my ankles, my shins, and my calves. When I exhale, I allow my muscles to become loose, limp, and completely relaxed.

Feeling even better now, I allow my thighs to completely relax. My legs feel comfortable and rested as I continue with this wonderful meditation.

I know that a relaxed body is a healthier body, so I enjoy the relaxing feelings as they move up to my hips and groin area, up to my lower back, and around to my abdomen. I allow all stress or strain in my lower back to simply fade away as I exhale.

As I breathe in again, I allow my upper chest and shoulder blades to let go of any tension. When I exhale, I allow my shoulders to drop even more. I feel even more relaxed than before.

My arms are resting peacefully now, feeling wonderful all the way down to my fingertips. My neck relaxes and is able to support my head safely without stress or strain.

I feel my scalp letting go of any tension. My cheeks are relaxing, and my ears are relaxing. I allow my teeth to part slightly and I relax the back of my jaw. I feel wonderful, rested, and at ease.

I scan my body to see if there is any stress or strain left in any of my muscles. If there is any place that is still not completely relaxed, I simply focus my attention there and give myself permission to release the tension or strain. All my muscles are now loose, limp, and relaxed.

I take a few moments to enjoy this feeling. My body seems to float on the waves of relaxation. (Pause for a moment.)

SECTION 3:
RECORDING PERSONALITY PHRASES

After you have recorded your relaxation script, use the following as a guideline to record your personality phrases/affirmations.

Now that I am completely relaxed, I will repeat these statements silently in my mind and allow them to be anchored as new beliefs in my subconscious. By doing so, I will also anchor them in my conscious awareness and all other levels of my mind.

(Your name)'s subconscious, I accept these new beliefs and anchor them in all areas of my mind. I also direct you to reinforce the positive phrases that are already current in my life. These new beliefs and reinforced phrases will become so strong that they will be second nature in my outlook and my expectations of life.

(Your name)'s subconscious, I allow myself to easily release any conflicting beliefs and emotions, and I direct you to release the old statements in a loving fashion.

(Your name)'s subconscious mind, know that I accept all of these phrases to be true and beneficial for our well-being. I accept each and every one of these statements because I know them to be true.

(Your name)'s subconscious, repeat these words in my mind after I say them and rewrite the old beliefs with these new positive beliefs.

Begin with your first phrase. Don't forget to use your choice of action words. Leave a few seconds after each statement so you can repeat the phrase in your mind. Then go on to your next phrase.

After you have recorded all of your positive phrases, you can finish the recording with the following paragraphs:

(Your name)'s subconscious, thank you for accepting all of these statements and releasing my old beliefs that no longer serve us well. Please make these statements so strong that they help guide me in all areas of my life. Please make them so strong that they become second nature to my being. (Your name)'s subconscious mind, thank you for helping me today to make this our new reality.

Now it is time to come back to complete awareness. Each number that I hear will bring more awareness to my conscious self and my eyes will open wide when I hear the count of 1.

5...each statement taking more hold in all levels of my mind and body
4...feeling refreshed and revived from my new outlook on life
3...gaining more awareness of my new outlook
2...eyes opening and allowing light into my life
And number 1...eyes completely wide open...ready to live my life with a new positive outlook and positive expectations.

PART TWO

My First Wish: A Roadmap for World Peace

CHAPTER THIRTEEN

THE PRINCESS RIDDLE
THE LAND OF EDEN, THE LAND OF FEAR,
AND THE LINE THAT COULD NOT
BE CROSSED

W E VISIT A PLACE *forged not long ago. The tribes who lived here cooperated with the land and cherished the natural bounty the Earth provided for all. As centuries rolled by, the old ways of peace were forgotten and conflicts arose in every corner of the realm. Wars ensued for time untold, and nearly wiped out the beings called tall walking men. For humans to survive, the life force knew it must change polarities to make way for a time when peace would prevail.*

The elders knew this. They spoke of a great change to come in the soon told times. It loomed ominously on the horizon. As fortunes spoke, the feminine energies would leave forever and clear a path for a new life force to enter our world. This new life force would be the masculine energy, neither good nor bad, and was expected to come without much delay. The future actions of the people would dictate the perception of this new force, so now it was decided to be the masculine perspective. The strangers set foot on this once peaceful land, as we now enter the time of kings and queens.

It was also foretold that a third transition would come, after the male energy dominated its era. Each life force was a stone for the other to build upon. Without the feminine energy, there was no reference for the male. Without the male energy, there was no reference for balance.

We now visit the transition from female to male, and from male to balance. Listen to the tale as the male ego grew strong. Listen and witness as time made way for the ego to leave and balance the land. Hear this now, a new change is on the horizon. It will bring peace to the lands once and for all.

The kings made their way from their depleted homelands. Their resources were exhausted from a twenty-year drought, so they gathered their remaining people and ventured far away to the unknown realm that lies beyond the uncharted sea. They had no way to know if they would survive the journey, but journey they must, if they wanted to live.

Courage was there, and the leaders were strong. They had to find a way to endure in the unknown. What was missing had been the insight to leave tyranny behind. The old ways gave them comfort in this scary new world. As much as they tried to escape from their past, they planted their old seeds and allowed them to grow.

In time, they began to argue which religion was right, which God to worship, and what money to use. They created laws without end to enforce their views. They took to the old ways and adopted a king. With a king on the throne, they gave up their right to choose, until the next transition would come to change life for all.

The first of the kings were good people at heart. They ruled properly and fairly as well as they could. But before they began, their hands would be tied. Fear soon crept in, along with ego and money, and religion separated even the greatest of men.

As time had passed, and king replaced king, fear grew stronger than the mightiest warrior. When the first king ruled with fear as his weapon, the downward spiral would continue until this cycle would pass. All of life cycles, and this was no different. It was disappointing to many, as it did not have to unfold this way. The kings could have easily chosen Eden instead of fear.

From one king to the next, each passed the torch to his successor. If a king ruled without fear, the noble courts, military, and religious leaders used that weapon. Soon it became easy to control all the people. Fear is more powerful than all the bombs and guns combined.

By this time, the kingdom had sprouted an economy, and businesses flourished well for a while. Money became entrenched in their lives for good. Town leaders and courts were established for control, and their hunger for power and wealth grew with the greatest of fury. At the top of the pyramid was the lineage of the kings, and the kings found ways to keep power in their possession. They saw the incredible force that fear had on people. They knew how to manipulate truth to cause great fear in the land.

The need for increasing power grew within the royalty. They met in secret councils, which included bankers, landowners, religious figures, and military leaders. They handpicked them because they had the same desire for power, and they did not want another uprising as before in their old land. The king told the council he would help keep them rich, as long as they allowed the king to remain at the top. Benefits would be given to all those who agreed, benefits the people would never know about.

The king who started the secret society declared all information must go through him first. All knowledge of the kingdom's wealth and security was to be censored and monitored, and it would be controlled and dispersed by handpicked town criers. If the town criers divulged too much, or they divulged uncensored information, they were banished for good, or worse, beheaded. The king used this power to manipulate and withhold important information, sometimes completely rewriting the truth, in order to keep the townspeople fearful and under control.

At one point, the king's people started to revolt. They, in turn, formed groups of their own, led by teachers and others with great courage. These teachers made great strides in the land by sharing the hidden knowledge of peace and love. These teachers embraced thinking and self-governing over memorization. They taught their students that we are all connected as one; they taught how we are connected to the land; and they taught how the Universe manifests our thoughts and feelings.

Well, this wouldn't do, so the king took over the education system and changed it completely. He forced the teachers to teach facts and not lessons of life. Only pre-approved information was to be taught. If students memorized well, the teachers were rewarded with money and land. This was part of the plan to keep true knowledge under control. Anyone who opposed this would be cast out of the system and treated as a threat to the welfare of man.

Since people received filtered truths from the king and his council, and education emphasized memorization alone, the next step was to entertain the masses. This would keep the people from thinking for themselves and remembering the truths about life and a way toward Eden. So the king and the secret council devised exciting games and visual entertainment. They knew if they could keep the masses entertained, the people would become spiritually and intellectually lazy. That was the final key to keeping power with the king and secret councils.

This worked well for hundreds of years. The people became like worker bees. And those not on the council worked for food, land, and a chance to gain a little more.

Eventually, the power and greed of the council grew to untold levels. And their power and lust for wealth depleted the resources in the land. It was now time to expand, time to invade the neighboring kingdoms for their wealth and bounty.

This brings us near the end of the masculine cycle. Seated on the throne at this time was King Tasqure. King Tasqure was a powerful man. His tall, lean figure was forged for battle. His reign had claimed many of the surrounding towns to quench the thirst of his own selfish needs. Any unneeded resources were given to the secret council as a means to keep them happy.

Befitting all kings of his stature, King Tasqure's castle was without question the most expensive and lavish of all. He inherited the castle from those who had served before him. He added on sixty more rooms and fourteen kitchens and had the main ballroom remodeled so that his prolific image looked down from every archway. The great hall was also remodeled with stained-glass windows, and, of course, a red carpet leading up the stairs to the throne. All of the passageways into the great hall, all but one with no angles and a single light above, were ordained with sixteen-foot double doors. Each of the doorways was guarded by no fewer than two guards at all times.

As King Tasqure sat on his throne on his 45th birthday, he wondered what his future would hold. He wondered just how long the rule of the kings would last. It was a life envied by most, but he knew there was more. He thought to himself, "Once all is conquered, what is left to do? What will be left when all our resources are used?"

During one of the many wars for more wealth and land, King Tasqure came face to face with his destiny and suffered a fatal wound. Tasqure's faithful son, Moirdan, was at his father's side throughout the entire battle, fending off all of the enemy's attempts to wield the final death blow. Moirdan's courage was unmatched by anyone on the field, and he nearly lost his own life more than once as he dodged arrows and spears. He did everything in his power to give his father more time.

The generals signaled to King Tasqure, looking for orders and his assurance of victory. But the king was in no condition to continue fighting. Blood escaped his wounds, and his body grew cold, as his life force slowly gave way. In Tasqure's final moments, he called for his generals to come to his side. He instructed them to follow his son from now on. "Look to Moirdan. Moirdan will lead you better than I. Did you see him fend off an entire legion just to give me a few more breaths of life? His bravery will live on in unending legends and song. When I am no longer here, my son will carry out my reign and complete all the good deeds that I was unable to fulfill. Be grateful for his leadership. Give him your allegiance and your respect."

The generals had seen Moirdan fending off the enemy without fear. They knew he was a skilled warrior and leader. He had always proven himself in battle and had led many armies to victory. The generals felt confident with their new king and knelt down before him. Each of the generals pledged his life to Moirdan and vowed to take the battlefield with full fury and force. They vowed not to leave until victory was at hand and every enemy had been slain.

Just as the last general made his pledge, the battle turned in their favor. King Tasqure looked up at his son one final time and smiled. "You will be greater than all those who ruled before me, and you are already much greater than I could ever be. I should have told you this long ago, but in my final breath, I tell you of my infinite pride in you, my son. I love you, and you are already a great king."

King Tasqure made a momentous decision during his final seconds of life. He decided not to pass on the secrets of fear as was done before him. For most of Moirdan's life, Tasqure had sheltered his son from the hidden truths and secret societies. He could tell that Moirdan would be the one to make a great change for the people of the land.

There King Tasqure lay, his last breath taken. The battle was all but over, and the young new king made his first command to all the generals. "Go, now, to your soldiers. Tell them the killing is over. We will not do as the kings of the past. No slaves will be taken, and no heads will be rolled.

Let those who survived go back to their homes with a message of peace. Let them go to their king with the news that a new age of cooperation is at hand. Go, now, tend to our wounded, respect the bodies of our dead warriors, and lend aid to the other side. Tell our surgeons to treat all the wounded as if they were their own sons."

The generals were taken aback for a moment by these encouraging words. They had grown weary of killing for land, wealth, and greed. Many had personally lost much while in service. Most had seen their sons killed during the many wars. War had taken its toll on them, as well. They were ready to stop fighting and dying for blind patriotism. They were ready to start in a new direction of peace.

Upon returning to their homeland, and with the old ways dying away, King Moirdan was coronated, and all hoped for a new life. The kingdom embraced their new leader with open arms. They had always liked Moirdan; he had a good heart, a loving soul, and wisdom far greater than those before him.

Many years passed in the newly revived land. The people were prospering from King Moirdan's generosity and leadership. During those great times, Moirdan decided to wed. He married a courtier whom he had known since he was a young boy.

After their first year of marriage, Moirdan and his new bride had a beautiful baby girl, named Elsira. Unfortunately, Moirdan's wife suffered complications during birth and didn't live to see Elsira come into the world.

King Moirdan was distraught over this terrible loss, and he vowed never to marry again. Instead, he would give his unconditional love and complete attention to Elsira, who would succeed him when Moirdan passed on his reign. She was to be the new balance in the unbalanced time. She would lead the new age from the male energy to beyond.

When Moirdan's reign began, the people in the land were still clinging to the old ways. They had been conditioned for generations to believe their former kings. It didn't matter what the king said, the people believed his words out of fear. As much as Moirdan tried, he knew he would have to wait one generation before the people would be able to change.

As time passed by, Elsira grew into a beautiful young woman. She had the best qualities of her mother and her father. Her knowledge, compassion, and love of life shined brighter than any star in the night sky. She was a true joy to the court and to all the people.

King Moirdan knew that, since he had no son, it was time to groom his daughter for her destiny as queen. When Elsira was eighteen, Moirdan approached her with an option that had never before been considered. Normally, a prearranged marriage to a prince, or other person of high royal position, would be in her future. But Moirdan wanted to give Elsira a choice, a chance to self-govern. This choice would break from all tradition and start a new way. Moirdan gave her three options: she could find her own suitor, she could have her father find a suitor for her, or they could do it together.

Elsira knew of her father's vision for the people to be able to seek their own truth without fear of reprisal. She knew her suitor must have the ability to do just that. She also knew that as the future ruler of the land, it was sometimes necessary to make personal sacrifices on behalf of what was best for the people, so she decided to allow her father to select her future husband. She wanted to be sure her husband would be capable of leading their people to the future that she and her father envisioned.

How would he choose a proper king? How would he find someone who would be worthy enough to bring the people into a new era? Would it be a contest of skill, or a test of courage? What test would set one person above the rest?

"Elsira, I am going to do something that I have never done before," the king said. "I am going to give you a command. I command you to find your own suitor, one who can pass a test of your choosing. This will anchor what we both are trying to do for the people. I will be here to guide you if you wish, but this is your life, and I want you to do what is right for yourself. Once your suitor has passed your test, I will step down as king and let you guide our people to a new era of peace, prosperity, self-governing, and truth."

Elsira didn't know what to say at first. She was so overwhelmed with love and respect for her father that she immediately knelt down before him. But before Moirdan could lay a comforting hand on her head, she jumped into his arms to give him a loving daughter's embrace.

It was one month later when Elsira asked for a special audience with her father. "I have devised a test that will help me select a suitor," she said, "and I want the information to be announced to all the people in the kingdom in the same manner as before." This puzzled Moirdan at first, but she continued. "The test will be very simple. If one person can attain the truth on his own and answer my question, he will be worthy of my hand in marriage

181

and worthy of becoming king. If someone can rise above the rumors and misguided information from the town criers, this person will stand out far above all others in the land."

King Moirdan beamed with pride. His daughter had surpassed all of his expectations. He rose and declared loudly, "My daughter will be the finest queen of the land, and I am proud to be her father." The servants also cheered, for they, too, loved Elsira and were anxious to see everlasting peace settle over the land.

Elsira told her father that she was going to ask the candidates one riddle. If any male could answer her riddle correctly, she would accept his hand in marriage. Her riddle was this:

I place the shadow of a long staff in front of your king.
Approach this line and bring your answer to him.
You must angle with no angles the shadow to a perfect view,
Then my heart, and kingdom, I will give completely to you.

Your soul must be clean, and your body filled with strength.
The line is no more than four cubits in length.
If you find the angle, you will find me,
And happy our kingdom will forever be.

So approach this line and look from afar.
The answer will make you shine like a star.
When your answer is acknowledged, then you will see;
Walk forty paces true, and you will find me.

The king and I wait in full anticipation.
You will bring hope to the citizens of our great nation.
When you walk the path of the enlightened son,
You and I will join, and through marriage become one.

Your words and actions will prove your great worth.
Your leadership and knowledge will give this land a new birth.
Please find the angle, but don't make it bent,
Then the kingdom I will share with you as a wife content.

I gave you the riddle. I gave you the rhyme.
Please find the angle of this line in time.
Only the worthy one shall approach and appear,
And the people will rejoice, and welcome, and cheer.

We will gather in the hall where the great one still sits.
When seven days pass, bring your answer, strength, and wit.
You get just one chance, so make it stand true.
It is time. I wish you luck, and I bid you adieu.

King Moirdan laughed. "What a great riddle," he thought. Of course, he knew the answer right away. He kissed his daughter on the forehead. "Much preparation is needed," he told her, "for in one month, you will be wed, and our kingdom will be one king too many."

Elsira was crowned a queen before the entire kingdom. Her rule would not begin until she was wed, but her station was to be secured before meeting her new husband. The people were happy for her and overjoyed for their future. They knew a new age of balance was at hand.

As Queen Elsira's first command, she instructed all the people to listen intently to the town criers one week from that day. Elsira declared, "Our criers will bring the most important message ever heard to all eligible men. Their message will be my message, word for word. Please take them literally, and follow their instructions."

On the sixth day, Queen Elsira met with her town criers in the great hall. She read her riddle aloud and asked them what they thought the line represented. When they told her it was a staff four cubits long, Elsira had already anticipated their answer and gave them each a staff to take on their mission. They were instructed to show this symbol to all the single men in the land. She said, "You are to hold it up while you read my rhyme. Let the men copy the staff in order to help them solve the riddle. Tell them this symbol is the truth. They have been programmed to believe you already, so you shouldn't have any trouble getting them to accept your message as my own. Before the sun sets today, begin your journey to all the corners of our land, and as the sun blinks a smile on morrow's morning, speak the riddle until every single male of age has heard your voice. One last command: If they try to bribe you, give them a false answer, take their bribe, and give

their money to the poor. Our kingdom requires an honest king, not someone who purchased his way to the throne."

As commanded, the criers went out to every town, shire, castle, and farm.
They repeated the queen's riddle word for word. They let the men examine
the long staff as much as they liked, and helped them measure and cut new
staffs with which to work during their long dark nights.

The men who heard the riddle came from all levels of society. They were
noblemen, farmers, religious men, warriors, cooks, apprentices, and masters of trade. They were horsemen, fishermen, woodsmen, castle builders,
barrel makers, and scholars alike. It didn't matter what station or status
they held in the land, if they were a single male, and of age, they were to
hear the rhyme.

As the riddle was told, most of the men were seen scratching their heads.
Many held the long staff, desperately trying to figure out the correct angle
in which to hold it before King Moirdan. They begged the town criers for
more information. "Just one more clue, please, give us just one more." Of
course, with this much potential for money and power, some offered bribes
to the town criers to divulge the answer. And as instructed by the queen,
the town criers took their bribes and distributed them to the needy.

It took the town criers almost two weeks to cover the territory and de-
liver the queen's message. With one week to go before the greatest of gath-
erings, every eligible man was consumed with working on the riddle. They
shunned their duties so they could unlock the clues hidden within. Some
of the men took their staffs and the riddle to neighboring kingdoms and
paid their scholars a handsome sum in exchange for help. As you can imagine, the riddle produced numerous solutions.

Some figured that the staff must be held with an angle that was upright
and true, pointing to their version of a God, the Supreme Being, and to the
Heavens above. They would present themselves as being faithful to their
God and to their truth. God would rule through them, and only they would
hear the words of God. If God told them to kill in His name, they would
take up arms against all who stood against their God and their kingdom.

Others decided that the staff should be held like a lance, ready for attack.
This would show the king that they were strong and willing to fight for their
kingdom. They would protect the queen, their people, the land, and especially the king's wealth and treasures. They were warriors, full of strength,
courage, and vigor. They would grip the staff fiercely, flexing their muscles

in an attempt to sway the king by their physical superiority. They thought, "It is strength of body, not of mind, that will lead our new land."

Some of the men decided to spin the staff, hoping to show they had vision of perception. As king, when faced with a difficult choice, they would be able to look at a problem from many angles. This would show the king that they were wise and open-minded. They worked up routines of skill, swinging their staffs above, below, and all around their bodies. Even if they were not chosen, their displays would certainly be very entertaining for King Moirdan and his court. They hired jugglers, dancers, and entertainers to help them come up with dazzling routines.

Some of the men decided to use words alone to answer the riddle. They felt that a sonnet representing wisdom and praise would honor their king and show him they had enough intellect to rule the land. They would approach and kneel before the line, then use their prepared speeches to angle the king's thoughts of approval toward them.

As the seventh sun rose in the east, the entire kingdom poured into the great halls of the castle to see their potential king answer Queen Elsira's riddle. It was a festival as never seen before by the people. Prior to Moirdan's rule, commoners had never been permitted into the castle, so just being there was a new step of hope for the people. Food had been provided for everyone, and drinks flowed forth like a mighty waterfall. The crowds were entertained by minstrels, jugglers, fire breathers, and acrobats. They saw feats of strength, kissing wenches, and puppeteers. It was a great day to be in the kingdom.

The trumpets heralded the approach of King Moirdan. He walked through the crowds, embracing all who were close to him. He shook their hands and acknowledged their cheers. The beginning of the red carpet was soon under his feet as the crowd took to one knee in adoration for their king. For Moirdan to step down while he was still alive was proof to the people that he was a king above all others. He was leading the people to a better life.

As planned, Queen Elsira was not to be seen throughout the entire festival. She would reveal herself only to the one who could answer her riddle. No one, not even her ladies-in-waiting, knew where she was.

The trumpets heralded again as King Moirdan took his seat on the throne. When the noise from the crowds settled down, King Moirdan addressed his people for the last time as their ruler. He assured them that his daughter's leadership, knowledge, and compassion were already greater than any prior king had ever shown. "I will be glad to be a royal subject of hers, and to continue my role as a supporting father when this day is done and she is wed. Let the first suitor approach, and good luck to all." With that said, the crowds erupted into a huge cheer, exalting their king and all the potential suitors.

The line to approach the king stretched far beyond the castle walls. With a chance to marry his beautiful daughter, and to become future king, there wasn't a single man in the realm that would pass on this opportunity. One by one, they approached the line, and one by one, they tried to angle the line in just the right way to answer the riddle. The crowd cheered for each suitor, wondering which man would become their new leader.

Hundreds had tried, and hundreds had failed. It was beginning to seem as if no one would solve the riddle. The people were getting anxious. They wanted to see someone become king. Even the men in the long line grew weary, especially the royalty. The princes, dukes, and earls, who still considered themselves above the rest because of their birthrights, took their losses especially hard.

The king called for a break. "We will resume after the dinner festivities. Make sure that every man in the kingdom is here and has given his best effort."

During the feast, one man in particular seemed to gather quite a crowd around him. He was in his mid-twenties, close to six feet in height, and his body was toned and very strong from working hard at his trade. He was well-loved in his town, and even people from the surrounding villages knew him for the quality of his work and for his good nature.

His name was Broden. If ever there was a person who should have been born into royalty, it was he. Everyone in his town looked up to him. He was skilled in his trade and always shared with his neighbors. If someone came into his shop with no money for clothing or food, he provided that person what he could. If the children stopped by after their chores, he would always take time to share a tale or two with them. He gave of himself and never asked for more than his share in return. He sat on the town council, and his contributions of knowledge and guidance were an inspiration to all.

Broden was a master blacksmith who specialized in making hoops for wine casks. He took great pride in his work and was a shining example for other tradesmen. He often traveled to surrounding villages to share his skills and make new friends. There was no place that he was not welcome. Many a drink and dinner had been bought for this good soul.

The trumpets blared again to resume the task at hand, but the line had begun to dwindle. Some of the men had already seen their answers fail when presented by others, and there was no reason to offer the same answers again.

The crowd became more jovial and festive, probably because of the abundant wine and spirits. As each man stepped up to the line, the chants of "King, King, King!" grew louder and rang through the great hall.

It eventually came down to the last two men, Malten and Broden. Malten went first. He took a mathematical approach, more like a scientist. He regaled King Moirdan with his knowledge of mathematic proportions and how they related to the qualities of a good king. The crowd grew silent, not knowing how King Moirdan would take to this approach. But King Moirdan smiled, as he had done for hundreds of others before him, and he thanked Malten for his efforts and bid him well in life.

The crowd looked down at the last man standing. They knew that if anyone could provide the answer, it would be Broden. They began to chant, "Bro-den, Bro-den, Bro-den, Bro-den!" On and on they shouted, louder and louder, as Broden approached the line before the king.

Broden was sure that there was nothing special to the riddle and that there was nothing he had to do before the king. He knew from his time spent on the town council that the next leader had to find the truth on his own. He recognized that for centuries the people had been programmed so they wouldn't think for themselves, and that they had been forced to believe what was told to them by their former leaders through the use of fear and torture.

Broden approached the line, and the crowd became still. Without saying a word, he bowed before King Moirdan, looked to his right, and looked back to the king for acknowledgment. At that moment, King Moirdan stood up and smiled as he had done for all the others before. The crowd gasped, and you could hear one of them say, "Noooo! Please let at least one man pass the test."

But King Moirdan didn't speak. Instead, he left his throne and came down the stairs. The people watched in utter silence. At the bottom of the stairs, Moirdan stood in front of Broden, placed a hand on his shoulder, and turned him toward the door on the right. "Go, Broden, walk forty paces true, and find your queen."

The crowd erupted in applause, yelling, "All hail King Moirdan! All hail King Broden!"

You see, the doorway to the right of the throne was circular, an open doorway with no angles and a light shining down from above. The only way to find the answer to the riddle was to forego the visual perception presented by the town criers. Broden listened to the riddle and chose to ignore the straight staff that was shown to him. He was used to working with metal hoops, and when you angle a metal hoop just right and look down upon it, a circle becomes a straight line, which also casts the shadow of a straight line. And the door to the right of the throne was a circular doorway exactly four cubits in height with the shadow of a straight line beneath it. He remembered the first line of the riddle:

> I place the shadow of a long staff in front of your king.
> Approach this line and bring your answer to him.
> You must angle with no angles the shadow to a perfect view,
> Then my heart, and kingdom, I will give completely to you.

Broden knew that a shadow is not always what it appears to be. A two-dimensional shadow can be created by a two- or three-dimensional object. So by looking at a hoop from more than one angle, more than one perception, you could easily get the shadow of a straight line. And as truth and perception are as individual as personalities, there was another truth besides a staff.

Broden walked forty paces, passing the only circular door in the great hall, the only door with no angles. The passageway turned slightly, keeping Elsira out of sight. When he met Queen Elsira, he knelt before her and asked for her hand in marriage. Elsira was overjoyed that she had found such a wonderful suitor. King Moirdan joined them, just as Elsira accepted Broden's proposal.

The three of them walked out to the great hall, Elsira's hand wrapped around Broden's strong arm, and King Moirdan happily walked beside them. "Good people of the land, I present to you your new king, King Broden, and Queen Elsira. We will coronate your new king after their wedding tomorrow's eve. Stay, enjoy, and come to know your new king."

Queen Elsira addressed the crowd after her father. She promised the people that she would help lead them into a new age of enlightenment, an age when people would once again be encouraged to govern themselves. She wanted truth to reign and not be limited to one person's perception. And she hoped that when two people's perceptions didn't match, they would still be able to love each other unconditionally. She vowed to always announce news in the purest form possible, and never to manipulate the truth for power or personal gain.

This was the beginning of change for the land. The female energy gave way to the male, and the male transitioned toward a new balance for all. Peace was at hand for all to enjoy.

CHAPTER FOURTEEN

A BEGINNING FOR CHANGE

L IVING ON THIS GREAT PLANET has been a blessing and an honor, especially in this particular time period. I, like many of you, have been fortunate to experience firsthand many of the great changes and advances the human race has achieved. It feels like we are living in a science fiction movie that has turned into a reality. I call it *science non-fictionality*. We are now capable of placing an order for Chinese take-out while skydiving, without being connected to a wall with a 13,000-foot extension cord. We can pull up information almost instantaneously on a small computer while driving down the Pacific Coast Highway to locate the famous wineries in Napa Valley. We can ride on a super train traveling over 350 mph in Japan while floating inches above the ground on a magnetic field. Who would have thought that our cars would be talking back to us? And subatomic particles, in a sense, can be transported instantaneously across a room.

It's amazing how fast change has happened. We have seen huge advances in all areas of science, technology, and medicine. We have witnessed astounding acts of charity, kindness, and forgiveness. We have also seen inconceivable acts of violence that most people consider terrible and outright inhumane. Our race is young and growing, and we have barely scratched the surface of our potential for knowledge, peace, tolerance, and cooperation. We have the capability to be so very kind, loving, caring, creative, bitter, and cruel all at the same time. And what is so encouraging to me is that it feels like we are getting ready to make an even bigger leap forward in progress for humanity's sake. We have the gift of freedom to decide as a race if this change will move us toward peace and happiness for all species on this planet, or if it will keep us bound to a life in which individuals and governments still control the masses with fear, dominance, and oppression.

CHANGES FROM CHILDHOOD

I was only four years old when the first person from Earth supposedly walked on the moon. At that time in our small town, you could still have milk delivered to your home. Some of you remember—the old-fashioned kind of milk in a glass bottle with the tin foil tops. It was a time when chocolate milk came from chocolate cows. People could leave their doors unlocked and not have to worry about theft or vandalism. Children played outside for fun. We rode our bikes, swam in the lakes and rivers, played hide-and-seek at our friends' homes, and we loved a good game of kickball. If we didn't have enough people for a team, we made up our own fun with creativity, desire, and whatever interesting stuff we could find in an attic or basement. A broom easily transformed into a knight's horse with a garbage can lid as a shield. With a little imagination, an old cardboard box magically became a spaceship or a castle for a princess. Life was simple and exciting at this early age. There was so much to explore and learn. It's time to let your inner child out again. Maybe today will be the day you will find a wooded area and take a new journey with a friend. Maybe tomorrow is the day you will drive to a new unexplored town. (This book will still be here when you get back. Go have fun!)

When it came time to change the channel on our small black-and-white TV, we didn't have a fancy remote that instantly switched channels, turned off the lights, and started the blender all at the same time. There were five children in our house, which meant there were plenty of bodies to walk over and turn the knob by hand. If the reception was fuzzy on our seven or eight channels, we moved the rabbit ears until the rolling lines disappeared and Walter Cronkite came in loud and clear.

I had a ball as a child. We lived outside the city close to a few dairy farms.

Across the street from our house was a sloping cow pasture. This steep incline made a great sled riding hill when the winter snows blanketed our town with the cold white water. During the spring and summer months, when the cows were not eating grass in the open pasture, their grazing fields created an awesome place for flying kites. There were no telephone wires to worry about or spy satellites falling from the sky, just little steamy piles of you-know-what to avoid when rescuing a downed paper kite.

Life was good without laptops, pagers, beepers, text messaging, and cell phones. Word of mouth worked just fine back then, and it still does today. If you wanted to tell your friend something, you got on your bike and rode to his house. If you were lucky, there was a plate of warm cookies in his family's kitchen to munch on. And if dinner was on the stove, an invite for supper echoed through their house with words of encouragement to stay and eat a home cooked meal. Talking to people face to face, seeing their reactions, feeling their emotions, and sharing a good laugh together are priceless, in my mind. You can't get that from an email or a text message.

Now don't get me wrong; I am not bashing our progress and electronic revolutions. The words you are reading in this book were typed on a lap-top with a word-processing program. This book would have taken twice as long to complete if it had been written before computers existed. Editing and moving text is much easier than before and doesn't waste reams of paper or cartons of correction tape. I am glad that this device is around, not to mention the ability to research vast amounts of information on the internet.

I have enjoyed the benefits of living a great life with, and without, these electronic comforts. I am finding a good balance with progress and us-ing these very tools to help others in their quest for happiness, peace, and balance. I know what it is like to have and not to have. I feel fortunate to know both sides of the coin. I am glad to know that life can continue with or without these creature comforts because we did this once before. I feel at balance with our progress, and I continue to balance myself as best as possible with our advancing technologies.

COMBINING TECHNOLOGY

One of my desires is to learn all the ways in which we could use technol-ogy without causing harm to another. I imagine we would all welcome technological advances a little more if they didn't hurt other people, plants, animals, insects, and especially the planet, in any way. If you don't take care of your house and all its inhabitants, how can the house and inhabitants take care of you? We need to take better care of our planet, but how? This is the knowledge that I, and many others, wish we knew. I believe we are moving in this direction, though. There is a much larger awareness for going *green* and helping the Earth to heal Herself from our previous mistakes, and She will heal Herself again if given a chance. We can stay here for a long, long time if we cooperate with our Mother planet. All She needs is a chance. If we don't give it to Her, though, I believe we are looking at our own demise as a species. Let's cross our fingers and hope we are moving toward a healthier Mother Earth.

NOTABLE IMPROVEMENTS
TO KEEP AROUND

If I had to choose only five comforts to keep that have been invented in the last 200 years and have made a huge impact on our culture, the top item on my list would have to be the refrigerator/freezer. Nothing beats a cold glass of milk to go with those warm chocolate chip cookies for a mid-afternoon snack. We all know how invaluable the refrigerator is for food storage and helping to alleviate waste. Without the refrigerator, we would be spending most of our lives again hunting and gathering food. The refrigerator gives us a chance to pursue other passions.

Along with refrigeration, we could also bring back some of the lost arts of salting, canning, smoking, and pickling foods for preservation. (Let's hear it for Betty and Mary's blue ribbon prize at the county fair.) Maybe there could be a better balance of refrigeration, hunting and gathering, and food preservation practices. I am not talking about all the preservatives and chemicals that are found in the majority of our store-bought meats, produce, and boxed goods. I am talking about the healthier practices of food preservation. These pastimes helped bring people together. While hunting, gathering, and preparing food, people were given an opportunity to know their neighbors and family. A lot of these practices were done as a community, and food was shared throughout the neighborhood. Nowadays, there isn't much time for these practices because of the pursuit of wealth and accumulating stuff to fill our closets, attics, and storage units. Doesn't it seem like most of our time is spent in cars, commuting to and from work, waiting in line at the checkout counter, or spending the night outside the football stadium waiting for season tickets to go on sale?

We're all aware of the benefit of knowing your family and neighbors. The better you know a person deep down inside, the more you care about them and wish them well. This creates less fear of the unknown and less hatred and anger. And when people feel comfortable around you, they also open up to you more. Think about it. No more secrets or fear of being judged. This, alone, would take care of the majority of fights and divorces in our country, and around the world.

I am not blaming the refrigerator for this, not one bit. And I am not saying that bringing back some of the old methods of food preservation would fix the world's problems. I am merely commenting on a proposed balance to help our species grow further in peace. Couldn't we bring back the parts of the old that were beneficial for the world and combine them with the new? I believe so. What do you think?

THE REMAINING FOUR

As I think about other notable improvements that would be keepers for a peaceful world, running hot and cold water in every home would be a contender for my top five. I enjoy the benefit of turning on a faucet and having instant access to water. As a child, I also liked hiking to get water from the river. Have you ever experienced what it is like to take a drink from a cold mountain stream to satisfy your thirst while exploring the woods? It's a completely different feeling when you get water right from nature. It seems to connect us with the Earth again.

Here is a part of the old that could be brought back to the new when talking about water. Fetching water at a local well or stream used to benefit a town because it produced a natural community center. This common gathering spot gave people a place to share news, share ideas, and form new friendships. Supplying water to a town or village became a community activity and built camaraderie and togetherness.

At this time, though, I imagine we are all glad that we don't have to walk outside, while trudging our way through five feet of snow, to bring back a pitcher of water. I, like many others, am still searching for a way to balance our need for water with how it fits into our society.

The internet has turned out to be a great tool. It's helped our world move to a new level of human connection that has never been seen before. Some have even said the World Wide Web has created a new means of telepathic communication between people and cultures. Information and knowledge are almost instantaneous. The vast amount of knowledge one can obtain from the internet has surely narrowed the gap between social statuses of older times. With entire volumes of encyclopedias, dictionaries, and what seems like an unlimited amount of resource material found at the push of a button, one cannot help but be amazed at the wealth of knowledge and possibilities that this invention has created.

If electricity and the benefits of motorized engines could be obtained without hurting the planet, this would also make my top five list. I have heard of numerous types of free energy, such as zero point, the field, scalar waves, dark energy, dark matter, and magnetic impulse. And let's not forget a force from a higher power: life force energy, chi, mana, prana, ki, and all of its other many names. We are already familiar with other types of free energy, too. We have solar power, power from the wind, power from the force of water, methane, and power of the mind. When any of these are not blocked by the need for profit, their benefits will be welcomed by the masses. We have made such incredible technical advances in the last fifty years alone. I have no doubt that we will be able to see at least one of these natural resources come into mainstream use for the benefit of all inhabitants of this planet.

I must admit that I have been spoiled with air conditioning and a thermostat for automatically turning on the heat. So air conditioning and heaters round out my top five. I have lived in the southern part of the US for the last twenty years. The average temperature in the summertime has been reaching mid-90s to 100s with stifling humidity that frizzes the straightest of hair as soon as you walk outside. Now, if I had to, I know I could go without air conditioning again. I grew up without any air conditioning in my home and survived just fine. We had a huge fan for the living room, and my parents had a window fan; that was it. If we wanted air conditioning, we started a good pillow fight to get the breeze moving. Our tiny bedroom, which housed three stout teenage boys, had a very small window that barely opened a crack, so there wasn't much help for cooling down at night. Our high school didn't always have air conditioning, either. It wasn't until I went to college that I became accustomed to air conditioning in the buildings. But once you get a taste of air conditioning, and notice the word *conditioning*, you grow accustomed rather fast to the comforts of a cool, controlled climate. Heaven forbid when the electricity and the A/C go out for good on this planet.

Speaking of electricity going out, I know that we could also survive all over again without power if we had to. When Hurricane Ike came through the Houston area on September 12, 2008, the Category 2 storm made landfall and wiped out homes and businesses, downed trees, and knocked out power lines. Hurricane Ike pulled the plug and turned off electricity for millions of people for days, weeks, and even months. At our house, power was out for one day shy of two weeks. Even without this creature comfort, I was still able to breathe, eat, and survive without any negative after-effects. I like the convenience of this wonderful resource, but I was still able to cook, clean, and entertain myself without having my plug-in toys. I also didn't use a generator. I had my grill for my fire, candles and lamps for light, my books for entertainment, and my thoughts mixed with friendly company. My time away from work gave me numerous opportunities to create new projects, complete old projects, help my neighbors, and find another level of appreciation for what I had and didn't have.

I also found a way to overcome the heat and distractions from my own discomforts by helping others. I spent a few days at the distribution centers handing out ice, food, supplies, and MRE's (meals ready to eat) to those people in need. If you want to forget about your own problems, help someone else with theirs. It was hotter outside in the blazing sun than it was at my house, but I didn't complain once about the heat at my house because I was outside helping others. I didn't care about air conditioning because I found a better internal feeling by giving my time and energy to help others who had it worse than I did. There were those who'd lost their homes, their clothes, their cars, their boats, their keepsakes, and in some cases, their health. So I felt fortunate and was glad that I'd been able to help.

OTHER NOTABLES

A few other notable inventions would be the microwave, deodorant, cell phones, toilet paper without pine needles, and mosquito repellent. Oh, and my wife just nudged me and said I should add antibiotics. I guess I need to add milk chocolate to the list, too. There are many more worth mentioning here, but there simply isn't room. I hope that these words brought back some good memories for you. I also hope this helps you decide what you cherish and would like to keep around for a while. Here are a few questions to think about to help your life move forward.

What would be your five favorite technological advancements?

Do you feel at balance with progress? How do you feel about the accelerated progress of technology?

What do you see changing fifty years from now that would make a difference in medicine, science, technology, or spirituality?

What technological toys could you live without if you had to?

Are you willing to let go of something old in your life to allow something new to come in? What would that be?

Is there an invention that is hurting you, hurting others, or hurting the planet that you can let go of?

AN ADVANCING WORLD

If we were able to use H.G. Wells' time machine to go backwards and forwards through time and talk to people from multiple eras, I think we would find a lot of people saying the same thing about advances in technology, science, weaponry, medicine, and humanity. Maybe not to the same degree as we have seen in the last fifty years, but certainly most cultures and time periods have witnessed great changes and advances that have influenced their lives in one way or another.

Traveling back as far as 100,000 years ago, fire was still the rage of the tribes and would be considered one of the greatest discoveries for humanity. (Barbecued mastodon ribs sounds pretty tasty right now.) If we moved forward to 3500 B.C. and visited Mesopotamia, the wheel was considered one of the greatest inventions ever made, and it remains so to this day. This, of course, is debatable with the party crowd who also thinks that brewing beer around the same time period might have been the greatest discovery ever.

Jumping into our time machine again and stopping in Korea just after 1000 A.D., we could have witnessed the beginnings of moveable type, which took on even greater fame around 1450 A.D. when Johannes Gutenberg used moveable type to create the famous Gutenberg Bible. Going backwards again 35,000 years, we might have danced the night away to the entertaining sounds of a pentatonic flute made from ivory or bone. Moving forward one last time to 1867 A.D., we might have been fortunate to sample something made by a Swiss confectioner named Daniel Peter. His great contribution was the process of using condensed milk to solidify milk chocolate, which was invented by Henri Nestlé in the early 1800s. Each of these events stands out as an incredible addition to an ever-changing and fluctuating world.

NEW DIRECTIONS OF LEADERSHIP

Just as discoveries and inventions have helped to change the world, so have leadership and government systems. The need to organize, create, control, and survive has given birth to numerous types of local and global management systems for hundreds and thousands of years. Rules, laws, edicts, proclamations, rituals, religions, and orders have been the norm since the beginning of the tribal leaders and the discovery of fried flesh. None of these previous ruling systems can be called primitive, sadistic, or outdated. (Well, they can be, but there are always multiple ways to look at these previous leadership systems.) As I see it, there is a bright outlook for having these ruling systems as part of our history. Each ruling government had its place and need in time. Each of these systems created room for growth. Sometimes the progress was imperceptible, and other times it grew faster than our known Universe. These old and current systems have helped our world move consistently toward a common goal of individual freedom for all races and species. We are not there yet, but this is the direction in which I believe we are headed.

For as long as our race can remember, there have been governing systems instituted by and for humans. Likewise, there has always been a natural system for governing nature. Each species has its place of importance in the larger picture. Take away too many species by extermination, eradication, domination, or extinction, and the entire ecosystem could topple with little or no chance of recovering. As an example, a recent concern voiced by scientists and conservationists pertains to our world's coral reefs. If the coral reefs completely die off in the oceans, this could radically affect the natural balance of the entire fish and animal kingdom—and the human race as well.

We know there is a huge population of small fish that coexist and rely on the coral reef to sustain life. Without these living coral gardens, the smaller fish, which rely on coral as a natural food source, would be gone in the blink of an eye. To grasp what these smaller fish might experience, imagine that all the food stores and markets in the entire country close their doors forever. No more food supplies. This would be rather frightening for most. Eventually, the smaller fish, like us, would have to find a new food source or die from starvation. And without their natural protection, the smaller fish would be exposed to predators and would die off rather quickly.

The medium and larger fish in the ocean know there is an abundance of smaller fish that live around the coral reef, so they feed there to help remove injured and older fish and keep the reef from becoming over populated. If you remove all the smaller fish, the larger fish lose their food source and die off as well. If the larger fish and ocean mammals die off, this affects the land-based animals, mammals, and people who also rely on fish as a food source. One small change in a natural governing system could completely change the balance and existence of an entire world.

Likewise, if one species tries to dominate, control, and monopolize all other species and inhabitants, this will also cause a huge chain reaction that will shift the balance and very nature of survival for all involved. One species can easily eradicate an entire food source and cause its own demise. This is one theory behind the almost instantaneous disappearance of the ancient Incan culture in South America.

At present, our current government systems and business monopolies are horribly unbalanced and are completely dominating our society. If you look at nature, you will see that each species requires a balance of freedom and cooperation to help keep the cycle from collapsing. One of my teachers, Dr. David Frederick, from Lancaster, PA, introduced this to me. He told me that Qi Gong "is a science which studies the energy of nature." By looking at our world from a non-human perspective, I was able to see that the freedoms of every species, including the human race, must be respected, and we all must be allowed to live freely as intended.

PERCEPTIONS OF FREEDOM

If you asked five people at the dinner table to write down a word that describes the opposite of freedom, I imagine at least one of those five words would be *slavery*. A good follow-up question might be this one: For someone to really know and appreciate freedom, would they first have to experience what it is like to be a slave? What do you think? My answer would be, "No, not one bit." Freedom can be achieved in many ways without being owned or having your rights or privileges completely stripped away. However, this extreme would certainly provide a broad spectrum of individual experience compared to someone who has never lived as a slave. And hopefully, anyone who has this extensive knowledge would use it to help enlighten others and expand their minds and perceptions. This valuable knowledge and perception could help an entire civilization avoid a path lived once before so it could evolve faster and without hurting others or the planet.

Of course, everyone will have their own opinions for what freedom and slavery mean to them. There is no way that one person could tell another that he or she is right or wrong. As an example, some people's freedom might be to give up their right to choose and no longer have a voice in the decision-making process. These people don't want the burden of making a choice and will live their lives content and happy under someone else's rule. At the same time, others would consider this loss of choice a major crime and travesty against society, and they would quickly form emotional hordes of angry mobs for demonstrations, rallies, marches, and even violence to voice their displeasure. Wars have started just as quickly because of minor differences of opinion over what freedom means and who is allowed to have it.

To put this into today's perspective, imagine asking your spouse what he or she would like for dinner tonight. The choices might be lasagna or raw three-week-old chicken, yet your spouse may still respond, "Honey, I don't care. You decide. I'll eat whatever you choose." This release of choice is a form of freedom for some people. They feel better with another person making the decision, while others, on the opposite side of the coin, feel better by taking the leadership role. These leaders, in turn, are helping those who desire this temporary reprieve from decision-making.

The great thing about freedom and choice is that they are malleable. Just because some people choose to give up control sometimes doesn't mean they want to do this for every thought, idea, or action. There can be an unspoken give and take with this type of freedom transfer, and people can easily switch roles. I know that my wife and I have switched this role many times. Sometimes it is a comfort to give up my choice when I am exhausted from a long day of teaching and serving the community. The last thing I want to do is decide what's for dinner. But on other days, I may feel very emphatic about the choices on our dinner menu. I didn't have to become a slave in order to appreciate this freedom. However, in some respects, we are all slaves and servants to one thing or another. Is choice the ultimate factor that determines whether one is enslaved or free? We will talk about this more in the next chapters.

REVOLVING GOVERNMENTS

The last section to cover before moving on is to discuss the history of leadership and government. When and where could the next possible step in the evolution of leadership for the human race take place?

I am speculating here, but it seems that the first government, or ruling system, a few million years ago might have established itself when one of the first tribes or clans of early humans instituted a leader. Or maybe an early alien ancestor of ours became the new government when they took control over a tribe with advanced technology. We don't have to look back millions of years to see this happen, either. All we need to do is pick up a recent newspaper, turn on the news, or look on the internet to hear about the same type of "prehistoric" acts of claiming power in today's world. (Isn't it funny how history keeps repeating itself until people get tired of it and welcome change?)

As I've said before, each ruling system has been a part of the learning process. Each system has had its time of glory in history. Power has shifted from the early tribal leaders to the standard economic—and sometimes power hungry—governments of today. And while there are still tribal leaders in our world, at one point in history, a shift toward other types of government and ruling powers began to take place. Some of these systems dominated the others with massive size and force, while others made their way through their own growth spurts, waiting to take their turn as the dominating force on the planet. But nearly all of them have managed to coexist at one time or another.

EXPANDING AND INTEGRATING GOVERNMENTS

Since the earliest of times, religion has always played a significant role in all levels of government. When the first deafening claps of thunder roared across the savannah in Africa, Gods and Goddesses spoke to the people of the lands. The early tribal leaders might have easily been influenced by nature's boisterous loud call. (The Gods and Goddesses might have also been aliens. But that is another book, too.) So I think it would be safe to say that this was probably the beginning of government rule being combined with religious beliefs. No one will know ever know for sure, unless we can borrow our time machine again and speak with early Homo sapiens, Neanderthals, and their ancestors, but the conclusion seems plausible.

Up to this point, we have gone from tribal leaders to tribal councils, monarchies, socialism, feudal systems, religious rule, democracy, communism, capitalism, socialism, and a few other isms that I didn't mention. We have been through so many different types of government and isms that the mind is left spinning around faster than a runaway merry-go-round. Each of these forms of government has shown its good sides and downfalls. Each government has had great leaders, not-so-great leaders, times of prosperity, and times of collapse. One thing has been plain to see over the course of our civilization: No one type of government has stood the test of time. Even our own democracy in the United States has its many mounting imperfections and visions of future collapse.

There is one more form of government left that I believe will be the single ruling system that *will* withstand the test of time. This will be the one that will take the human race to a new time of peace, happiness, and prosperity. This type of government, which I will discuss in great detail in future chapters, is the one type of government that has been explored but never mastered. I will not let the cat out of the bag just yet. There is a little more to introduce before the answer can be revealed in Chapter 18. I believe it is a possible solution to the problems of current forms of government, though maybe not the only one, and maybe not the right one for all. But after exploring many options, after spending days, weeks, and countless months going over possible solutions and objections, after meditating and spending many sleepless nights trying to help our race move forward, I believe that this is one type of leadership that could help our planet return to a healthy state of production, cooperation, peace, rejuvenation, and love.

CHAPTER FIFTEEN

CHANGE OF MIND, CHANGE OF HEART, CHANGE THE WORLD

I N THE EARLIER PART OF THIS BOOK, I spoke to you about releasing identities that could alleviate separation from others and help strengthen your connection with your family, your friends, your neighbors, other civilizations, and the world as a whole. By willingly releasing identities, you can also help yourself let go of personal fears and create a state of happiness and contentment for yourself and for those around you.

I bring identities to the forefront once more because these next few chapters could help you find a new inner peace while helping humanity evolve to a new level of cooperation and acceptance. What a huge benefit this would be for all inhabitants on this planet.

There are many ways to achieve this lofty goal, and I am aware that this method is not the only one, but it is a very successful method. I am living proof of these results, and I have seen many positive changes in others who have followed a similar path. Personally, I have found more peace in the last few years than ever before. As I live in peace, with much less fear or stress on my plate, my energy field and my heart field are helping those who can't escape their own fears and worries at this time. I am helping these people find balance by being at peace with myself.

Just like water can balance another wave of water without destroying the existence of water, so can emotions balance each other while creating a neutral and peaceful existence. We all know that a mother's smiling face and consoling hug can instantly transform all feelings of hurt and dry up her baby's tears faster than the searing heat of the Mojave Desert. Another great way to change a bad emotion to a good emotion is to laugh out loud or even laugh at oneself. This can be the best medicine of all. Laughing can change the mood of a room or transform an awkward moment quicker than my rabbits can hop to me for a treat. (They are really fast when they want to be.)

RELEASING IDENTITY IN YOUR TIME

This is very important, so I will say it again. I want to make sure that you hear this loud and clear. In no way, shape, or form am I telling you to release an identity, or any group of identities, from your personality until you decide it's the right time for you. This will always remain your choice, and you have the freedom to decide if and when this will happen. When you do feel the time is right for you to release an identity, do it. You can always regain an identity that you've let go. The benefit of reclaiming an identity after you've let it go is having a broader perspective to see life from inside and outside your identity.

In short, keep your identities and belief systems until you are ready for a change. Keep them until you are tired of them and your identities no longer serve you or your life's purpose. Keep them until you grow old and die if you like. You may never let go of an identity for your entire life, and that's OK. Many people are born into a religion and never change. Many people are born a nationality and never release their heritage. Keep your identities for many lives if you wish. And when you are ready, try a new identity, or stay neutral without adding any more to your plate.

If you don't feel comfortable making the choice on your own to release an identity, or if you don't trust your own instincts and inner guidance, consult with a trusted friend, your spouse, your teacher, your spiritual guide, or pray if you want. Go to Vegas and roll the dice if you feel lucky and it makes you feel better to leave the decision to chance. Talk with those you respect and admire. Do what feels most comfortable for you. And if you release an identity, replace it with something positive that will promote peace and happiness. The Universe hates a void, and it's much better for you to decide how to fill in a hole than allowing chance, outside circumstances, or someone else to decide for you. This is one time when it helps to make a well thought-out decision.

You may be asking yourself again, "How do I release an identity?" The answer is easier than you think. People change identities and belief systems as easily as they change their socks. Sometimes this task is as easy as forgetting, forgiving, or appreciating your new thought process. Think back to a time in your life when you were part of a team, a club, a school, or a group of people. If you no longer associate yourself with any of these, did you have to consciously release those old identities? Think of your elementary school years. Are you still carrying that identity around with you? Do you still carry the same connection with your class pet turtle? You probably didn't make a conscious effort to let it go; you just changed naturally. You made the transition to a new identity or let the old identity go and created more peace in your life. And, of course, we've already covered other ways to do this earlier in the book. This is just a reminder of how easy it is.

Before we move on, know this: There is nothing written in stone that says you have to remove an identity, or group of identities, in order to find peace. This is only one way that many people in the world have accomplished this goal. I, myself, have found more inner peace simply by releasing my own classifications and labels and moving towards a sense of *Oneness* with all life on our planet.

CAN YOU RELATE?

In my current belief system, the more identities that I kept in my life, the more I felt disconnected from the whole, the source, you, and the rest of the world. For the most part, I didn't need these identities to show who I really was inside. Most of the time, my previous identities were simply window dressing. I played the parts because I didn't know any other options, or I found myself trying to fit in to a predetermined social screenplay of accepted lifestyles. Society seems to need individuals to classify themselves one way or another, but people don't need to do this to live happy lives. Do you have any identities that you feel comfortable releasing right now?

To function in today's financial structure, we are more or less strong-armed into identifying with a title or a group just so we can do business. It feels as if we have to keep certain identities in order to keep peace in the workplace. However, what I found out for myself was that I was not keeping the peace at all. I was only adding to the tensions of the existing ruling systems that taught us we need identities to function as a workforce.

By exercising my freedom to let go of my identities, I found a new inner-strength that helped me release buckets full of fear, worry, anxiety, frustration, and pain. With every identity that I willingly released, I gained a closer connection to more people around me. I became vast and diverse all over again. My spirit grew larger than anyone could imagine. I was no longer bound by my skin color, my social status, my name, my country, my spirituality, my education, my financial status, or my occupations. When all was said and done, I was just me, and I felt better for it. And now, I feel great! I like being connected to others again. I don't know why I gave that up in the first place. Actually, I do. We are taught to accept identities from the moment we are born. And there is nothing wrong with having multiple identities. Identities can be fun and rewarding. Identities help people to learn, grow, separate, build an ego, and experience parts of themselves that they wouldn't know about if they didn't have an identity.

If you study the second law of thermodynamics, the part that explains entropy, it says that the more options you have, the greater the chance for disorder. This can also pertain to identities. The more identities you have, the more chance there is for disorder, fear, and especially separation. The less identity you have, the less you fear, and the less you need. You find yourself living life for the moment and not for what you, or others, feel you need. With less identity, you connect with others on new levels of awareness and cooperation. Confidence in one's own ability also seems to grow when identities are released willingly.

As we wrap up this portion, I feel fortunate for all my life's past experiences. I cherish them. I lived them until they no longer gave me satisfaction or tranquility, and then I knew it was time for me to move on. It was time to help others find a different type of security, balance, and inner peace. I am here to help, through the energy of this book, any person who chooses this new path in life. Whether you have an identity, or you have less identity, one is no better than the other. The grass is not necessarily greener just because you release a few identities. Peace still takes work, sacrifice, growth, patience, tolerance, and especially, love. If you decide to go this route, before you know it, you could suddenly find yourself living with less stress, less worry, less fear, and much more enjoyment. So, if you are ready, here is a way that I have been able to start peeling away some of my own layers of social training, political programming, and expected patriotic behaviors.

SPECIAL NOTE: If you are a proud American and part of your identity is to stay a proud American, or stay proud about any other nationalities, religions, or cultural belief systems, you might want to skip the remainder of this chapter, and the next two chapters, and move on to Chapter 18. You will still gain all the information you need if you decide to forgo reading these chapters. In addition, no disrespect is intended toward anyone in this country, other countries, or any other time periods in which people have lost their lives in the pursuit of true peace and freedom. Armies have been used for good and for evil, and one person's evil is another person's good. My descriptions are not meant to form a finite judgment one way or the other. This is simply how I was able to release the identities that separated me from you. Use this information to strengthen your current beliefs, or use them to give you options for shifting your perception.

In addition, the following content is only shared as a means for those who willingly choose to remove or replace identities to help the world reconnect with everyone again. Oneness is still my personal goal, and I will not force my beliefs on any of you. It is my personal goal to find my inner peace and happiness.

My best recommendation is to read the content, see how you feel about it, and let it strengthen your own thoughts for finding inner peace and tranquility. You may or may not agree with any or all of the content you are about to read. I am not trying to make you see it my way, or convert you to the Michael religion. We have enough religious dogma already that divides the world. I have faced my fears, released my identities by choice, and I choose to share this content as a means to help those who want at least one more option for finding *world peace.*

STRIPPING AWAY
SEPARATION OF LAND

I have always been curious why we separate ourselves from others because of where we were born, what school we attended, or what our religious beliefs are. The human race has done the same thing for centuries based on what sex we were born, what our parents do for work, or what our financial status is at that moment.

In our current society, if you talk to people who have run into bad luck serious enough to affect their credit scores, they will tell you stories of being instantly blackballed, labeled, and shunned by nearly every financial institution they approach. We have seen the headlines that say a bad credit report can hurt a person when they apply for a job. These are still good people, but they have been labeled in a negative way because of changes in their lives, changes that they might not have been able to control. Maybe there was an immediate loss of income in the family due to death or injury, and these people could no longer pay their medical bills. Maybe there was a major catastrophe and the family had no insurance. Maybe their financial trouble was due to identity theft or a divorce. Someone else's perception of what is good or acceptable affects another's life in a negative way—all because of money. People are judged by their bank accounts and not by their potential, their kindness, their generosity, love, or their ability to forgive. People are judged on their past and not on their potential. Isn't it time we make a conscious change to allow people to grow and show their true inner selves? When we have grown to the next level and are able to alleviate money and barter systems, we will see this positive change.

Have you ever noticed that when we are born in a specific country, we are automatically bound to cultural constraints and laws that have been passed down for hundreds of years, long before we even took our first breath? And the worst part is that this national identity automatically separates us from our brothers and sisters across the sea, over the mountain range, or sometimes right across the street from us. I like the people in other lands. I like the people across the street. I want them to know they have a friend who will appreciate them as human beings and won't consider them different just because they were born over there, or speak a different language. I am a human being who happens to be born here and not there. I feel no different than my sisters and brothers with different colored skin, different religious and spiritual beliefs, or different cultural heritages. Do you have any of the same feelings?

The more I recognize diversity, the more opportunities I have to release my fear that other people may be different or that they may see life through different colored eyeglasses. What a great opportunity for us all. Variety is a gift to be cherished. Maybe opposites do attract for many reasons beyond our conscious perception.

I know this: We all have a heart, liver, lungs, five fingers and toes, and the same slippery guts as the rest of the world. I am you in another land. I am you experiencing life in another body, in another part of the world. We are only separated by our inability to remember that we all came from the same stardust that formed our planet nearly 14 billion years ago. We all came from the same early subatomic particles that were scattered over billions of light years and vast amounts of space as a result of the Big Bang. We are all part of the same cosmic soup. (Maybe a good bowl of cosmic chicken soup will help heal all the hurt and separation in our Universes.) And I want you all to know that I welcome your existence and respect your beliefs. I am just a temporary human being, experiencing what it is like to be a Caucasian male at this time. I am a spirit in temporary flesh playing the part of a human. In my next life, I may be Hindu, Egyptian, Irish, Australian, African, Swedish, or French. I may be Venutian, Martian, Aldebaran, Pleiadian, or become a Hathor. I may come back as your dog, your cat, or your pet ferret (so treat me nicely or I'll bite). My pets may be my sisters and brothers from a different time. I am doing my best to treat everything as if it were a part of me and a part of my family.

You most certainly don't have to do the same thing. I am only offering possibilities for you to consider. Live your life and find your own peace. I respect your opinion, and I don't need you to agree with me to satisfy a fear. Live and be free, my friend.

THE BEGINNING OF WORLD FREEDOM AND LAW

I believe that all souls who come to this planet are born with a natural birthright of freedom. However, based upon the location or the country into which they are born, or the spiritual path they follow, some people seem to have more freedom than others.

There will always be those who view laws as a means of keeping order and control, and others who believe that laws restrict people's freedom to live and express themselves to their fullest potential. Personally, I believe that our laws have become unbalanced, and that our lawmakers are out of control. (Our current lawsuit epidemic is a great example of this.) Furthermore, I have long felt that the laws and restrictions automatically placed upon us at birth have taken away our natural birthright of freedom; we have become instant slaves. As individuals, we are not privileged to decide if we can make changes to the laws at hand; we have to go to someone else first to see if a law can be changed or removed. *So much for freedom!* At this point, the only choice we have is to follow the law or face a consequence.

In our current law-driven system, we are not free to function as free sentient beings because of fear and control. We are still bound by the previous ideologies of past and present politicians, self-imposed kings, presidents, and military leaders. To this day, the lawmakers—some of whom have long since passed away—still bind our freedoms with their perceptions. Why do we have to continue to live under *their* perceptions of *their* law and order? Just because one human being decides an idea should become a law doesn't make it right, moral, or helpful for this time period, or for the entire human race.

You and I were not asked if we agreed to these present-day laws when we were born. I know of no one who has been given this choice. And unfortunately, I, like all of you, am forced to abide by these laws. This shows how little humans are trusted and how our birthright of freedom has been stripped away. Our birthright of freedom disappeared as soon as our bottoms were slapped and we cried in the hospital. Multiply this by billions of people in the world, and not one person is living freely anywhere. There is not one country exempt from this. We are all bound to laws set up by others wherever we go on this planet. There seems to be no escaping the fear and control of others at this point. If there were any place on the planet that offered a land of peace and freedom for all, I would go there in a heartbeat. Are you also looking for that place? In time, with help from those who also seek freedom from greed, ego, fear, and control, we will be able to create a new land of opportunity. America was given this chance, but it was stripped of its resources and taken down another path by a few who clung to the old ways. But this may be changing soon.

We all know that we don't have the right to ignore or deny these fear-based laws without violating them and suffering a consequence. If we did, we would find ourselves eating breakfast, lunch, and dinner in the county lockup. I have no doubt that some of our lawmakers and politicians are upstanding people, but their belief system should not bind everyone to their ideologies. Our lawmakers and politicians do not represent me, nor was I asked for my opinion. Doesn't that make me a slave, in some respects? I thought the Thirteenth Amendment abolished slavery.

As individuals, we also did not get to develop the governmental system that enslaves us today. We were born into it and told to make the best of it. I have to wonder, who are these people to say what is right for humankind? Who are they to say that you and I have to make the best of it? I certainly couldn't decide what is right for another. I can only do my best to govern myself and help others in the process. I can only do my best to heal my own pains and create inner peace around me. I can only do my best to share, teach, and provide for my fellow human beings. And there will be those who will tell you that you can change a law. But the process to remove just one law can take decades, and the law can be reinstated by the money-driven legal system before you walk out the courtroom door.

I have tried, but I have been unsuccessful in finding the exact number of laws that bind our freedom today. There are thousands upon thousands of city, state, federal, and tax laws on the books in our country alone. Even as I write this sentence, more laws are being created. Multiply this by every state, province, and country in the world, and there is no way to gain true freedom. *There are so many laws telling us what we cannot do that freedom has become strangled by the lawmakers.*

If we were truly free, we would have the choice to agree or not agree with the laws at hand. We would have the freedom to agree and abide by our own self-imposed guidelines to help our planet and species coexist in peace. If we release fear, laws become obsolete. I know we are not ready for this type of freedom, as we are still evolving and mastering fear and ego, but I can still hope. It may be in our near future. (I am crossing all my fingers and toes that I will see this within my lifetime.) When we are able to govern ourselves and not harm another, maybe our species will have grown enough to enjoy this type of freedom and remove restrictions imposed by fear-based lawmakers. Wouldn't it be great if the only things a person would feel growing up were love and acceptance, not slavery?

If you could make a choice today, would you rather continue living with all the laws, taxes, and restrictions imposed by others, or would you rather live knowing you are always loved and accepted for who you are? I choose love and acceptance.

TODAY'S LAWS

Living in America today, if you challenge the law, you are instantly labeled an outsider, a troublemaker, or an anarchist. An FBI file would be started on you faster than you could say "rubber baby buggy bumpers." Thirty years ago, you would have been called a communist. And today, you would be called a terrorist. Aren't these really just more labels that people use to make themselves feel safe and secure because they are afraid? Fear not, my friend (no pun intended), peace is still my ultimate goal. And although I am not perfect, I am doing my best to accept and respect all opinions. I still have my own demons to transform, and my own fears and ego to release. I am a work in progress, and I support those who also choose this path of peace and freedom in life. I look forward to a world where everyone is free.

MEANING BEHIND LAW

I have spent many hours in deep thought about laws and why they were created. My conclusion should not be very surprising to you. I believe that laws are a true byproduct of fear. Almost every law can be attributed to someone's fear of an outcome that does not meet his or her perception of how life should exist. If a person feels he is not getting his fair share, a true byproduct of ego and fear, he can express his fear by running to the existing governing body to create a law in his favor. If these people gather enough influence, or give large enough donations, a law will be passed to ensure their fair share in the form of remuneration, compensation, wages, salary, or taxes. Besides taking care of our basic needs, our ego also dictates how much money or services we should receive for our time, energy, and thoughts. The more ego a person has, the more money and remuneration he or she demands. "If he gets this much, then I deserve this much—and more." The cycle has continued since the beginning of ego. Money has never been the problem; money is neutral. It is the ego and fear connected to our current monetary system that seems to have created so many problems.

On the other side of the coin, there have been laws that try to ensure a fair compensation in the form of a minimum wage, but even these laws were still created as a result of fear. If business owners didn't fear having enough money, they would pay a fair compensation for services rendered.

Here is another example: If someone is afraid that words or prayers could hurt another or infringe on personal rights, laws would be passed to ban specific types of speech, even in a land where free speech is touted as a right of the people. The First Amendment has been challenged time and again.

"Congress shall make no law respecting an establishment of religion, or prohibiting the free exercise thereof; or abridging the freedom of speech, or of the press; or the right of the people peaceably to assemble, and to petition the Government for a redress of grievances."

Does this sound like our country? I can think of many examples in which this does not represent our country at all. Others have expressed to me that *"We the People"* are not free to speak our minds whenever or wherever we choose. There are places where free speech is completely forbidden, and other places where one needs a permit just to address a group of people.

Our current court system is a great example of where people are not allowed to speak freely. In court, one must follow a system of protocol established by others decades, and even centuries, ago, without having any say in the process. If you question the process in court, or say something that the judge doesn't like, you can be held in contempt of court, fined, and even thrown in jail. You may have certain choices in our current legal system, but you are certainly not allowed freedom of speech.

Throughout the history of our country and many others, governments have taken away the right to speak freely, especially in times of war. A person speaking out against war at the turn of the 20th century would likely have found himself looking through the bars of a prison window. The Espionage Act of 1917 and the Sedition Act of 1918 (an amendment to the former) were created from fear and the need to control the masses' freedom of speech. It's been said that Woodrow Wilson, our 28th president, signed these acts into law because of the mounting dissention toward global war. Speaking out against this conflict, the government, the flag, the military, or patriotism would have resulted in your mail being suspended and possibly yourself being imprisoned. If you published any periodicals, newspapers, or magazines that spoke against the government and war, the postmaster had the freedom to remove your material from distribution. Thousands of people across our planet have been jailed, confined, ridiculed, persecuted, starved, and tortured for speaking out against blind patriotism, greed, and useless killing.

I could go on and on about laws that are created as the result of fear. Here is one final example, and the hardest one to accept or change. For those who fear death, laws were created to prevent another from taking a life. (Unless of course your country declares war on another—then, killing is perfectly legal.) If we examine the reasons why a human being will take another human being's life, it usually comes down to a point where that person feels there is no other option. The act of killing another becomes a last resort action for the person who has fallen victim to fear. So, even the law protecting life itself is still a result of fear.

The first time I proposed a land without binding laws, those afraid of dying and murder were quickest to speak out. They asked, "Aren't you afraid there would be more murders without these laws? Do you want more murder?" Of course, I don't condone murder or senseless death. If peace and self-governing are the goal, and fear is transformed into courage, then murder would become obsolete, a thing of the past. All these people could envision were gangsters running amok and killing defenseless babies. Humanity has done that for centuries, and we call it patriotism and history. Having laws has not stopped people from committing murder or starting wars (which is the same thing in my book). War is still murder! What has changed is our appreciation for life and abundance. This has transformed society more and more as time has progressed, and that is so admirable. The more fear a person loses, the less that person desires to kill. A fearless person no longer fears having enough. A fearless person no longer fears needing what someone else has. A fearless person knows he can create what he needs, survive without it, or allow someone else to help provide it. A fearless person no longer clings to a temporary human shell; he doesn't fear what will happen in the afterlife. When fear is transformed into courage, there is no need for law. Once fear, hate, need, and desire are transformed, obsessions become less influential in daily life. If, and when, we are ready for this as a society, it will be a phenomenal transformation.

BEST SYSTEM TO DATE

As I have studied many different cultures and time periods, the most impressive cultural belief system I have encountered has been the Hawaiian Huna system. The content of Huna has been both questioned and taught by native Hawaiians, so it is hard to know if it was actually practiced by many on the islands long ago, or if it was created by a haole. (Haole is the Hawaiian word for Caucasian, or someone who is not native Hawaiian.) If we had our time machine again, we would be able to transport to the beautiful tropical islands at the time when Huna began. We would be able to see this great system in action. Whether Huna is a factual system or not, the concept is still awe-inspiring. Let me explain.

The Hawaiian Huna system has a simple concept at its core. The concept is this: *No hurt, no sin.* How great is that? This was set up as a guideline, not a law. People lived life freely and without imposed restrictions. They lived to explore, learn, grow, and cherish others. Their main goal was to excel in life without harming another in the process. It is such a great concept that it is worth repeating again. Say the words as you read them—*No hurt, no sin.* Boy, that feels refreshing. Take a moment and let those words sink in. This concept would wipe away 99.99% of all laws today. Talk about renewed freedom. This can happen all over again as we instill self-governing, cooperation, and tolerance.

Imagine driving through the Iowa Corn Belt. The corn has just been planted and there are no stalks above the ground. While driving on a road that passes through the fields, you are able to see for miles and miles in all directions. There are no obstructions, no hills, no valleys, no trees, just fertile black land as far as the eye can see. Clearly, no one is around your car at all. You are taking a peaceful Sunday drive to admire the great feeding grounds of Mother Earth. The weather is perfect and your windows are down as well, so not even a smeared bug on your side windows could impede your vision. You drive up to a stop sign and no one is there. It is completely deserted. No one could possibly be hurt by your decision to continue on without stopping your car. You are free to govern yourself. You make your choice and can see that no one could be hurt as you drive through the stop sign. In the Huna system, no harm was done, and no laws were broken. But today, spy satellites would be aimed on your car to catch you in an illegal act, and you would soon find yourself surrounded by fifty police cars and a few military helicopters. OK, the spy satellite is a little strong, but you get the idea. In this example, no one was harmed in any way. The only reason that this type of law exists is because of fear. Someone fears getting hurt or losing property; furthermore, this law provides a lot of money to the cities and states in the form of fines.

In the system of *no hurt, no sin,* you can instantly begin to see the possibilities of freedom. Could this be a reason why those who crave power claimed Hawaii illegally and took away the rights of the Hawaiian people? (We will cover this in Chapter 17.) In the Huna system, people are no longer bound by the constraints of another. People would be able to choose, grow, and learn cooperation all over again. Yes, this would take time to master, and there would be growing pains, but the rewards would be so much more gratifying than remaining slaves to the current legal and financial systems. I have heard many people say that our current legal system doesn't work. Laws don't deter people from committing terrible acts. The overcrowded prisons are proof of this. The ones who are really harmed by these restrictions are those who choose to live for peace. We have thousands upon thousands of laws that tell us what we are not allowed to do in a land that boasts liberty and justice for all.

I ask you again: Which system would you like to live in? Which system would you like your children and grandchildren to grow up in? Would you like for you and your children to have the freedom to choose, based on a system of no hurt, no sin? Or would you prefer others, who claim superiority over you, to continue creating laws that restrict our natural birthright of freedom? Neither answer is right or wrong. It is your choice. I respect your decision and the reasons for your choice. And I hope you can, in turn, respect others' decisions that are different from your own.

Additionally, Huna is not just about *no hurt, no sin.* Huna has so many benefits and possibilities for creation, life, and manifestation that I could write entire volumes on the subject, but that has been done already. I may do this in the future, but right now my energies are needed elsewhere. If you decide to research Huna further, there are a number of books and websites available to get you started. You might begin with the works of Max Freedom Long. His work brought the forgotten practices to light again in the early 1930s. It is well worth researching.

CHAPTER SIXTEEN

DEFINING PATRIOTISM

A S I HAVE RESEARCHED different societies and cultures, as I have gathered information about various government systems and leadership roles, and as I have examined the progress the human race has made toward peace, I have learned a great deal about the use, misuse, and need for patriotism. There are evident reasons why our government and economic leaders require us to be proud of our heritage and country. Our present-day government leaders pound national pride into our education system, the media, sports and entertainment, and other venues, in order to influence us from the earliest of ages all the way up until the time we die. This is done for a few obvious reasons—control, control, and more control. Patriotism can easily be viewed as brainwashing and coercion. Before you've even had a chance to fully develop and make decisions on your own, you are standing in a classroom saying your country's pledge (and in Texas, your state's pledge, too). You are taught to honor people from your country's past without knowing the whole picture of how your country was formed. Past and present military and government leaders, who killed and wiped out entire cultures just to obtain money, land, power, and resources, have been turned into heroes. The needs of a few individuals have governed the actions of the many for personal gain and greed. There are those who have seen this happen and are ready for a big change. Many of us in this world are ready for a life of peace and cooperation, and

219

we are willing to step away from the old practices of manipulating leadership and blind patriotism.

It is true that patriotism can have a positive purpose. A country with pride can move mountains and rescue countless lives. A proud nation can act as a single entity and help neighboring countries overcome drought, famine, and disease. But on the darker side, a proud *angry* nation can be driven to commit genocide, unspeakable and inhumane tortures, and subjugate entire races just for wartime profit and the benefit of a few leaders. This has happened time and again in history. WWI, WWII, the Spanish Inquisition, the American-Indian wars, the Crusades, and many others are prime examples of this misuse of blind national and religious pride. Just about every war in our history can be linked to profit, fear, anger, misunderstanding, greed, and ego.

On a brighter note, another positive benefit of exhibiting national patriotism has been the slow evolutionary process toward freedom and equality for all. Although we don't have this in any of our countries yet, our society is moving ever closer to this goal. Wouldn't it be great to experience this within our lifetime? We have the ability to make this happen if we agree that peace is an important goal for all on this planet. I vote for now, instead of waiting fifty, a hundred, or a thousand or more years in the future. If we all stand up and say, "Enough is enough! We will no longer follow our money-driven governments and will create a world of peace right now," we could make this monumental change happen overnight. I support a movement for peace and freedom with every breath in my body.

Even in our current millennia, barriers have been breaking down more and more regarding noble birthright, financial birthright, and education birthrights. Just because someone is born into a noble lineage, this no longer guarantees her a place of leadership in her country. Just because someone is born on Rodeo Drive in Beverly Hills, it doesn't guarantee she will be wealthy and have good money sense. And just because someone was born a child of a scholar doesn't mean she will be smarter than all the other children in school or deserve more attention. Equality is growing stronger in our world. This is a natural occurrence as more people remember who they are and where they come from. There is a change happening. It is slow, but it has happened steadily over the centuries. We have all seen it. Do you feel the change happening? Do you support this change?

PATRIOTISM FOR WAR

When I was a young boy, the United States found itself deeply involved in another conflict, the Vietnam War. I never knew what it was like to be in a real war. I only knew about war from watching the censored news and the Saturday afternoon movies that made Hollywood actors into American heroes. Throughout American history, the media has turned US soldiers into heroes and men of good character. In a WWII movie, the Americans were always the good guys, and the Germans and Japanese were portrayed as the bad guys. In a western movie, the American Cavalry would swiftly gallop over the hill with a trail of dust in their wake as they came to the settlers' rescue, while Native Americans were made to look like ignorant savages. In movies about the Vietnam War, the North Vietnamese and Chinese were our worst enemies and were to be feared.

My feelings and thoughts were in conflict because fighting and patriotism became synonymous. I thought fighting was bad. Isn't fighting the opposite of peace? How could the Americans be the good guys if they were fighting, too? Most of these conflicts were not fought for the good of all people; they were fought to obtain money, land, and power for a few at the top.

Even as a young adult, I could see the patriotic programming that the movies and tilted news reports tried to instill. Anyone who fought and killed the enemy was considered to be courageous. If a soldier jumped on a grenade, or rushed a machine gun nest, he was given a medal. People are respected when they kill the enemy. Defending or dying for your country became an act of courage and respect. People like being respected, so they became patriotic and went to war.

In the eyes of military leaders, to be a good soldier, you have to follow orders without question. This also means having to kill without questioning morality. I spoke to one Vietnam veteran who told me he didn't have a choice whether he wanted to fight. He was drafted and sent to another country full of people he didn't hate. They had done nothing wrong to him. He was placed in situations that forced him to fight just to survive. He didn't want to kill, but he also didn't have the right to refuse without receiving a major consequence and losing his freedom. He killed a perfect stranger, and now he suffers from post-traumatic stress disorder. He killed because some government and military leaders gave an order that he had to follow, or be killed himself.

HUMANITY VS. PATRIOTISM

I was reminded of an inspirational story that recounted the very peaceful nature of human beings during one of the worst of global conflicts. I am talking about the Christmas Truce that occurred during WWI, also known as the Great War and the War to End All Wars. (WWI was considered to be one of the most horrific wars, with 10 million to 50 million killed, depending on the source.)

I have heard this humane tale more than once in my life. This true epic tells us that people are inherently peaceful and kind in nature, not killing machines and warmongers. People would rather live in peace than fight. It is only for the benefits of war, profit, and damaged ego that we are taught by a handful of political and military leaders to hate others. The masses become brainwashed by political tactics and emotional uproar and kill without knowing their enemy.

The event that is said to have triggered this world war was the assassination of Archduke Franz Ferdinand of Austria on June 28, 1914, by Gavrilo Princip, a Serbian nationalist. Germany immediately declared war on Russia and France, and England joined the war when Belgium was later invaded. During this war, new weapons of mass destruction were developed, new military tactics were devised, global fear increased, and trench warfare became a new military science that killed hundreds of thousands of soldiers at a time for mere yards of dirt.

Each side thought the war would be over within a few months, but they were sadly mistaken. Battle lines were drawn, and the trenches were dug in heavily along the Western and Eastern Fronts.

During the winter months in the first year of the war, soldiers on both sides of the Western Front were becoming less aggressive toward their enemies. The soldiers' desire to kill waned as they fought off their own deaths from frostbite, trench foot, and other diseases. As the soldiers began to regain bits and pieces of their humanity, and a desire to live peacefully again, new propaganda campaigns were launched by the governments to rebuild the animosity between all sides. The purpose was to make each country fear and hate each other so much that the soldiers wouldn't think twice about killing the opposing Russians, Germans, French, English, Americans, or whoever participated in the war. (This sounds very familiar in today's news and media. I can't count how many times the word *terrorist* has been used to drag America into another conflict or war during the late 20th and early 21st centuries. Fear has been used again and again by a small group of government leaders and media to ensure as much public support as possible for each deadly engagement.)

On December 19, 1914, an attempt to boost wartime morale became one of the deadliest military offenses to date in the War to End All Wars. This backfired miserably on the military leaders, and morale sank even lower due to the huge numbers of deaths and casualties. (I can't imagine how killing another human being could boost morale.)

As Christmas neared, both sides received gifts, food, letters, pictures, and warm clothes from home. This also made the soldiers homesick and helped to bring back their natural sense of humanity. Their desire to kill was growing weaker by the day. Those in the military headquarters knew this could happen and sent word to the leaders at the front. They warned the commanders to keep up morale and continue fighting.

As the story goes, on the eve of Christmas, the German troops along the front began to decorate their trenches and placed candles on pine trees. (Decorating Christmas trees was not yet a practice common to the rest of the world.) The German soldiers began singing *Stille Nacht* ("Silent Night") and other Christmas carols in celebration of the holidays. The Germans knew that their singing would give away their positions, but they did it anyway. This act must have reminded the Germans of the peaceful human beings they really were.

At first, the Allied soldiers were confused and a little wary of the songs they heard only a few yards away. They feared this might be a German trick to lull them into a false sense of security before a new enemy offensive. Not surprisingly, though, humanity won over in a big way, as peace is still stronger than hate. Eventually, the English soldiers began singing along in their own language. Music became a peacemaker. (In fact, music is considered to be a universal language that all races can appreciate and understand. The words matter some, but the meaning and emotion behind the words, the melodies, and rhythms, speak a language understood by all. You don't have to know a different language to hear uplifting emotions and peaceful meanings in a song. Music can transcend the most diverse of languages and cultures.)

History records that one brave German soldier crossed the enemy line into No Man's Land bearing holiday cheer with a Christmas tree in hand.

The soldiers on the other side took aim on the lone German. They were ready to shoot at the first sign of trickery. However, there was something different about this brave act. Maybe other forces were at work here. If there are Angels, one of them must have had its wings over this fellow. What a lucky guy.

The soldiers from either side never fired a shot. They began to trust in the possibility of goodwill toward all mankind. They began to release their fear, and they put down their weapons. They watched as this lone man started a new chapter of peace.

When this happened, a few of the Germans on the other side began calling out to the soldiers across the way. They called to them in a friendly manner and encouraged them to come and visit. Against orders, the English troops made their way into the former killing fields. They walked cautiously at first, but when they saw the sincere intent of the Germans for a peaceful meeting, they put away their aggressions and dropped their guard. They met as equals, humans, brothers from a different nation, instead of meeting as soldiers.

While in the famous No Man's Land, small gifts were exchanged and games were played. Cigarettes, cigars, chocolates, whiskey, and other personal items made their way into the hands of their new friends. It is even written that a game of football (or soccer, as we know it) was played. Kindness and generosity were the feelings on these bloodied grounds, not hatred and slaughter. Fallen comrades were gathered and given burials, and kind words were spoken by both sides for the deceased and dying.

These men were given a chance to see that their temporary enemies could also be their friends, their brothers, or their fathers. They were just like themselves—farmers, mechanics, cooks, teachers, musicians, and more. These young men shared common interests and dreams. They missed their families, their loved ones, their girlfriends, wives, and children. They missed the life they'd had before guns were thrust into their hands to take another life. This was a true sign of social evolution for humankind.

Unfortunately, not all the soldiers welcomed or participated in the temporary truce because some had lost close friends and they held onto resentment and hatred. But this show of humanity cannot be denied. These young men didn't hate each other before the war. They were taught to hate each other, they were taught to kill each other after the war broke out. Given a chance, people will inherently choose peace and cooperation over war and fighting. People will find a way to work out their differences and cooperate. This one remarkable event shows the very nature of humanity: peace before war and death. No war has ever lasted, and peace will always prevail.

If you have not heard this story before, you should know that the non-violent actions of these brave men were considered an act of treason by their leaders. Peace and humane acts are considered illegal in times of war. (Do you hear how silly that sounds? Peace is considered an act of treason that would have brought about court-martial and possible death by firing squad or hanging. It makes me wonder who should have been leading the world governments and military units.) In reaction to news of these kind acts, the English command warned that any unofficial armistice was specifically prohibited.

Unbelievable, isn't it? One would think that peace would always be the ultimate goal. At least we're making progress in that direction. It is growing stronger with every generation. People just need to be tired enough of killing, tired enough of fear, and tired enough of ego and blind national pride to make the huge shift in social evolution. This is evolution worth cheering about. Even the identity of war can be shed.

NOT SO EVIL AFTER ALL

In the last chapter, I made a brief statement about the so-called savage Native Americans and the so-called evil Germans and Japanese. I don't believe that they were all evil, or our enemies. In our history as a people, and as a country, anyone opposing a specific political or monetary national ideology has usually been twisted rather quickly as an enemy of the current political groups, the military, and the public masses.

Right before the Japanese attack on Pearl Harbor on December 7, 1941, I find it impossible to believe that every Japanese citizen felt hatred for the Americans and their Allies. I can't believe that the Japanese rice farmers hated the corn farmers from Iowa so much that they wanted to cut their heads off before the war started. The Japanese were not born with a natural hatred for Americans. People on both sides of the ocean were taught to hate the other. They were taught to hate and fear their new enemy. Each side was pressured to be patriotic and to murder a new global threat to their leader's proposed way of life. Propaganda, twisted truths, and lies about other cultures and societies made their way into mass media, pamphlets, and radio messages overnight. People were manipulated or coerced into fearing the other side for what they might do to our women and children. Patriotism, for the benefit of helping a few people in command, has killed hundreds of millions of people throughout our history, and this was no different.

As we revisit the trenches at the Western Front, the temporary armistice was broken by a need to continue the war and win for pride's sake. Unfortunately, not all of the soldiers on the front were privy to this cease-fire. The story goes that the cease-fire was ordered to end immediately, and fighting should begin without delay. It may have only taken one bullet for peace to be forgotten. Fighting broke out again and lasted a few more years. On the following Christmas, fearing another repeat of peace, an order was given to shoot any soldier that made a friendly gesture toward the enemy, or anyone who crossed into No Man's Land to show the same holiday cheer and goodwill toward men. Once again, peace and humane acts were considered acts of treason and were punishable by death. Despite urges to show peace, the war continued on until fighting ceased on November 11, 1918, and the Treaty of Versailles was signed on June 28, 1919. Other treaties followed, but not until millions of lives were lost, and our planet suffered dearly from blind patriotism.

MULTIPLE PERCEPTIONS

I will stop here to interject an important point. For those who believe in the multi-life theory that everyone chooses their future experiences before birth, if you wished to experience the atrocities of war for the purpose of expanding your perception and appreciation of peace, then the people responsible for the continued carnage would actually have done you a huge favor. These people—soldiers, military, and political leaders—although not conscious of why they were doing so, or not at an experience level of peace for all, could have played a very important part in your soul's evolution. In the belief systems that adhere to the multi-life theory, these people should be thanked over and over again for agreeing to play the bad guys for you and for the world. As always, you decide.

Even as a child at play, I can remember sacrificing my own desires and playing the role of the bad guy so my friends could play the roles of the good guys. I didn't like doing it, but I did it as a sign of friendship. I sacrificed my needs for the benefit of others. We took our turns playing different characters, and some were better at being the good guys, while some were better at being the bad guys. Remember, without a bad guy, how do you define a good guy? Without hate, even on the smallest of levels, how do you know love? Without fear and control, how can one be a hero and know freedom? These opposites rely on each other to provide multiple and infinite experiences. Our lives are one big perception, with each of us at the helms of our own ships. Let the winds of perception fill your sails and allow you the vision to reach your destination.

This is not an easy concept to accept if you cling tightly to life and the lives of others. I can empathize with both sides of the coin. I know that in life, and with life's hardest and most challenging lessons, not all parts of the picture are easy to accept. If you have been affected by any of these wars or losses of life due to military or political conflict, or any loss of a loved one, I wish you the best of speedy recoveries and hope you will be able to forgive and release the pains of these past experiences. Holding onto pain and anguish can affect the body, mind, and soul, and could lead to further suffering.

The choice is always yours. Hurt until you are tired of feeling hurt. Hold onto pain until you are ready to let go. Then move on to a new experience and find peace. You can always place yourself in similar situations if you wish. Have you ever found yourself repeating life's hardest lessons again and again, or witnessed other people placing themselves in similar situations over and over? Most of the time, as my clients have taught me, this is done on a subconscious level. People repeat lessons until they are ready for something new. People develop habits without knowing how to release them. We can repeat these experiences and habits until we are ready for a new lesson or a new challenge. And hopefully, when we are ready, we will choose to refill the void of change with new experiences of love and acceptance. For myself, I am not tired of chocolate yet, so I continue to place myself in situations where there is plenty of chocolate. I like this much better than repeating war. If we do need war, can't we use chocolate bullets?

SOLUTIONS FOR WAR
(BESIDES CHOCOLATE BULLETS)

If you believe in the multi-life theory, then there will always be a need for war. For example, let's say you are a soul that has lived 100,000 happy lives, and you are ready for a new perspective. You've become bored with living happy lives all the time, so you decide one day, while floating in spirit, that you want to know what it is like to be a prisoner or a casualty of war. You would go to your spiritual family, friends, and counsel, and ask them to sign you up for a life at a given point in history to experience the atrocities of war. That seems pretty simple to follow.

However, even if you believe in this solid theory, you can still experience peace without war, too. A little argument or disagreement with another person can be the opposite of peace; and war is nothing more than a larger argument filled with guns, tanks, airplanes, and bombs that rip your enemy into tiny little shreds. There are many levels of peace, with an infinite number of possibilities for the opposite of peace. Climbing the evolutionary ladder of peace becomes easier to see. War and peace are only a larger extreme which gives you a larger perspective.

If you don't believe in the multi-life theory, what are some possible solutions for bringing war to a permanent end? The obvious answer is, of course, don't do it, but that hasn't seemed to work yet. Since the earliest of battles at Megiddo—known as one of the major battlegrounds of the world, and also the proposed spot where Armageddon will take place and end all wars and usher in 1,000 years of peace—wars have raged on this planet in one location or another because of pride, ego, power, fear, greed, money, love, misunderstanding, and control.

In most of the schools I have taught in, if students started a fight, or participated in a fight, they were usually suspended from school. They lost their privilege of being a student for a few days. I propose that this same policy be used with our political and military leaders of the world. If our president, congressmen, and generals support these disciplinary actions in schools, shouldn't they also follow the same rules and be prepared to lead by example? If our politicians and military leaders choose to act like children and go to war, then their ability to rule should be suspended until they grow up and learn to cooperate with their neighbors.

In more recent times of world history, delegates are sent to other countries to keep good relations open and commerce growing between neighboring governments. If the governing leaders are not talking directly with each other to resolve differences, their delegates are given power to do this in their place. If the government leaders and delegates are not able to come to a peaceful solution and avoid war, then maybe they should step down, move over, and let a new team of leaders and delegates resolve their issues. It is ego and pride that keep people in these leadership positions. Even if you have to go through 100 million different leaders and delegates until you are able to resolve differences and avoid war, then it is worth every minute of power exchange to reach a peaceful solution. If I were a delegate, and I couldn't come up with a plan of cooperation, then I should step down and let someone else try.

The majority of people have no desire to go to war or kill another human being. Here is a great experiment to affirm this truth. Imagine walking up to someone on the street and asking them to pick out a name from a bag containing all 6,000,000,000-plus names of the people on our planet. After this person picks a random name out of the bag, which is most likely someone they have never met or seen before—a complete stranger—ask them if they want to kill this person right now on the spot. Except for a very, very, very small percentage of people who like to kill and control others, I would bet that over 6,000,000,000 people would probably refuse and say, "NO!" They would probably say something along these lines: "Why should I kill this person? I don't even know him. He has done nothing wrong to me. Live and let live, I always say." I rest my case.

I am sure that you have figured out that my generalities of the government and military only pertain to a few individuals, those intent on killing, manipulating, and using fear and hatred as a means of control. There are many, many good people in every level of government and military, and I fully support a defensive-only military. It's a shame that people have to be afraid of standing up to someone higher in the chain of command when they don't agree with decisions for killing or suppressing another culture for the means of more land, more money, more power, or a religious belief system. That is why so many people have chosen to go to prison instead of fight. Many people in many lands have been imprisoned for standing their ground and opting for peace. These people have shown great courage in the midst of plain stupidity, and I applaud them. Once again, this lends weight to the idea of *no hurt, no sin*, self-governing, and the choice of living in love and peace.

BEYOND WAR

As I write this, I am easily reminded of the vast amounts of progress we have made as a species. We have made improvements in technology, science, and medicine, but the one that's most impressive is the tremendous progress we have made within the human spirit. Look at how far we have come as a race, and look in your heart to where we are heading as a species. We have been stripping away slavery, racism, and religious and spiritual separation over the centuries. We are moving towards equality of sexes, sexualities, single-gender partnerships, and social status. It may take hundreds, or even thousands, of years to complete this honorable task, but we are doing it. We are making huge strides as a people to become *one* again and accept all of life.

Do you see the progress we are making? And it's all because of good people like you. You are playing a huge part in the world as a whole. Without your puzzle piece, without your presence here on Earth this very moment, the picture of the world would be incomplete. When it is your time to move on to other realms, your energetic space will be filled in by another, or left to the guidance of the Universe to fill in as needed. But while you are here, I thank you for striving to be the best you can be. Experience and remember the wonders of it all. And move on in peace when you have had your fill of life and perception.

CHAPTER SEVENTEEN

A NEW DIRECTION,
A NEW UNDERSTANDING

L IFE SEEMS TO TAKE PEOPLE on incredible journeys of happiness and sadness, accomplishment and defeat, and growth and suppression. One way to look at each new and old experience is through appreciation. By accepting the bitter cold temperatures of winter, you can appreciate the warmth and new life of spring. When you experience acts of hatred in your life, you have a solid reference point for love and tolerance. All of these lessons, which produce broader spectrums of perception, can be called a *path of enlightenment.*

Recently, I made a conscious choice to seek out enlightenment. Some people have labeled this as a spiritual path, some have called it enlightenment about reality, and others don't know what to call it yet. Enlightenment is only a word, another badge of self-imposed identity. I imagine your journey is certainly not defined by a single word, and has been an interesting and event-filled passage into new realms of understanding and peace. In my mind, this path doesn't make anyone better or worse than his neighbor; it is simply a different path, a new experience, a new lesson in life. I'd had my fill of greed, worry, fear, climbing the social ladder, and trying to fit in because that is what was expected of me. Then I remembered what I was sent here to do, and now it is time for rebirth, a new direction, a new reality.

I am here to help others transform fear into courage and teach others about new possibilities, to release their ties to finite answers, and to accept options and alternative solutions. I am here to help the Earth get a chance to heal Herself again.

OTHER FORMS OF ENLIGHTENMENT

For those who like money, enlightenment might mean "brightening their mint." Get it, en-lighten-mint? This gives new meaning to a shiny penny. It also makes me wonder about the word *government*. Government feels to me like the politicians are governing the mint. Govern-mint seems to care more about governing money than helping people learn how to govern themselves. If people were taught how to govern themselves and transform fear, pride, and ego, we wouldn't need money, or our government, in its current form. Could this be a reason why they don't teach this?

I prefer to think of enlightenment as shedding new light on the mint of the mind. Wisdom and understanding will outlast a dollar over the course of time.

Remember, I said there are good people everywhere, and there is nothing wrong with people filling their coffers or making a shiny penny. People will use money until they are tired of it and wish to explore other options. I, myself, am tired of living in a system in which greed, control, and capitalizing on the misfortunes of others are the main focus. We live in a capitalistic society. When I looked up synonyms for capitalize, I found words such as: take advantage of, profit from, and exploit. When people capitalize on others, they are taking advantage of a situation or a person, they are exploiting them. That has such a negative connotation to it. I prefer to help someone instead of capitalize on them.

I, like you, am ready for more options, and I am creating solutions for this possible existence, which will free us from the need for cash and the echoes of cha-ching. But for now, I am still bound to a money system as long as I choose to stay on this planet to help others. I believe we can transcend this if we choose, and I have an answer that I will present in Chapter 18 that is a real, workable solution for a world without money and barter systems.

Can a monetary system still provide peace? Can we make a conscious effort to change our thoughts about money? Can we decide to use money more wisely and with a purpose that is greater than our own personal needs? Are we at a point in our evolution where we have outgrown a need for money as we release more ego and fear?

I have to tell you, I wasn't always like this. I, like the rest of you, grew up with a need for money to function in our society. I was brainwashed that way. I also didn't wake up one day and say, "I am enlightened," or "I am tired of money." I'm still looking for the light bulb of the soul to say, "I am enlightened." As I have heard many times before, and most recently by my friend, Dr. Dave, "Gradualness leads to suddenness." This has been a gradual change over many years of my life. This has been an ongoing process and will continue to be an ongoing process for most of my life. This progression took time, patience, experience, and learning as much about other people, other belief systems, government systems, and history, as possible. Then I realized how I had changed. It was well worth the wait and the journey.

I started as a child remembering what life was about. Life was about happiness, love, and acceptance. And then, somewhere in there, I forgot. I fell into the trappings of an expected future for a young American boy. Then I remembered all over again, thirty years later. I can still recall standing in my front yard at a very early age, maybe around eleven or twelve. I stood there and thought to myself, "Is life only about going to school, getting a job, raising a family, and retiring with a gold watch and a pension plan?" (This shows how outdated those childhood thoughts are. Pension plans and gold watches are becoming things of the past.) I was distraught by my mind's answer. I didn't have any other options at that time. So I went to high school, college, graduate school, got a job, paid my taxes, and lived like a good American was supposed to live. I coveted my paycheck and searched for ways to improve the status of my life. I looked at the Joneses and saw their success as a goal. I was inspired to have wealth, a great home, and a wonderful family because that is how I, how we, were programmed. Then it happened. I can still remember the day and where it happened. It was like a switch was turned on and a voice said, "Remember!" Life has never been the same since. Thank goodness. Thank God, thank Allah, Vishnu, Krishna, the Goddess, Yahweh, the Easter Bunny, and anyone else that helped.

As many have found, objects and toys do not create happiness. I have also found this to be true. These items only helped to alleviate the symptoms of my true desires. They were a temporary fix until I accepted the real lessons and goals of life. People of wealth are sometimes the saddest and loneliest people in the world. Not all of them feel this way, just some. And on the reverse side, some of the poorest people I know are the wealthiest in happiness, health, and love.

Recently, I began to clear out my closet of past creature trappings and began donating them to worthier causes. I donated my entire music library, and a good portion of my personal instruments, to a local university because I had moved on from teaching music in public school to teaching people how to transform fear and create new futures. My filing cabinet full of music served its purpose when I was a musician and teacher, but life changed, and my boxes of percussion music didn't help my clients. One day, I thought to myself, "Music is meant to be played, books are meant to be read, and toys are meant to be played with. How 'bout I give them to others to read, play, and enjoy?" I would rather have someone play the music that I donated than to have it collect dust in my filing cabinet. When I had let go of the old, I allowed new energies and opportunities to come into my life. It will also make my moving bill cheaper when it becomes time to move again.

A MAN WITHOUT A COUNTRY

After I forgot who I was at an early age, I had succumbed to the temporary loss of memory and grew up a good Catholic American boy. I accepted blind patriotism and my religion because that is how we are programmed in school, at church, in the newspapers, magazines, movies, and TV. I knew that Hitler and the Germans were bad people because that is what I was taught. We were never taught about the good deeds performed by the German people, the humane acts, or that not everyone in Germany hated Americans. I was taught that the Native Americans were savage, and the Pilgrims and Cavalry were the good guys. I was taught that the British wore red coats and despised the Colonial Americans. I was taught that our forefathers were like mini-Gods and could do no wrong. Our past presidents and military leaders forged a country on the principles of equality for all. The words "*We the People*" seemed to be real and the way of life for everyone on the northern continent. I grew up sheltered in our tiny little town in western Pennsylvania.

Then I started to learn about the things that had not been taught in our schools. I didn't want to believe them. I didn't want to lose my identity as a patriotic American. Fear set in. If I weren't an American, who would I be? What would become of me? Would I be run out of the country because I no longer sang the praises of our past and present countrymen? If our forefathers were not saints, what would that make me? So I began to do research. I wanted to find out if what was being said about our past was true or not. I found out a lot about our country and how it came to be.

What I discovered was staggering and life changing. My previous perception of our country turned around 180 degrees, and I was OK with this. I was no longer the proud, flag-waving citizen because of what I found in my research. How could I be proud of a country that did so many horrible things just to obtain land, rape the planet's resources, and subjugate others? How could I be proud of our presidents that still owned people as property? Eight of our presidents owned slaves while they were serving as president. Furthermore, slaves were owned by twelve of the presidents all the way up until the late 1800s. (Not all of them owned slaves while they were in office, and some people argue that there were thirteen presidents who were slave owners.) How could I be proud of a government created by our forefathers that counted people (slaves) as only three-fifths of a human being for taxation and voting rights in the House of Representatives? This was written in the US Constitution and occurred eleven years after Thomas Jefferson wrote in the Declaration of Independence that "All men are created equal."

And let's not forget the Thirteenth Amendment, which states:

"Neither slavery nor involuntary servitude, except as a punishment for crime whereof the party shall have been duly convicted, shall exist within the United States, or any place subject to their jurisdiction."

Financial slavery, which we are in right now, is still ignored by our government, court systems, and the presidency. As a microscopic example, we are not permitted to give away money or services without being penalized by the IRS. We are forced to live in a monetary system with no individual choice. When you take away too many choices, you create a slave.

I don't regret letting go of my national pride in any way at all. I am free again. Free, I tell you! I am closer to others around the world than ever before. The stories of our history contain so many truths, fictions, guesses, and rumors that a true picture of America may never be known. It would help if our government actually shared the truth more often than once in a while, but that is not the case. So I will share a little of what I've found that helped me gain freedom from my expected blind patriotism and granted me a freedom that our government could never provide.

I promise you, my goal was never to remove myself as an American, and it still isn't. I am not trying to remove you as an American, either. I am only trying to be the best person I can be as I transform into a messenger of peace and help others find freedom. I am *pro freedom*. If releasing my need for a national identity helps me find peace and freedom, then I hope you will support my endeavor, just as I will support you if you choose to stay a proud American.

I started to live with a new belief system. If you wish to be a proud American, great! How can I help you be a better American? If you need to be a proud Australian, great! How can I help you be a better Australian? If you need to be a proud Canadian, great! How can I help you be a better Canadian? No matter what you believe, I hope you'll be able to achieve happiness in your pursuits without requiring anyone to convert to your belief system just to appease your own fears. I will not make a promise, as promises cause more problems than good at times. I will do this instead: I will give you my best to help you achieve happiness and not require you to believe the same things I do. Stay who you are for as long as you like. This is my wish for you.

MANY ATROCITIES IN OUR HISTORY

Every continent has its history of poor decisions, suppressions, annihilations, and massacres. While Mohandas Gandhi was sharing his views on nonviolence to free India from the tyrannical rule of England, a terrible massacre took place in Amritsar, India, on April 13, 1919. A group of fifty English Indian soldiers, under the orders of a British Brigadier General, opened fire without warning on 10,000 unarmed men, women, and children in the Jallianwala Bagh (garden). The majority of people were there to celebrate a Hindu festival, and none of them had committed any acts of violence. In a horrendous act, the soldiers fired for almost fifteen minutes straight, using 1,650 rounds of ammunition on the unarmed group. They fired until they had no ammunition left.

The crowd had nowhere to go as the gates were locked and the firing soldiers had blocked the only exit. In a scramble to avoid the horrible slaughter, frightened people jumped into the public well and drowned. There is a plaque there which states 120 people were taken out of what became known as *The Martyr's Well*. According to the British, the death toll was 379 killed and over 200 injured. The Indian National Congress reported approximately 1,000 dead and over 1,500 injured. The death toll and number of injured could not be accurately confirmed because a curfew was placed in effect, and no aid was given to the wounded by the general and his troops.

This is only one of many terrible acts committed by man against his brothers and sisters because of blind patriotism, fear, pride, and ego. I believe in a nonviolent solution. I support nonviolence. So did the people on the receiving end of the bullets at Amritsar. If a change is to be made, this is how I believe it will happen. Nonviolence, or better said, intended peace, or just *peace,* will be the energy that creates a new world of hope. I believe in what Gandhi proposed for a peaceful solution—nonviolence. I believe more strongly in intended peace. I believe in peace and self-governing.

AMERICAN MASSACRES

Our country has also experienced countless horrible massacres within its own borders against anyone who stood in the way of land and resources for the government and a few in control. In doing research, I have counted *hundreds* more than I care to share in this book. One of these terrible events took place near Wounded Knee Creek, South Dakota, on December 29, 1890. The Sioux (Lakota) Indians were surrounded by 500 soldiers of the US 7th Calvary. The account goes that while the federal troops were forcibly taking away the Indians' firearms, after the American government had broken another treaty with the Sioux, a deaf member of the tribe, named Black Coyote, did not hear the order to give up his rifle. This event escalated into 500 soldiers opening fire on the defenseless Sioux. Different sources list the dead from 150 to 350 Indian men, women, and children. Twenty-three members of the 7th Cavalry were later awarded the Congressional Medal of Honor, also nicknamed Medals of Shameless Honor, for this senseless slaughter.

I take no pride in our government's actions of suppressing another culture just so the United States could have more land and resources. And not just any land, land that was already occupied by another race. The military arm of our government has done a good job of running out any Mexicans, French Canadians, and Native Americans that stood in the way of resources, profit, and ownership of illegally-seized land. This does not even scrape the surface of all the offenses that have occurred in our country and around the world.

In an attempt to keep this book moving toward the resulting solution for a peaceful world, I will only share two more examples of why I do not consider the actions of American history good enough to warrant blind patriotism. Yes, there have been good acts committed by individuals linked to our government, military, and corporations. Individual actions will always stand out as shining stars. Good for those who rise above blind patriotism and help others with kindness and compassion. I will never tell you that there weren't any of these actions taking place. What I am saying is that I will not give in to blind patriotism so I can be used to kill another human being for greed, money, or world domination. I willingly released my patriotic identity so I could not be used as a weapon of war against another entity on our planet. Will you do the same?

Peace can be obtained without blind patriotism. Don't let anyone tell you that you have to be a proud American to maintain peace in our world. The American way is only one way; it does not make it the right way or the wrong way. I can easily see why other countries dislike America because of the self-imposed police actions and some of the strong-arm tactics that our representatives have imposed on others worldwide. Having the gift of perception allows one to ask these questions: "Who are the Americans, past and present, to say they have the only path toward a peaceful coexistence? Who is the American government to say who can and cannot have weapons of mass destruction? Who are the Americans to set world policy?" The American military, under orders from the US president, was the only one to ever drop two nuclear bombs on an enemy, killing up to 140,000 people in Hiroshima, and up to 80,000 people in Nagasaki, Japan (another example of a terrible massacre linked to American history). With this type of history, who is the American government to make decisions in world policy? I have to say, I can't argue with these questions from others around the world.

I know there will be people who will say that dropping the atomic bombs was the only way to stop WWII. Hear me out. If blind patriotism didn't exist, the German people would never have followed Hitler, and he would have had no army to invade other countries. If blind patriotism did not exist, the Japanese would never have followed their emperor and bombed Pearl Harbor. If blind patriotism did not exist, American soldiers would not have driven Native Americans from their lands and gone to war with many other countries. So many atrocities would never have taken place if blind patriotism were not taught by our governments and militaries. If you take away blind patriotism, then there are no armies left to fight their wars.

And it's not just blind patriotism that has caused our world conflicts. The cowardly act of our government, and other governments of the world, instituting and enforcing a draft that forced people to fight for the cause of a few misguided leaders, is the true act of a primitive leadership system. Most people did not want to fight in these wars. They were forced to fight or face punishment, torture, or be sent to prison. (The Vietnam War was a great example.) Should we continue to allow our governments and military to teach blind patriotism and institute a draft to force people to fight their wars? If our president and Congress want to go to war, send the president and Congress to fight. (See how fast they change their minds if they are the only ones fighting.) Leave all the others who want peace out of the picture. If you stop blind patriotism, you stop the majority of war.

When our government and world leaders begin leading with world peace as the main goal, I will support them. But for now, that is not the case. Our world governments still govern for money, land, religious rule, and resources. This will always create natural conflicts. There are only so many resources. A simple shift from ego to peace is all it takes.

I also hope that when we get to meet visitors from other realms, they do not seek out our government and military leaders first. Our politicians do not represent me, the nation, or the world. I hope that our new visitors will meet first with a loving mother who is working three jobs so her children can eat and go to school everyday. I hope these visitors meet first with the humanitarians and those who are ushering in peace for our world. I hope these visitors seek out teachers and spiritual leaders. The last people on the list should be the politicians and military leaders.

TROPICAL PARADISE LOSES FREEDOM

On November 23, 1993, President Clinton signed Public Law 103-150. This important act signifies the "Apology Resolution" to the Hawaiian people, recognizing the illegal overthrow of the Kingdom of Hawaii 100 years earlier. This illegal annexation of the tropical islands into American rule has been a highly controversial subject. (There is also a debate about Texas being illegally annexed into the United States, but I will let you look that one up on your own.) This information was not taught in any school that I attended, nor is it generally taught in most schools in our country.

In January of 1893, Queen Lili'uokalani was replaced by a provisional government that was made up of American citizens, with protection and security provided by US Armed Forces. Queen Lili'uokalani refused to recognize this self-imposed government, also known as the Committee of Safety, and did everything in her power to remain the ruling leader of Hawaii.

President Grover Cleveland's administration commissioned the Blount Report, which stated that the removal of Queen Lili'uokalani was illegal, and sovereign rule should be given back to her immediately. Queen Lili'uokalani's strength was not to be denied, and she wrote the following on January 17, 1893:

"I Lili'uokalani, by the Grace of God and under the Constitution of the Hawaiian Kingdom, Queen, do hereby solemnly protest against any and all acts done against myself and the Constitutional Government of the Hawaiian Kingdom by certain persons claiming to have established a Provisional Government of and for this Kingdom. "That I yield to the superior force of the United States of America whose Minister Plenipotentiary, His Excellency John L. Stevens, has caused United States troops to be landed at Honolulu and declared that he would support the Provisional Government. "Now to avoid any collision of armed forces, and perhaps the loss of life, I do this under protest and impelled by said force yield my authority until such time as the Government of the United States shall, upon facts being presented to it, undo the action of its representatives and reinstate me in the authority which I claim as the Constitutional Sovereign of the Hawaiian Islands."

President William McKinley won the presidency in 1896. With President Cleveland out of office, Queen Lili'uokalani's support was said to be gone. The story goes that McKinley met with the leader of the Committee of Safety and others to talk about annexing Hawaii under US control. The real debate after this rests on the fact that the United States Government, or any part of the government, has no legal standings in a foreign country. Since Hawaii was a foreign country, under the illegal rule of a provisional government made up of American citizens, Hawaii could not be legally annexed into the union.

It is written in some accounts that money—in the form of sugar—had been the reason behind this movement to take over Hawaii. Not to mention that the strategic location of the islands made a great buffer between the larger continents. We would need more replacement batteries for our time machine to witness history as it was made. If the accounts are true, this strengthens my decision to willingly release blind patriotism.

To date, no land has been returned, and no compensation has been given to the people of Hawaii. All they received was an apology. No land has been returned to the Native Americans, either; they are still waiting for their apology.

REMOVING BLAME

I have heard about numerous conspiracy theories that secret organizations of financial leaders are behind much of our world's history and are to blame for our current financially dominated society. Who can say for sure? There are so many conspiracy theories and groups blamed for this social control and financial slavery that the list and stories can go on for days. To name a few alleged conspiracy groups, with no intent to support the claims of conspiracy or wrongdoing, there are the Illuminati, the Freemasons, the alien conspiracy (Reptilians and Greys), the Anunnaki, the Bilderberg New World Order, the Rosicrucians, the Knights Templar, and more. I do not blame any of them, and listing them here does not make them conspiracy groups, either. Could our current problems be a result of poor choice and misused power? Could it be a combination of both? Is it time to stop blaming others for the world's problems and look within for a solution? We can create peace today if we all decide this is a worthy cause. We can do this!

In my own history, I have hurt others by poor decisions alone. It was not my intention to hurt another person. I didn't wake up in the morning and say, "Hmm, who could I hurt today?" But unfortunately, it happened. Afterward, I did my best to apologize and make amends where possible. There are those I may have hurt without knowing that I caused them any ill will. I am still doing my best to live out my days without harming another, and there are many other groups that share the same philosophy.

As we look at these conspiracy groups, are any of them to blame? Perhaps we should look within first and say to ourselves, "We can make or break our present, and our future, right now if we work together." If peace is the true goal, couldn't we make a change as a group? I believe so. If everyone agrees that peace is a common goal, we could change our world *today* instead of *tomorrow*. We wouldn't have to look to a government to bail us out, or to give us the OK message. All it takes is a conscious group of people and a little effort to change how we live. If 340 million people in India could do it under Gandhi's leadership, so can we.

The tiniest of creatures know this already. Ants can move mountains of dirt for their size when they work together. Schools of dolphins and whales, who work together, can create a huge fish ball to help feed the entire group. Study and mimic the good parts of nature, and all could change in a blink of an eye.

Going back to the conspiracy groups, these unverified financial monarchs are said to control our government leaders and our world militaries as if they are marionette puppets on a very long string. I am not here to add fuel or fire to either side of these conspiracy theories. I have seen and read evidence to support both sides. What I find interesting is an unconfirmed correlation between an objective for peace for the entire world and a religious tool that could block such a movement toward world cooperation.

If any of these groups are behind the trappings of world freedom, they set up one heck of a good plan and conspicuously placed content in a very popular religious text that has controlled billions for centuries. Think about it. If you could control government and the military, you would also want to control as much religious thought as possible. This makes sense since the majority of the world practices one type of religion or another. Fear is a very strong tool. And if fear could be used in religious teachings, that would help control the masses.

But remember this, tools get old and break. This is great news for you and everyone else. I have seen more people become tired of fear as part of their own personal identity and release their worst fears almost overnight to live a happier and more productive life. Many of my clients have done this. Their success is no surprise. When people are ready to move on in life, they let go of the subconscious blocks that no longer serve their purpose. Being controlled by another will get old in time. Those who rule with this type of power have never stood the test of time. Tyrants may control for a while, but peace will always prevail in the end. And when people are tired of living in peace, the cycle will begin all over again. Such is the gift of living in duality and perception in this extremely diverse world.

THE STORY THAT BINDS PEACE

Suppose you are part of a group that wants to keep control over the masses. You would need to come up with a great story that makes as many people as possible afraid of any movement toward world peace. You would want them to be so afraid of any leader that promotes nonviolence and a peaceful existence that they cringe at the very thought of world unity. Anyone who hopes to conquer and transform fear in any country, or give self-governing a rebirth in the world, will be labeled the next Anti-Christ. If there is truth to any of these conspiracy theories, this will make sense of what I am about to tell you.

A great fear factor for many religions in this world has been related to the Book of Revelations. According to John of Patmos, also known as John the Apostle, the Anti-Christ and Armageddon are linked together better than strings of bratwurst. John states that before Armageddon wipes out most of our planet, Satan will return as one of us. Satan will take the form of a charismatic leader who will unite all nations with the intent of world peace. But this evil leader does not want world peace. This unidentified satanic leader is planning complete world domination and the demise of God and all souls on the planet.

Talk about a great set-up. If anyone tries to promote world peace, he or she could easily be twisted by anyone, including members of these conspiracy groups, believers of Christian faith, or even our current political leaders, to be the next Satan. You know, the Satan who plans to take over the world and cast all souls to an eternity of ice cream without hot fudge, hot dogs without ketchup, or crackers without cheese. Fire and brimstone is on the menu for all souls for time without end. No more pools with water, no more electricity (but you live in a room full of electronic devices), and the stray cat never leaves your bedroom window as it sings into the night for eternity.

Rest easy, fellow readers, I am no Satan. It's true that I want world peace, but I also checked in the mirror, and I have no pitchfork as my writing tool. Dominating the world takes too much work, and I am not that motivated to control you. I want self-governing in all the lands, not domination. I have too many bits of my own ego and fear to strip away. This is a lifetime's work for me. I am here to help others. As I help others find peace, this allows me to live in peace, too. It may take more than one lifetime to accomplish this great feat, but I have nowhere else to go. Eternity is a long time.

I like to think of it this way: You could spend all your energy trying to control your own destiny and help all those around you find peace and reach their destiny, or you could spend all your energy trying to control and dominate others just to make yourself feel good. Trying to control the entire planet is like trying to catch all the raindrops from a thunderstorm and keep them from hitting the ground. It may be fun at first trying to catch the droplets in a bucket, but the rain will become overwhelming and act as rain is meant to act. Rain falls freely where it was supposed to fall. People will become free to be who they were meant to be without oppression, control, or domination. Give it time; our world will shift naturally as more people become tired of money, greed, and oppressing governments. People will begin to explore their passions, and their passions will ignite a new world of love, acceptance, and self-governing.

THE GREAT EXPERIMENT THAT ALMOST WAS

In my mind, "America the Beautiful" was the right set of words to describe our country. (Well, it was before it was overrun by Pilgrims who stole the Indians' seed corn, robbed their graves, and pushed them from their lands.) When the first settlers landed on the northeastern shores, there was a great opportunity for creating a new continent without a monetary system or corrupt government and to establish peace with their brothers and sisters in a new land. There was a real chance for A-Merry-Ka.

I looked up the meaning behind the name America, and I couldn't find a definitive source. There are a few theories behind the actual meaning of America, but no one seems to know for sure how the name came to be. I also came up with my own theory. If you break down the word into three phonetic parts—A-Merry-Ka—you come up with this definition. Ka, in some texts, is the Egyptian word for "the soul beyond the body's soul." Why not have a happy soul? Why not have countries where all men and women are created equal and free to pursue their passions? Why not create a haven for a happy spirit? A-Merry-Ka, A-Merry-Soul, might have been named subconsciously for a reason. This land has so much potential. It is the breadbox for the entire world. There are enough resources here to feed everyone on the planet and still have leftovers for tomorrow, and the next day, and the next millennia. If money and over-farming, and the need to spend billions of dollars on the military, were spent on better cultivation and shipping of extra food stores to our neighbors, if we could release our fear of everyone attacking the American way of life, we would create so many friends that we would shift the energy of the world today.

See this in your mind: If you met a snarling, teeth-gnashing, growling, starving dog, and you fed him, and fed him again, and fed him again, and fed him some more, you would create a trusted friend for life. Your one-time enemy, who would have bitten your face off twice, would now be your best buddy. You would have a loving new friend who wags his tail and licks your face until it is dripping with slobber—all because you were kind to him. Your new pal would be there when you are down and out, when you are feeling ill, and when you are ready to go play fetch. Your new friend would be by your side at all times, just like Joe's dog, Duke. I may not want all my neighbors to come up and lick my face, but I sure want them as my friends. Maybe we could stop spending so much money on offensive/defensive military weapons and keep a *defensive only* military. I support the defensive actions of our military, but not the offensive actions. Offensive actions are for money, land, and greed.

Furthermore, we have enough bombs and bullets to kill all the inhabitants of the world hundreds of times over. How many times do we need to kill a dead body? This doesn't seem to stop a few of our government and military leaders from discovering more ways to kill people faster and in greater numbers. How many ways do we need to kill someone? Isn't it time to stop making more bullets and share the bounty of our harvest?

If everyone in the world did the same thing, created a *defensive only* military, there would be no offensive military to defend against. All the tanks and planes would be parked in the garage and hangars with nowhere to go. All that money could be spent on food, distribution, and other efforts to help feed the world. If I were a starving person in another land, I would be so thankful to those who helped me get back on my feet again, that I would do my best to help my helpers succeed and continue helping as a way to say thanks. What a great role model this would make for our country. Inspiration would spread faster than melting butter on corn-on-the-cob that just came off the grill. That is a plan of action that I would support. Couldn't we be the first to do this? If America wants to lead the world, why not do it with love and giving?

MIXED INTENTIONS OF A REVOLUTIONARY WAR

I learned in grade school that the beginning of the Revolutionary War was fought to free the American colonists from the tyrannical rule of the British monarchy and establish a new government. What they didn't teach us in school was the possible underlying reason for starting the war in the first place—money. This may not be the only reason, but it is listed as a major contributor. The Stamp Act of 1765 was enforced by the British Parliament on the American colonists. This act required all legal documents, permits, commercial contracts, newspapers, wills, pamphlets, and playing cards to be taxed under a new Stamp Tax. (Thank goodness they didn't tax toilet paper then. That would have been a crappy decision.) The Stamp Tax was said to be created as a means to pay off debt accrued from the Seven Years' War and to maintain a military presence in America. Needless to say, this taxation, along with a famous tax on tea and other goods, created a huge uproar within the colonies. "Taxation without representation!" could be heard in the streets and town halls.

As you look at the underlying reason for the Revolutionary War, was it really *freedom* that these people wanted? Were they going to the King of England and demanding freedom from English law because of monarchy rule? Or were these colonists mad about *MONEY* as a result of a monarch's ruling? Maybe it was a combination of all the above. Once again, we need our time machine to see the real reasons before we can make an educated statement about the cause behind the war. No matter which side may have won, there is still greed and money involved as the means to control people. However, we do know who won, and money and greed prevail to this day. We gave up a monarchy rule for a presidential rule. Are we any better off? There were also great kings and queens who provided for everyone in their land. We have had great presidents and those who went bust. Have we made new progress in humanity because of democracy? I believe we have made great strides in humanity. Democracy is only an experience in our history of evolution. We are continuing to change toward freedom for all, and that is incredibly optimistic.

INTENTIONS OF A POST-REVOLUTIONARY GOVERNMENT

I am making my best educated guess at the real intent of our freedom as our new government was formed. I have been trying hard to make sense of the direction of our forefathers. If unity, peace, liberty, and freedom were the intentions when the foundation of our new government system was being drafted, why would they allow opposing parties to be created? That seems to scream non-agreement. To this day, it is the Democrats against the Republicans. Throw in a few extreme liberals and conservatives, and it's no wonder that nothing can get done in this country without a long, drawn-out struggle. (Maybe the conspiracy groups did come over here and set that one up. Where is that time machine when you need it?)

The reason given for the creation of a two-party system was so that no one party would gain an advantage or supreme rule over the other. If you ever watch the news, you can see how the two opposing parties are jostling to gain the edge of voting power over the other in today's system. Did it work? NO!

I look at it this way. A true team effort will not set up an opposing team within itself. Read that again. A true team effort will not set up an opposing team within itself. A team effort works best when all team players are working toward the same goal. Imagine what would happen if that goal was *peace*. To continue with my confusion over our forefathers' decisions, if you have ten men, and their goal is to push a boulder up the hill, you wouldn't have two teams with opposing goals. You wouldn't have a team of five guys pushing the boulder up the hill, while the other five guys are pushing the boulder down the hill. This makes perfect sense. Our Democrats are pushing uphill while the Republicans are pushing downhill, and the other parties are pushing sideways. If the goal was peace, they could all push in the same direction.

I have to wonder, was the goal of the government to provide peace, freedom, and good will toward all men and women, or was it for a different mode of control with money as the controlling tool? It seems like you can't have both at the same time. Greed, power, control, and domination are opposing forces of peace, freedom, and a loving way of life. Maybe the true intent was to give freedom to the masses. I still believe this type of government was a step in the process. Democracy needed to be explored to show that it has good qualities. This could be said about every government system in our history. There is good and bad with everything. Perception is what makes the difference.

Let's look at some of the earlier famous texts and drafts and see how the intent looks if you interchange key words.

OUR US CONSTITUTION

We have earned more frequent time machine miles, and a few extra bonus perks, as our time machine lands in 1787. America is beginning to grow as it moves from a monarchy rule to a presidential rule. Here is the preamble to the US Constitution, adopted on September 17, 1787.

"We the People of the United States, in Order to form a more perfect Union, establish Justice, insure domestic Tranquility, provide for the common defense, promote the general Welfare, and secure the Blessings of Liberty to ourselves and our Posterity, do ordain and establish this Constitution for the United States of America."

I took certain key words from this historic text and inserted words from their definitions. This is the same preamble to the United States Constitution with definitions replacing the following words: justice, domestic, tranquility, common, welfare, liberty, posterity, and ordain. I also rewrote the word *We* to include all races, belief systems, sexes, and cultures.

"All people of any race, sex, religion, or financial status, living together in America, will be treated with fairness in action and decision-making. Your homeland will be free from commotion, anxiety, or agitation. The defense of the nation will be for the people. The government will promote conditions where people are healthy, safe, happy, and prosperous. The government will secure freedom from racial, religious, or financial slavery. The government will secure this for all generations to come. This the government establishes as law."

That sounds pretty good. They did a great job of writing. Do you feel that this sounds like the America we live in today? This text is over 200 years old. If, in your mind, this does not describe our current living situation in the US, what are we waiting for? We cannot blame the government for everything. We must look at ourselves as well. If we decide on common goals, such as peace, self-governing, acceptance, and tolerance, we can become a great team working toward similar goals. I vote for a team effort with a common goal of peace and acceptance. What do you want for yourself and your children's children? If you had to choose between our current monetary system that only benefits a *few*, and a world of peace for *all*, what would you choose?

Now mind you, when the preamble was written, "We the people" did not include slaves, women, the American Indians, or the Mexicans who lived in the southern and western portions of North America. "We the people" seemed to stand for a few male leaders with wealth and a white powdered wig. Some of our forefathers were still slave owners at that time—both financial slave owners and racial slave owners. A few of these men—and many more political leaders to follow, with the help of the military and blind patriotism—continued to take land away from the Indians and the Mexicans for over 100 years.

With democracy reaching a possible end, is it time for self-governing? Has democracy run its usefulness to allow us to grow beyond giving up control to others in power? Are we ready to accept our own mistakes, the mistakes of others, and use love as a means for teaching and redirection? Can we love someone instead of retaliating with hate? Can we let go of ego and fear, which will also alleviate the need for control, power, and our monetary system? No doubt there will be challenges. I am constantly working on changing my negative thoughts to thoughts of acceptance and peaceful resolutions. It may take time, but it is time well spent.

PROGRAMMED SEPARATION

Let's look at one last part of our culture in America that promotes separation from our neighbors across the borders and seas. As long as we continue to see ourselves as Americans, and separate from other nations, such as Mexico, Japan, Korea, Germany, China, Russia, Canada, and France, there will always be room for fear, hatred, and doubt. Is it time to view our world as a world filled with living water, living earth, living plants, living animals, living insects, and living people of all races, all living in equality for the good of the all? People are not born Communists, Democrats, Republicans, or Socialists; people are forced into government ruling and laws because of where they were born. The masses don't make the decisions to go to war. Most people just want to live and be happy. The majority of people want a roadmap for a better existence. Many roadmaps have been provided for centuries by influential, and not-so-influential, people of our time. And unfortunately, those who speak for world peace are usually killed because of greed, money, and fear. I may die in the process, but I stand for peace, freedom, and equality for *all people*.

WHERE THE HAND GOES

It is time to look at familiar words that have been spoken time and again. As soon as you entered kindergarten, these words were drilled over and over into your brain until you could recite the words in your sleep. Here is our pledge, not to world peace or world unity, but to a single country. I can see good intent behind this pledge; our government wants America to be unified. Maybe we are ready for a larger picture, though. Maybe it is time for a world unity pledge.

PLEDGE OF ALLEGIANCE

I pledge allegiance to the flag
of the United States of America
and to the republic for which it stands,
one nation, under God, indivisible,
with liberty and justice for all.

As before, I've inserted definitions for a few key words.

I pledge loyalty to a symbol representing a group of fifty states
and other provinces,
under a name for a spiritual being, where the land cannot be divided,
where everyone has freedom to think or act without being
constrained by necessity or force, with fairness for all.

No doubt about it, some of these words have good intent. Are we living these words today? If you cling to personal identities, those same words could be rather insulting or separate you from the whole. As an example, if you don't take offense to the word God, you are in good shape. If you find that offensive, because it does not represent the name of your spiritual leader or entity, you might feel separated. If you chose world unity over a unity of only fifty states, you might feel separated. If you feel that the land was taken away without honor from those who were here before, you might feel separated.

The last line is the one that stands out most: "Where everyone has freedom to think or act without being constrained by necessity or force, with fairness for all." If you stand against the money-driven govern-mint, you are considered a threat, a terrorist. If the govern-mint even thinks you are a terrorist, the military arm now has the right to detain you indefinitely without cause. Freedom is now a fleeting memory. It went up in smoke and will never be seen again as long as we live under these money-minded leaders.

I have to wonder, who gets to make these decisions? Who are these politicians to say what is right or wrong? They are no better than you or I. I say again, the government and military leaders do not represent me. I am only a slave in their system. Slavery still exists as long as we do not have the right to choose and govern our individual selves. I did not put them into power, and I do not have a right to change the system unless I go to them first. If it looks like a slave, and is forced to submit like a slave, it must be a slave.

As we look at the last line again, what is fairness for all? One person's fair is another person's unfair. What if the word *fairness* was changed to *peace*? Would this give us better direction for our country and our world? "Where everyone has freedom to think or act without being constrained by necessity or force, with *peace* for all."

A LAST LOOK AT TODAY

In our current world, I have had others tell me that they feel we are living in financial slavery. Financial slavery does not discriminate between color, sex, religion, or race. We are the property of the system. I wish I'd kept a list of all the people who have told me that they are ready for a change and are ready to give up this monetary system for a chance at a peaceful existence in which they could live their passions and not be constrained by money. My list would equal and surpass both of Santa Claus' naughty and nice lists combined.

There are those who will say "We have the right to vote." But the leaders we put into the system are trapped by the system. Voting is as ineffective as betting on a dirigible to break Mach 1, the speed of sound. The politicians' hands are usually tied. If they hope to get re-elected, they cannot go against the large corporations and banks that fund election campaigns. My understanding is that it is political suicide for a politician to do good for the people. Ask a politician if he will start a new campaign to change Social Security. If he does, he would kiss his career goodbye faster than he could kiss the next baby for a photo opportunity.

People are brainwashed to accept taxes from the earliest of ages. It's a nail that most people are forced to live with. If this was also a brainstorm of the conspiracy governments, they pulled another good one over the masses. People say, "There are three things you can count on in life: taxes, death, and more taxes." And there are those who ask, "If we don't have taxes, how do we expect life to continue as we know it?"

When I pay taxes, I have no say in how the money is spent. I would rather help a neighbor build a home than pay a tax that supports corrupt government, world separation, or an offensive military. I would rather help someone fight a fire in their home, farm, or business than pay a tax to support the same points from above. I would rather help mend a road than pay a tax to a government where I have no voice in how or where the money goes. I would freely give my time to teach others and help them conquer fear, rather than continue paying taxes. And I can go on and on with this list. At least there would be a choice, a freedom, as opposed to no choice at all. (Maybe I'm one of the forefathers reincarnated and destined to help America, and the world, obtain true freedom that was meant for all.)

I remind you again, I am not making judgments on any one person associated with the government. There are good and bad people in all areas of life and in all occupations. I am pointing out that the old system, and the current system we are using, still does not provide freedom and equality for all. It is a personal viewpoint, and I respect your views as well if you feel that our current system is a perfect system and is running like clockwork for everyone on our planet.

I ask you then, what can we learn from this part of our world history? Is there a common denominator that has been repeated over and over again by other nations and people for hundreds and thousands of years? Maybe we should be looking at the systems we honor and the titles we bestow upon other people. I believe we should honor people and not their titles. Should we keep our blind patriotic allegiances to kings, queens, caesars, presidents, pharaohs, popes, flags, and military heads of state? Or should we keep our allegiances to people, the planet, and its inhabitants? Is it time to usher in self-governing?

It seems almost inevitable that we are in for a major shift. Our population is forecasted to be greatly reduced, or wiped out all together, by any number of impending manmade or natural disasters. My hope is that after the dust settles from any one of these world disasters—some of which we helped to bring upon ourselves—the survivors will not repeat the same organizational mistakes of a one-ruler military system. My hope is that they will be able to conquer fear and shift from a self-serving society to one of giving, sharing, and caring through self-governing.

You might also be ready for a change. You may also want to know of a way that this can work. I will give you this roadmap in the next chapter.

WORLD UNITY PLEDGE

I really admired the efforts of Mohandas Gandhi. I never met this motivational soul, nor do I know of every action or deed that he performed in his life. What I have learned from this man, whom I have worked to emulate, is to act in the best efforts of others and to do it with nonviolence. I still like the words intended peace, or *peace*, better, as this already states a desire in action. I see us living for each other. I see us cooperating and loving others. I see our acceptance of others growing more and more each day. My cup is no longer half full. My cup is no longer half empty. My cup is full of potential. My cup is full of world peace.

What Gandhi did for India is what I hope to contribute to the entire world. Gandhi made a huge step forward for the human race and showed nations worldwide that a group of people, working toward a common goal of freedom, can change the old ways of a monarchy rule. I am not Gandhi, and at this time I am not able to get an entire nation to move toward freedom and peace. If I go on a hunger strike as he did, that just means more pizza for my neighbors. This won't hinder or stop my efforts, though. The best way I can help at this time is by finding inner peace, releasing my demons, and helping others release ego and fear.

A simple change to our Pledge of Allegiance could move our world toward a unified goal of peace. These words will speak very loudly and clearly as to how we can achieve this unified goal. It all starts with a wish, an idea, or a desire. In time, a desire becomes a belief. Beliefs lead to bigger possibilities. Bigger possibilities grow into stronger probabilities. Stronger probabilities turn into the beginnings of reality. And new realities turn into new life experiences. Voilá. Before you know it, a new world history has been written.

I ask you to read over this World Unity Pledge three times before going on in the book. Read the words and see how they feel to you. I did my best to include everyone and everything in these words. I went through countless drafts to make the words as simple, positive, and as full of potential as possible. Enjoy.

WORLD UNITY PLEDGE

BY MICHAEL J. RHODES

**I pledge my best to other people,
to the planet and all its inhabitants,
to promote *freedom* and *equality* for *all* races,
species, and genders,
One world, cooperating and sharing,
with love and acceptance for all.**

By choice, I have been saying this pledge instead of our country's pledge. I have the utmost respect for those from our past who have given us this opportunity to say such things without being dragged off to jail or being stoned to death. I honor their actions by helping our species move forward in the next evolutionary process of world unity and peace. I thank all those before us for their bravery, courage, and fortitude. With this intent, I say this new pledge again.

I pledge my best to other people,
to the planet and all its inhabitants,
To promote *freedom* and *equality* for *all* races,
species, and genders,
One world, cooperating and sharing,
with love and acceptance for all.

SUCCESS!

When I made the decision to say this pledge in place of our country's pledge at a networking event, I was questioned by the person next to me, and glared at by another. The person next to me mentioned that he heard me saying a different set of words. I kindly told him of my ideas of world cooperation and world unity. I shared with him that I respect the actions of those who came before us, and I am simply *acting toward our future*. I shared with him the content of my pledge, and he smiled. As I have shared this pledge with many since its conception, I have been given high-fives, hugs, handshakes, words of approval, smiles, blessings, words of encouragement, and requests for permission to repost the pledge on websites and in books. No one has expressed to me that they do not like this new pledge. I can imagine that the only ones who would not like this idea so far would be those who cling to an identity of being a proud American, and those afraid of losing power and money. I respect your identity if you wish to remain a proud American, and I will not force these words on you in any way. I want you to stay a proud American and say your pledge until you are tired of saying it. Live and let live in peace, choice, harmony, and potential.

In the state of Texas, all public school students recite a pledge to the Texas flag in addition to the American pledge.

"Honor the Texas flag: I pledge allegiance to thee, Texas, one state under God, one and indivisible."

Some of our community functions and networking events have also adopted the same practice. I know they are not doing this consciously to promote separation from the rest of the country, but if you were going to pledge to something, why pledge to a flag or a single state? If given a choice, would you rather pledge to a flag, an individual state, or to world peace? I choose world peace any day of the week, and the next week, and the next year, and you get the idea. Thank goodness I wasn't sent to jail because I did not say the pledge to the Texas flag, but I was met with a few dissenting eyes. I thought to myself, "Maybe we are not ready for this type of freedom yet." I keep believing, though. Belief becomes possibility. Possibility becomes probability. Probability becomes reality. Reality becomes life experiences and forms our history of peace with all.

UNIVERSAL PLEDGE

This pledge is a work in progress, and hopefully can be used as a roadmap for world cooperation. I also have another pledge that goes beyond this one. When some of my open-minded friends spoke to me about the potential of life elsewhere, they thought this pledge might not include the entire Universe. I was prepared for them, as I am also open-minded and believe in life elsewhere. I already had a second pledge in mind. For those who do not have an identity of a human being and believe they are spiritual souls living many paths of life, and believe in life elsewhere, enjoy this one:

UNIVERSAL UNITY PLEDGE

**I pledge my best to all entities, existing in spirit,
body, or other forms,
To promote freedom and equality for every type of species,
All consciousness, cooperating and sharing,
With love and acceptance for all.**

These pledges can be said at the same time as the American pledge, especially the World Unity Pledge. Your posture and hand position do not have to change, and the cadence is almost the same. If you believe that your emotions can influence another human being, then your intentions will flow to your neighbors and your neighbor's neighbor. You can also point your open palm to the world and place your non-dominant hand on your heart. It's been said that your dominant hand is your giving hand for energy. So if you are left-handed, you would place your right hand on your heart and point your left palm out toward the group to send them your heart energy of love and peace. Your hand would look like you are giving the universal sign for hello, not like you were saluting Hitler.

A NEW DIRECTION

The sixth-century B.C. philosopher Lao Tzu said, "Knowing others is intelligence; knowing yourself is true wisdom. Mastering others is strength; mastering yourself is true power." As we usher new possibilities into the future of our existence, self-governing may be the answer to changing our world. Add in tolerance, patience, and love, and we could create a paradise amongst the stars. I am glad to be in such good company with others who feel the same way.

CHAPTER EIGHTEEN

DISCOVERING
A NEW WORLD

GROUP OF EXPLORERS, assembled by the last surviving super powers, set out on an expedition to reach the uncharted lands of our planet. The mission for this special task force was to find and gather the remaining storehouses of natural resources, as the planet was running low on food, fuel, and clean drinking water. Their funding and supplies came from the few lingering corporations, banks, and military strongholds that refused to give up control. The explorers were well equipped with all the latest camping gear, technical devices, medical supplies, and weapons. Almost everyone in the group was made up of specialized forces from different branches of the government and military.

The world was already turning upside-down. Nobody believed that a single centralized power could fix the mounting problems that society was facing. Death tolls were on the climb from disease, and starvation was becoming commonplace in every city. Natural catastrophes were also causing mass destruction, as tornadoes, hurricanes, tsunamis, and earthquakes rumbled through the major metropolitan areas.

By now, most of the forests had been cut down, and the top soil depleted beyond repair from over-production and poor farming practices. As a result, the majority of land masses were experiencing terrible dust storms, which resulted in global famine. The world had been raped of resources for the last 200 years. The natural barriers of protection fell, and the planet became vulnerable to massive storms that blanketed out the sun. The weather conditions looked like a repeat of the Dust Bowl in America during the 1930s, but on a much larger scale. This time it was worldwide. Soon after, crops failed, water supplies were ruined, and riots began breaking out in most cities.

People were hoping and praying for an answer to this nightmare. The populace knew that they had also contributed to the planet's demise in one way or another and prayed for a second chance. In an effort to make things right, they began searching for possible solutions so they could help the Earth heal itself and get civilization back on its feet again.

OPERATION RESOURCE

With command at the ready, the members of the special task force began their journey. The team leaders were given their objectives and were provided with coordinates for potential target areas. Their mission seemed a little futile, though, as the industrial super giants had already reached just about every corner on the globe and exploited the land, forests, oceans, and fresh water supplies for profit.

The team members wanted to help humanity and did their best to remain optimistic. Their intentions were not to control people, but to bring what little hope and food they found to as many of their countrymen as possible.

The first few days produced no new discoveries of fresh resources. Whenever the task force came upon starving or sick people, they gave as much aid and comfort to these families as possible. They made a group decision to ration their food and share what they could. If there was a piece of equipment that would help a family, they left it behind. Both parties knew that these sincere acts of kindness would continue to raise hope.

A full week passed, and the team's travel brought them closer to one of the major coastlines. Unfortunately, there was still no progress to report to command. They set up camp and decided to move inland in the morning, using an uncharted river as their guiding star. The team leader called in their position and requested river transportation be delivered by chopper, along with fresh supplies.

As the sun crested the lifeless ocean waters, there were two boats float-ing a few hundred yards away from their tents. By the time the sun came into full view, the entire campsite had been broken down and the mem-bers were boarding the boats. Their spirits were still high and remained positive.

The land expedition turned into a river expedition by mid-morning. Moving cautiously through the uncharted winding river, the explorers made slow headway as they did their best to avoid piercing the bottom of the boat on an unseen boulder or being stuck on a sandbar.

The closer inland they got, the more they began to lose radio contact. All new messages were coming in garbled and filled with static. They had their best radioman, Adam, on the job. "Sir, I think I got it. I was able to boost the signal and pick up an incoming message. There is a severe weather warning in alert. An 8.8 magnitude earthquake occurred a few hundred miles from here in one of the ocean's abysses and caused a huge tidal wave to form. They are not sure, but they think it is heading our way," said Adam. The commander took action immediately and told the crew to secure all supplies and bind the two boats together. He knew they couldn't afford to be split up.

Before preparations could begin, all sounds on the river's shores and tree lines stopped suddenly. The eerie silence became so intense it was al-most deafening. All life became still, and everyone on the boat froze. Team members glanced at each other. They didn't know if they should be afraid, run for cover, or continue with preparations.

A rumble could be heard off in the distance, interrupting the chilling si-lence. It came from the direction of the ocean and grew louder and louder. The ominous growl sounded like an entire squadron of helicopters coming over the ridge. The group thought that they might be picked up before any danger could happen to them. They looked, and looked, and looked again in the direction of the ocean. They were sure they would be rescued. But the next sight they saw would frighten the bravest of men. A wall of water, towering higher than most buildings in New York, sped toward the boats with the force of 1,000 rocket engines. Before they could react, both boats were submerged and jettisoned along the flooded waterway. The tiny boats were tossed around and smashed with tons of debris from the intense speeding wave. It would be a miracle if anyone survived this onslaught from the natural disaster.

Moving further inland, the wall of water pushed all the way up toward the base of an unexplored mountain range. The entire forest range below was devastated and almost completely submerged under water. Only a few remaining treetops poked out of the new water basin.

Days passed, as the water receded back into the ocean from where it came. The land began to dry out and reveal the path of destruction from the ocean shoreline all the way to the base of the hills. Neither of the two boats was found, and all attempts to locate survivors from the group seemed hopeless.

A NEW DAWN

Light began to shine into Adam's eyes as he regained more consciousness. Slowly, bits and pieces of his surroundings were coming into focus as he found himself lying on a bed in a strange room. He was disoriented, but he was alive, and that was the best news of all.

"Ow, my head is hurting."

"Easy, Adam, take your time. You are lucky to be alive," said Lilith. "We have waited patiently for three days for you to regain consciousness."

"Three days! What do you mean, three days? What happened? Where am I? Are there any others still alive?"

"Our gatherers found you washed up along the mountainside. Your name on your torn uniform told us who you are. We found five others alive and scattered throughout the valley. All are fine and healing well. They suffered a few broken bones here and there, but nothing life threatening. Here, take this. You still need your rest." Lilith gave Adam an herbal drink to help his body heal through the night. "We will be watching over you, Adam. You are still recovering, so drink this and rest, and we will talk more tomorrow."

In the morning, Adam woke again in the same room. His headache was gone, and so was his uniform. Lying on a chair next to his bed was a beautifully handmade pants-and-shirt set. Underneath the chair was a pair of custom tan leather sandals in Adam's size.

The room that Adam was in was simply stunning. Woodwork, tables, and chairs of the finest craftsmanship filled every space and corner of the room. The most eye-pleasing artwork hung gracefully on the walls. Fresh flowers and plants also brightened the room and gave it a pleasant, homey feeling. Adam got dressed and walked to the door cautiously. He didn't know what to expect and was very curious. He was also a little weak from his ordeal. When he reached the door, he noticed it had no lock, and he opened it slowly.

Sitting in a chair outside of Adam's room sat a warm, inviting figure. "Adam, it is good to see you standing," said Lilith. "You must be hungry. Come, your friends are waiting for you in the dining hall. Here, let me help you get there." She gently raised her arm for Adam to gain support.

"Who are you, and how did I get here?"

"My name is Lilith, and it is a pleasure to meet you. There will be plenty of time to explain everything. Tell me, do you feel you can walk all right? How is your strength?"

"I'm fine, thanks. Where am I?"

"You are in our village, and you are welcome here. All who come are welcomed, supported, and loved. Come, let us go and meet your friends."

Lilith led the way as they walked down the decorated hallway to the front door. When she opened the door, Adam was treated to visions that could only be described as paradise. Cultivated flowers and vegetable gardens, waterfalls, ornate houses and buildings, fruit trees, and wildlife all completed the picturesque scene. "Adam, this is our village. Here we live in peace and harmony with each other, our neighbors, and with nature. We coexist in love and acceptance with all in the land we share. I know you have questions, and we will answer all of them in time. How do you like your clothing?"

"The pants and shirt fit me perfectly. The fabric feels like the finest ever made, and the workmanship is incredible. Who made these clothes? These are better than any tailor-made suits I have ever owned."

"Adam, the clothes you are wearing were made by apprentices when you arrived. They are still mastering their craft."

"Wow, if this is the work of apprentices, I can't wait to see the work of their teachers."

"You might be amazed by the work of everyone here. We are living our passions and are able to put our best efforts into our creations to please all who use them."

"You mean nobody has to work here?"

"We do not understand this concept of work as you know it, Adam. People grow up here encouraged to live, experience, and create for the community whenever they are ready. We live for peace, first and foremost.

It might seem foreign to you, as we have seen your society as it exists, but you will see how we are able to make this work and how we are able to make it last for generations to come."

"How old is this village, Lilith?"

"As far as I know, the village has been here for over 200 generations. Each generation has contributed to the future of the next by shedding ego, fear, and the need for control."

"Why haven't I heard of this place before?"

"That's a good question, Adam. I guess one reason is that no one ever wants to leave. We all have the freedom to come and go as we please, but we enjoy living our passions so much that we all choose to stay. The other option would be to live in your mainstream society. Tell me, Adam, do people get to live their passions and dreams where you come from? Are you living your passion now?"

"Actually, no, I am not living my passion. I became a radio operator because there was an opening that provided more pay. It's a job, nothing more."

"Adam, if you could live your passions without worrying about money, what would you do?"

"Wow, no one has ever asked me that before. I have always enjoyed farming, but farming was taken over by the government systems and it became impossible to run your own farm. That is, unless you wanted to live in poverty. How sad is that?"

"It does sound sad, Adam, very sad. Let me share with you our philosophy.

"We believe that when a person is forced to perform an act without love and passion, then the act is not done to his best ability. We believe there is an emotional energy to every action. We also believe that everything in existence is based on a vibrational structure. Your science calls these standing waves and string theory. If people are permitted to live their dreams, without fear, ridicule, judgment, or coercion, then they increase their chances of being more productive, and what they produce is of a much higher quality than if they were forced to work. In our village, for example, people can produce a particular type of food, clothing, or entertainment for the village. They may become great builders, caretakers, teachers, or students. Whatever they are doing, they create their own personal vibration of peace, contentment, and happiness, and it shows in their work.

"Tell me, Adam, have you ever walked into a room right after a couple had a big argument?"

"Why yes, I have. You could tell something negative happened in the room."

"Then, Adam, you know that emotions can be felt from an action, not just felt as a reaction. So when people are able to explore, learn, and live with peace and love as their main goal, they create an environment of tranquility for others and the planet. Are you beginning to understand?"

"Yes, but I have so many questions, Lilith. What have you done about government, laws, religion, and taxes?"

"These are all good questions, Adam. We will talk more after breakfast. We are at the dining hall."

REUNITED

As Adam and Lilith walked into the circular building, the survivors from Adam's team caught sight of him and waved from their table. "Adam, you're alive!" said Tom excitedly. "It's great to see you. Are you feeling better?"

"I am, thanks, Tom. Is there any word about the rest of the team?"

"No, not yet, but the surrounding villages have their trackers looking for them. You look pretty good for having been out of commission for three days, and I see you have met Lilith. She has stayed by your side the entire time. She is one of the town's physicians."

"Yes, she has been very kind to me," Adam said, as he looked her way with a thankful smile. "I am sure I owe my life to her."

"Here, sit down and try some of this food. It's fantastic! Everything is fresh and made by the village chefs. Did you know they apprentice for years while they master their craft? And there is no pressure for them to become a cook, either. If they choose, they can continue with their training, or start an entirely new craft. Heck, a lot of these folks live more than one passion at a time," said Tom. "Some of the master chefs spend their free hours apprenticing to become artists, builders, and craftsman. If the other villages need a chef for a while, they practically jump at the opportunity to help their neighbors. Everyone seems so happy here without the pressures that we experience everyday with money and job obligations."

"I'm beginning to notice that, Tom. There is a peaceful environment in this town that I must say I have never felt before. It's very refreshing."

After breakfast, Adam asked Lilith if they could meet with the town leader. "Adam, we have no town leader or government system."

"No government? Sounds like paradise. What about mayors, judges, lawyers, or laws? How do you make decisions that affect an entire community?"

"Adam, I have someone in mind that could explain this better than I can. I would like to take you to Isaac. He is one of our elders, and he can answer your questions regarding our ruling system here. Why don't you all come and ask Isaac your questions?"

MEETING WITH THE ELDER

The group took a short stroll through one of the flower gardens, which led them to a refined-looking gentleman who sat underneath a tree. His posture gave the appearance that he was meditating. "Isaac, pardon me. These are the people we helped rescue from the tidal wave. They would like to talk with you."

"Of course, Lilith, I would be happy to share with them." Isaac looked toward the visitors. "I understand you have been through quite an ordeal. How can I assist you?"

Adam spoke first. "It is a pleasure to meet you, Isaac. Can you please tell us how your village came to be? How do you operate without a government or laws?"

"Ah, a grand question, Adam. It has taken our people a great deal of time, patience, and many adjustments to achieve this type of peaceful existence. It did not happen overnight, and we encountered many challenges along the way. It is not a perfect system, but the desire for our serene environment makes all the challenges worthwhile."

"But, how did it start? How were you able to achieve what a lot of others would call *paradise?*"

"Adam, it all started with a desire for peace. Peace above all else. Once peace was established as a goal, everything else began to fall into place."

"Can you elaborate? How did you do this without a government?"

"Adam, our greatest joy in life is to govern ourselves, and one of our greatest challenges is never to govern another. As we continue to release fear and ego, and as we use peace as our motivator, most people are able to achieve their dreams without needing an appointed leader to make decisions for them. We also make decisions with the help of a council, much like the Native Americans did on their native lands."

"This all sounds great, Isaac. But I still don't understand how this works. What prompted this?"

"As it was told to me by my father's father, as it was told to him by his father's father, long ago in our village, before peace was established as our goal, people began to fear making decisions for themselves. They feared this because some of their decisions had caused bad feelings within their own hearts, between family members, and with their neighbors. Without peace as a true goal, people began to argue, fight, and carry grudges more easily. Pride and ego soared higher than the mighty condor in those days. Eventually, our forefathers began relying on others to make decisions for the community. And soon after, people began choosing sides, voting in leaders, and starting debates. Tempers eventually flared, and unfortunately, caused a few skirmishes and wars. The more people had others make decisions for them, create laws, and then pass judgment, the more people lost what they cherished most—freedom. Our ancestors eventually lost their right to self-govern. Once they realized this, they made a conscious effort to change."

"Change? How did they do this? Was the change to gain back their freedom?"

"Adam, our ancestors realized it was easier to forgive another than to forgive themselves. We have noticed that people tend to be much harder on themselves and more critical of their own mistakes. Self-criticism often turns into subconscious negative feelings, like guilt, fear, regret, and remorse. These subconscious beliefs kept people from being open and truthful with others about their true feelings. Their inner fears kept them from making a choice, or sharing their thoughts. Mostly, they were afraid of being ridiculed, chastised, and shunned for being honest and pursuing their ambitions. So in time, people allowed others to make decisions for their families and for the community."

"Wow, that sounds so familiar, doesn't it, Tom?"

"All too familiar, Adam. It's almost scary how much that sounds like our current society. Isaac, what were the leaders like back then?"

"Most leaders in our history did their best to serve the people, much like your society today. And only a very small percentage took advantage of the power that was entrusted to them. There were many leaders who did great things for a larger cause. The more time our ancestors spent in this governing system, the more people kept looking to their appointed leaders to fix all the problems. With people taking less responsibility and wanting more, there was no way that any one leader could solve all of life's major challenges. Eventually, the violence grew too much amongst the people, and this type of governing system collapsed. It almost destroyed our forefathers completely. As darker times came upon the land, people made a shift in consciousness and decided it was much better to face their fears, take responsibility, and govern themselves rather than kill their neighbor. I guess you could say that our forefathers got tired of killing and released their identity as warriors and patriots."

One of the others in the group spoke up. "Isaac, was there one major event that caused the shift?"

"Well, my dear visitor, to answer your question, there was no one single event that changed how things were developing. What happened was a conscious choice by enough people to make a positive change. You could always call choice the major cause, but it was not a single event; it was a series of events that led to this wonderful transformation. People became aware of their own fears and conquered them one by one. Once you face a fear, it no longer has control over you. After this conscious change took place, people just got tired of having others making decisions for them. People knew they could be responsible and self-govern if peace was the ultimate goal."

Adam jumped right in. "Surely there must have been conflicts. How were decisions made in your community?"

"We are always striving for a peaceful resolution to any goal or conflict. The most sought-after solution, of course, is for all people to be happy from any decision that may cause change. We achieved this most of the time. If an agreement could not be made, many of our people would simply put aside their desire until the time was right. Harmony prevailed in this instance over individual desires. And as you would expect, sometimes the most peaceful resolution to a conflict might result in an argument or a fight. We are still human, with human emotions. With our priority on harmony above all else, though, we seem to have fewer arguments and wars than in your current society."

Isaac continued, "You see, when a situation arises that offers multiple outcomes, our people have learned over the years to sit down with each other and discuss what would be the most positive outcome for all involved. With less ego and pride, and without a need for a monetary system, there is less conflict. It is not a hidden secret. Our success is attributed to a group of people working toward a higher cause than individual needs, ego, or the accumulation of things and wealth.

"Adam, one of the main differences between our village and your society is that we have a concentrated group of people with the same goals in mind: peace, acceptance, tolerance, and love. Your society is capable of the very same thing, once you make a conscious decision to move in this direction. The more people band together into communities with the same peaceful intentions, the more you will see the same changes and benefits in your world."

Tom asked, "So you still have disagreements? It was beginning to sound a little unrealistic."

"Oh yes, we still have our disagreements, but our disagreements are not over who owns what, who gets paid what amount, or over financial gains and wealth. Our arguments are not created by jealousy, lack, or pride. As everyone is given the best available food, clothing, shelter, care, and love in our villages, we no longer have a need to covet trinkets and bobbles. Instead of spending our time gathering wealth, we spend our time making others wealthier in happiness from their accomplishments. Our time is used to increase the wealth of a person's ability, not their bank account. We decided long ago to give up pursuing money and greed and made a conscious effort toward pursuing the potential of the human spirit.

"We are always growing, changing, and trying to improve the path of life for ourselves and our future grandchildren. As we have watched your society mature, we have witnessed the growth of your nations and government systems. We have noticed the positive progress you have made. We believe you are searching for an existence like ours where people are able to live their passions without fear of ridicule or persecution.

"As a guideline, our village agrees to keep the population small enough so everyone knows everybody else in the village. If the village gets so large that you don't know your neighbors, we believe that it becomes harder to care for them on a deep personal level. We have seen the same thing in your communities. People support each other more when they are in direct contact with their family, neighbors, and friends. They seem to try harder to help and encourage each other when they have a personal interest and relationship with that person. As an example, we have seen your concern over the depleted population of polar bears. If polar bears existed in your community, and people enjoyed their contribution to the cycle of life, the chances would increase that everyone would take more care in making sure that the polar bears' habitat was unharmed by human activity. Likewise, if someone is suffering from a life-threatening illness in a neighboring community, and no one makes a fuss about it where you live, it is not because your village is an uncaring, emotionless group of people. The underlying reason is the person's illness did not affect anyone on a close personal level. People still care about other people and want them to be healthy and well. It seems natural to care more about those who are in direct relationship to their lives. Does this make sense so far?" asked Isaac.

"Yes, it does," said Tom. "Please continue."

"As our village population increases beyond our ability to know everyone on a personal level, the village makes preparations to expand by starting a new sister community. The townspeople help find a new location for this sister community that will be in harmony with the surrounding villages. Supplies are always shared with the new sister community, and all other neighboring communities, as they are all still considered family members.

"Recently, one of the faraway neighboring communities began their expansion, but they were unaware of our village's location. They began establishing a new community higher up the mountain near the main fresh water supply for the valley. Their runoff created health issues with members of our community and the other surrounding villages. Upon hearing this, and with harmony as their main goal, they apologized and asked for assistance. All of the communities below theirs pitched in for months to help them establish a brand new living facility, even better than the one they left. The people were ecstatic. They didn't want to harm anyone else, and they had all the help they needed to create a new living center that would benefit them and everyone around them. With no jobs or money obligations to keep people from helping their neighbors, work schedules opened faster than a new flower bud on a bright spring morning. Everyone was happy. No egos were bruised, harmony was the intent, and peace prevailed. With that type of help and care available, and with peace and harmony as a goal for all communities in this area, who could say no to that type of help?" said Isaac.

"Without the need for money, I could see that working. What do the children do while all this is going on?" asked Tom.

"We have adopted what many tribes have successfully practiced from around our planet. Our elders, the ones with a passion to teach and guide, gladly watch over the children while the parents pursue their passions to create the basic needs for the community. All of our children are treated as if they were a part of everyone's family, so they all receive love and acceptance from the moment they take their first breath. We are not just a village; we are a large family.

"Our younger adults realized that they have a gift of youth and energy that can better serve the community while they are still strong and able. They also realize that the elders have more experience in life and welcome their knowledge as it is passed directly to their children. This has increased our children's understanding of nature, love, and living in harmony with others in our world. Everyone benefits. All of our adults also have the choice of who helps raise their children. With less fear in the community, people are not afraid of differing lessons or content of knowledge. And as the elders are respected and cherish the opportunity to be useful in the community, everyone wins.

"Tell me, dear travelers, could you see yourself living with peace as your goal?"

"Not speaking for anyone else," said Adam, "I would love this lifestyle where there is less fighting, greed, and fear. It would be awesome to explore my passion instead of working a job to meet the mortgage payment."

"Me, too!" added Tom. "No taxes, no money to worry about, and cooperation and tolerance as the main focus. I already feel healthier just from talking about it. We would no longer have to deal with the stress we have to endure on a daily basis just to make ends meet. No wonder people live longer here than in our society. Are you inviting us to stay?"

Lilith smiled. "All who come are welcomed, supported, and loved."

Adam remarked, "We know there will be some adjustments on our part. We would hope that the people in your village would be patient with those of us who choose to stay. It will be obvious that the system we've grown up in is far less tolerant than the one you have established."

Lilith replied, "Adam, we do our best to respond to every action with love. If you were to make a mistake, wouldn't you want support instead of criticism? If you were to fall and hurt yourself, wouldn't you want a helping hand to help you stand tall? If you were to strike another in anger, wouldn't you want forgiveness instead of a returning hateful blow? This is part of our teachings and philosophy. We show patience and love in all of our teachings, with love being the emotion we show most often. Tolerance and cooperation are the cornerstones of our foundation. Love is the binding emotion that fuels our desires and helps our community live as *One*. We believe we are all made from the same stardust and carry the same building blocks of potential in each of our souls. You are a part of us. Whether you choose to stay or return home, you are one of us in another body. And the greatest gift we can offer you is freedom of choice. You will be loved either way."

"What about our families and friends back home?" asked Tom.

"They are all welcome here as well," answered Isaac. "Don't you see? You are our brothers and sisters from another land. If they decide to come and live here, we would be able to welcome home our long-lost family members into the community once more. As it would be your choice to stay, it would also be their choice to come and live here. Some will journey, and others will choose to stay in their current lifestyle. We do not force this on anyone. And we will show an abundance of patience and love while those who join us release fear and ego and begin their pursuits of passion and happiness."

All the members of the team looked at each other with smiles and nods of agreement. "We are all staying," said Adam. "Thank you for inviting us home again." And a new chapter of history was about to be begin.

CHAPTER NINETEEN

COMMUNITY INGREDIENTS

THE MOST IMPORTANT INGREDIENT for a perfect community soufflé would be a great cross section of freshly picked people, with a side of warm passion sauce drizzled on top. You might think this would be a hard order to fill, but while going into the communities to do my research and interviews for this book, I received overwhelming positive responses from huge numbers of people who want to live in this type of society. I have heard from mothers, fathers, children, business owners, students, employers, employees, young, old, and people from all social and financial groups, all of them voicing their excitement over the possibility of a society where people could pursue their passions without being bound to a monetary system.

As you have just read, finding people to start a workable, realistic society where people can pursue their dreams will not be a challenge. If you go to a typical corporation and ask the workforce if they are living their passion in their current job, what do you think they will say? While networking in my business neighborhood, I often ask people if they are living their passion, and I am not surprised when they tell me "No!" As a matter of fact, I have very few people say "Yes," and these are mostly self-employed people. What does this tell you so far? Many people are looking for a change and an opportunity for this type of community.

TEN PASSIONS

The best reaction I have received is when I ask people what they would do if they did not have to worry about money. You should see their faces light up. I remember one gentleman who told me he was currently working as a contractor for a construction and oil company. I could tell this job was not his main passion, and he confirmed this for me. I know there are plenty of people out there who love to build things. I also like to build things and use my hands to create, but this was not his burning desire. When I asked him what he would do if there were no financial obligations, I barely got to finish my question before his excitement got the best of him. He told me that his dream was to be a fishing and hunting guide. He loved the outdoors. He loved spending time showing other people where the best spots are to catch fish and how to bring them into the boat. He loved sharing hunting and tracking tips. He loved putting food on the table. He went on for a good while sharing his excitement and dream with me. I loved every minute of his enthusiasm as he continued sharing his passion, and I could tell that he was inspired by our conversation. Who knows? Maybe our talk will bring him one day closer to living his dreams.

While attending another business meeting, I asked a financial advisor if he was living his passion. He looked at me, smiled, and said, "No one has ever asked me that question before." Without missing a beat, he went on to explain how he would love to continue working with animals, specifically dogs and cats. He adopted a few dogs from an animal rescue center and enjoyed the experience immensely. He told me he would love to continue doing this as his dream occupation.

I had the pleasure of working with a very talented choral director years ago in South Florida. He was a good teacher and had an exceptional voice. We often talked about desires and passions besides our teaching careers. Although he enjoyed teaching, this was not his driving passion either. His real desire was to make religious recordings and go on tour. He wished to inspire others with his motivational lyrics and pleasing melodies. In time, his courage grew, and he left the public school system to pursue a successful adventure as a performer. I am proud of him for making the leap of faith.

As I was shopping one evening, I saw one of my friends who is a manager at a well-known office supply store. He is a pleasure to visit with because of his infectious high spirit and great attitude. I don't think I've ever seen this guy in a bad mood. I told him I was still gathering information for this book and asked if he would mind telling me what his passion was if money were no longer an object. I also asked him to tell me his three wishes. He was ecstatic and shocked as he told me no one has ever asked him what his wishes are in life or what he would like to pursue as a passion. He has a great job, but he did not wish to be a store manager. His main dream was to create physical fitness programs for children and continue mastering his ability for building strength and endurance for marathons.

A casino pit boss from Louisiana got misty-eyed twice when I asked her to share her passions and wishes. Her original plans were to attend college and write an inspirational book, much like this one. She wanted to help people rediscover their dreams. She also has a desire to become a healer. Unfortunately, she was forced to leave college when her funding ran out. She ended up working in the casino to make ends meet. Before our interview ended, her spirits were raised again, and she found a new drive to inspire others.

Every year, I have to renew my yellow-page ads for my hypnosis practice. I took the opportunity to talk to my new sales rep and share with him the content of my book. As you might have guessed, he was not living his passion, either. He has a degree in psychology but did not have the financial means to develop a practice. Instead of being able to help patients with severe depression and other mental disorders, he was forced to go into sales so he could eat. I could hear the inspiration building inside him as I shared more of these ideas.

Most recently, I picked up my wife's car from the tire repair shop. While getting a ride to the repair center from their complimentary shuttle service, I had a great conversation with a young man about life's passions. He mentioned to me he was thinking about this very topic before he picked me up. (Can you say synchronicity?) I asked him if he was living his passion right now, and he said "No." His dream was to become a martial arts instructor and present the benefits gained from the philosophies instilled in these disciplines. He told me that he'd had to give up his dream because of a lack of money. While at the shop, I asked three managers behind the desk if they were living their passions, and they also responded "No." One gentleman wanted to be a marine biologist, another wished he could pursue sports and fishing, and the third just wanted to be a better father and be around his family more.

I could fill volumes of books with countless other stories like the ones you've just read. I know that you are not completely surprised by these reactions, and hopefully, if you are not already living your dream, you are creating a driving force within yourself to move closer to that blessed day.

PASSIONS OF NEED

I know I have been focusing on finding your dreams and passions and then living them to create harmony within yourself, which in turn will help create harmony with your neighbors. I also know that you don't have to have a passion to feel good and create a vibration of peace. Sometimes all it takes is for a person to feel needed or important. Give people the chance to feel needed, and they can move mountains, build roads, and feed hundreds of hungry people without thinking of their own desires. It may not be your dream to dig a hole, but if digging a hole helped your children, or served the community, that feeling of pride and accomplishment can satisfy the greatest of basic wants. If you were asked "Will you please help us dig this hole for our community to survive? We *need* your strength and help," what would you say as a member of that tight knit community? How would that make you feel to be needed and asked to be a part of something? Imagine the feelings of appreciation you would receive during and after the hole was dug. Those feelings alone make a community like this one worth all the effort.

As I have helped others discover their passions and encouraged them in their ability to succeed, I have been able to live my passion as well. I truly enjoy helping people release their fears and old subconscious habits that no longer fit their purpose. I love teaching and sharing knowledge about possibilities of the mind and the human spirit. I love inspiring others to pursue their childhood dreams and find personal peace and contentment. Without students, it is hard for me to be a teacher. I am blessed that there are so many out there searching for possible solutions to their goals.

Please take a moment and answer these questions to yourself:

Are you living your dream job or your passion right now?

What three passions would you pursue if money were no longer a factor?

What passion(s) could you pursue that would benefit a community?

Is there something you could do that would contribute to the needs of a community?

PASSIONS IN ACTION

Isn't it wonderful that there are people in this world who are already living their passion, and they are doing it without taking residence in a community like this one? You probably can think of more than one person right now who is making her dream come true. You are one of those people, aren't you? My hat goes off to you. Your courage is an inspiration to many, including myself. Please keep going and never look back. The more people like you who do this, the more our world will change to a peaceful place overnight.

I am speculating again, but I imagine the more people serve others first, the more they enjoy what they are doing. Schoolteachers come to mind as a great example. Teachers sacrifice countless hours to prepare for classes, grade papers, write lesson plans, attend staff meetings and parent conferences, attend school functions, and find creative ways to teach and challenge their students. They receive no paid bonuses for work above and beyond the call of duty. There are no major pay raises that one might experience in the corporate world. And unless you want to be an administrator, there is no corporate ladder to climb. Ask teachers why they continue in this challenging field, and they will tell you they like to give, share, and help others reach their potential.

The best pay I ever received as a teacher was when a student, who had already graduated from the school I taught in, came back to thank me for all the extra time, support, and lessons I had given him. A special bonus came my way when his parents also made a special trip into my band room to thank me for helping their son get into the School of the Arts. That made all the extra hours and effort worth it.

There are numerous other occupations and people who serve society before they serve themselves: nurses, doctors, counselors, volunteers, band parents, sports parents, boy scouts, girl scouts, nature and animal activists, moms, dads, grandparents, relatives, and those working in the nonprofit sector. These are just a few of the inspirational people that give more than they receive. If I did not mention your occupation or relation, please make sure you pat yourself on the back. You deserve it!

MEASURING CUP FOR A GROWING COMMUNITY

We've added our first ingredients to the baking dish: people and passion. It's a sweet and spicy mix for sure. The next few questions that come to mind are these: How many people do you need for this type of community to function? Is there a number that is too big or too small for a society of peace? Is there a population that is too large for everyone to know their neighbor?

Of course, there is no absolute answer to these questions. Land, resources, stable climate, and food availability all have their influence on how many people can flourish in one location for any length of time. Creating and maintaining social relationships is also a major key for unlocking the secrets to developing a harmonious society. If there are enough community interactions, or social interests, the community increases its chances of living together in peace. Fulfilling the basic needs of food, shelter, growth, spiritualism, and entertainment will easily satisfy the bulk of community interests.

I realized long ago that people care about others who live close by, and they also care for those who live far away. They care an incredible amount. I also noticed people tend to do more for others in times of need when these people are within a certain circle of personal familiarity. The more you know someone, the more you care about him or her. The more you care about them, the more you are willing to help them in times of need, even if it means a major personal sacrifice on your part. If a community gets too large, or if there are fewer community activities, the opportunity to know your neighbor gradually decreases, and a higher degree of chaos exists. It sounds like entropy has shown its familiar face again.

It has also been suggested the size of the neocortex, the largest part of the brain's cerebral cortex, has a direct correlation to the size of a cohesive group. The neocortex is believed to be responsible for the brain's higher functions. Language, conscious thought, reasoning, cognitive and social skills all owe their abilities to this slice of grey matter.

According to Professor Robin Dunbar, the director of Oxford University's Institute of Cognitive and Evolutionary Anthropology, his studies suggest that the size of the neocortex in primates directly relates to the size of a socially cohesive group. His formula, when used for humans, produces the number 147.8 for a maximum group size. Not surprisingly, this number has shown up throughout the world in various cultures and institutions. When Dunbar looked at different hunter-gatherer societies from around the world, he discovered their average number per village was 148.4.

Other studies have suggested that humans can keep common interests and know their neighbors well enough to support 300 people, twice the number of Dunbar's findings. It would be fair to say that the size of a community can vary to a degree based on the ability of the people to stay connected with one another, or by having a stronger belief system, such as peace.

I recently heard of a community in the United States with over 1,200 people living together in harmony with a 0% crime rate. Their main system, which helps bind them together, is based on meditation and following the Vedic way of life. They gather twice a day in a community center to meditate together. Their schools also implement meditation into their curriculum. That's amazing to me. Good for them. Can you imagine the calm energy of this place?

I believe that if peace is the binding belief system, communities can also break the 150-person barrier. As long as a common belief system, community activities, and desire for a peaceful existence prevail, who knows how large the community could grow? It could grow worldwide. That would be an experiment worth pursuing for sure.

BASIC INGREDIENTS

Whether your community is stationary or nomadic, a few basic needs must be met. People tend to function best when they have food in their bellies, fresh water to quench their thirst, and an opportunity for a restful night's sleep. People increase their comfort level if they have clothes to protect them from the harsh elements, shoes for their feet, and a roof and walls for privacy. They are even happier if they have activities to stimulate the mind and opportunities to strengthen their muscles. And people are ecstatic when they can play, create, entertain, and be entertained. As people follow their individual passions, surely one or more of these basic needs will be met.

As most people in our country have been forced and programmed to function on a monetary system, it may be a little strange to think of fulfilling these needs without money. I'm here to tell you, though, that it can be done very easily. Yes, there will be challenges, but challenges keep things interesting. Remember, if you think it will be easy, you increase the chance that it will be easy. If you think it will be hard, then you increase the chance that it will be hard. Your thoughts make all the difference in the world. Perception is the greatest game that is still free for everyone on the planet.

Imagine yourself already involved in a community where people govern themselves, peace is the ultimate binding belief system, and money is no longer a concern. What do you see yourself doing that could contribute to the needs of the community and create harmony within yourself? As I go through the basic needs, see if any of these fit your desires.

FOOD FOR THE SOUL

There are so many people in the world who love to grow fruits, vegetables, and grains. Their thumbs are as green as the lucky shamrocks found on the rolling hills of Ireland. There is something very magical and gratifying about growing and eating your own food, and better yet, having others appreciate your efforts as you share your harvest with them. There are so many uses for plants, ranging from food sources, to oils, to raw materials, that anyone with this green-thumbed passion will be welcomed and treasured.

Maybe you could be one of these people. You could grow one, two, or twenty different types of fruits and vegetables that will fill the dining room tables for you and your neighbors. Maybe you could grow a special herb that instantly alleviates headaches. Maybe you have the desire to grow entire crops of cotton or hemp to make clothing, paper, baskets, and other necessities for your community and surrounding communities. Your positive intentions and energy alone can help grow bountiful crops.

If growing crops is not your cup of tea, maybe you have a keen sense of where the tasty wild fruits and vegetables grow. Maybe you are a natural tracker and know how to find honey, roots, and herbs for medicinal use. It's exciting to come across an entire batch of wild blackberries for jams and pies. Or maybe you could stumble across a pear tree with the branches bending down to offer you a bountiful sweet harvest.

What if your ability was scientific in nature and you discovered hundreds of useful ways to use a plant or vegetable, just like George Washington Carver did with the peanut and sweet potato? Your discoveries could potentially alleviate any need for harmful chemicals, pesticides, and wipe out hunger around the world. That would be awesome.

You might enjoy raising animals on a farm, herding goats, milking cows, or tending to those cute fuzzy yellow chicks. Your skill might be as a master woodsman with special skills in hunting, tracking, or fishing. You might be the boat maker who helps fishermen to catch fish in all depths of water. You could be the metalworker who creates a better barrel for a hunting rifle. Or your skill may be in mathematics and engineering where you create a better design for an oven, an improved irrigation system with reduced evaporation in the fields, or a new arrow that flies straighter and farther to bring in the turkey. All of these occupations contribute to food production for the community.

Once you bag the turkey, now it is time to prepare the food. You can see how this cycle is beginning to help everyone involved in the process. If someone spends time and effort producing the best ingredients and meat for a meal, then the chef will naturally take a huge amount of pride in his work, and create the best meals for everyone to enjoy. Passion produces more passion. Good feelings produce more good feelings. Peace produces more peace. This is a true snowball effect. This community system will catch on very quickly, especially when the money system, fear, and ego are transformed. Remember, there is no dark or evil, there is only perception and opportunity.

Without money as a driving force, suitable farming and agricultural techniques can thrive once again. Crops can be rotated properly and allow the Earth to naturally replenish the soil with the necessary nutrients and fertilizers. Our bodies will be healthier without all the contaminating chemicals and pesticides that are currently used on our crops and in livestock. Animals will no longer be treated inhumanely while waiting to be slaughtered and slapped on a bun, just to increase stockholder dividends. It has been suggested that the cellular memory of an animal that is treated inhumanely through torture, poor housing, and painful butchering carries on into those who partake of its flesh.

As seasons change, there will be a need for long-term storage of spices, herbs, and perishable foods. A builder can help by constructing a new canning room, creating a new smokehouse, or designing a better storage facility for grains and other types of plants. Canning, smoking, pickling, and drying returns with a force and creates community involvement. You can see how food production creates community projects very quickly. Everyone needs food, and food can become one of the cornerstones for maintaining a community of peace.

BEYOND FOOD

By some unseen natural process, as I gathered data on peoples' passions, each basic need for the community was met in one way or another. There were those who could help produce food by growing, hunting, and fishing. There were those who enjoy building and architecture. There were people who wished to help others by teaching, giving medical assistance, making clothing, researching, providing entertainment, and more. All of the basic needs could be met by allowing people to decide for themselves what passions to pursue and how they could help their community grow when money was no longer an object.

We have barely scratched the surface for the major basic necessities when addressing the need for food. Perhaps you saw yourself pursuing a passion to produce food, cook food, store food, or help create new ways to maximize food potential with your abilities. Even if you did not see yourself being a part of the food production process, you are still pursuing a desire for food by consuming a plate full of tasty morsels. Unless you have evolved to a point where your body no longer needs food, you will have an appreciation for food and the efforts shared by those who helped provide it.

Besides food, there is a need for clean drinking water, water for personal hygiene, plants, fire prevention, and recreation. The process can be as simple as designing a working waterway for irrigation and consumption. You could help dig a hole, move dirt, place piping, create piping, help with heating or cooling water systems, or manufacture hoses, nozzles, or faucets. Your creative process can lend a helping hand to one or more of these needs. Most people desire clean water to come out of their pipes, and if you were a part of this, you would be helping an entire community with this important basic need.

Think of all the things that are needed for water to be used by everyone in your community. See if there is anything that can be connected to your passions or ways in which you could help a society like this one flourish. Here is a small list to help get you started: manufacture shovels; grow trees/wood for handles; find metal for shovel blades, drilling equipment; design power systems for drills; create material for pipes and hoses, molds for metal fixtures, machine shops, paddle/water wheels, water run-off systems for waste, heating and cooling systems; develop pressure systems, dowsing, water purification, water preservation; develop water resistant-fabrics and materials, water storage, irrigation for plants and animals, washers for seals, umbrellas; and anything to do with recreation in or on water. And don't forget balloons for water balloon fights. This is just the beginning. There are many other needs associated with water. Were you able to match a passion? Were you able to see something you could do that would help yourself and a neighborhood with water needs?

If food and water supply are not on your passion list, maybe you enjoy sewing, weaving, knitting, braiding, or mending. If modesty is still part of the human psyche, people will need to cover up with attractive clothing and footwear.

You might be wondering, "Where would I get the supplies and cloth to make the best dresses and suits?" Well, someone's passion is to grow cotton and other plants that can be used for thread. Someone may want to raise silkworms or sheep. Someone's passion might be to create a machine that helps separate cotton fibers without a cotton mill or cotton gin. Someone's passion is to spin the cotton fibers or create a machine for spindling and weaving. And while they are creating these materials and fabrics for you, you are creating the incredible outfits for people to wear. You don't have to do it all on your own. The natural process of selection will take care of the rest. And if there is a need for something that is not there, someone will rise to the occasion and fill in the gaps. If peace is the goal, all things work naturally.

ROOF OVER YOUR HEAD

OK. We have covered three basic needs so far: food, clothing, and clean water. Another basic need is shelter. This is where it becomes even more fun. Without money to bind someone to a 9-to-5 job (or more likely, a 7-to-7 job, with commuting and work preparation), people are free to help others if a new shelter, home, recreation center, bakery, or barn needs to be built. This is the old-fashioned barn raising, where communities came together in the 18th and 19th centuries to build a barn and home for a new family who moved into the area. The Amish and Mennonite communities still practice barn raising to this day.

If you aren't helping with the actual building, you are still helping by providing food, clothing, raw materials, building plans, or other activities to enrich the community. There are no schedules to keep people from giving their best effort to complete a new home. There are no profit sheets to worry about. If someone helped build my home, and he gave his best effort to protect my family, when I help build or produce something for him, I am inspired to give my best effort. And remember this, as people are pursuing their passion, they are also perfecting their skills and becoming masters at their craft. I welcome a master builder to come build my home. In return, I will cook my best batch of baked beans for them, which have been labeled by the government's new pyramid of nutrition as its own tasty food group.

NATURAL TALENTS

Some of you are really excited by what you are reading so far. Good for you! I am excited for you. I love seeing potential at its best. I love seeing potential in action even more.

What if you are one of the people who say "Mike, I'm really not into cooking or sewing." What if your natural talent is strength? I say, "Great! Talk about possibilities!" You can help people stay in shape and healthy with motivation, fun exercise activities, teaching, and living by example. Your strength can help protect individuals while gathering food and natural resources. Maybe you can create and maintain a *defensive only* organization to protect the community from predators and other hostile forces. Your ability of strength can be used for entertainment, recreation, sports, and show of skill. Your strength can help in so many ways. The only limit to positive use of strength is self-imposed.

Other natural talents that are vital to personal growth, and offer valuable contributions to a community, are entertainers, writers, poets, composers, artists, musicians, actors, mathematicians, and the list goes on. You might provide a soothing melody with your cello that sets an incredible mood for an evening meal. Your inspirational words could provide the one statement that helps a community transcend fear and ego and instills peace for all people on Earth. Your ability to process mathematics could provide the next version of the Phi ratio, the mathematical formula used by the world's most famous artists and builders. The works of Leonardo da Vinci, the builders of the Parthenon in Greece, and the Creator of plants, animals, and insects used this magical ratio for the building blocks of aesthetic beauty and amazing abilities.

Some people have a natural talent for sacrifice. They gain their inner peace by sacrificing their desires to meet the needs of others. Volunteers are a great example. I have had so many wonderful band parents sacrifice time and energy to help their children's band program grow. The band became a binding interest for the students and parents. This community works. A little shift from band parenting toward a community of peace is easy. All it takes is enough people to step away from their current programming of money, jobs, taxes, and fear. All it takes is a new *Freedom Code*.

Remember, if you think this will never happen in our lifetime, you increase the chance that it will never happen. If you believe this could happen, you increase the possibility of success. A possibility becomes a probability. A probability becomes a stronger belief. This strong belief turns into a reality. We can do this overnight if we want. India did it with nonviolence and gained its freedom. We can do the same thing if we all band together with a desire for peace and a world without financial slavery.

THE LIST GOES ON

The possibilities are growing faster than I can put words on paper. Without seeing all the potential passions that can help a community thrive, you are probably thinking about how your passion will create an environment of peace within yourself. Peace inside grows outside. Peace is projected outward. I believe that our bodies carry our internal thoughts and express them through our internal and external body parts. I believe that a healthy, relaxed, and stress-free mind and body creates a healthier, stronger mind, body, and soul. My health is an outward expression of my inner thoughts. Happy thoughts create happy bodies. If you believe you are going to be sick, you increase the chance that you will become sick. If you believe you will be healthy, you increase the chance that you will be healthy. If you believe in success, you increase the chance of success.

I believe this community is a roadmap for peace, so I am increasing the opportunity for a peaceful world.

Look at this next list of basic necessities. As each community will always need something more than another, see how your passions and abilities could contribute to the inner peace of yourself and others.

Food: and all that goes with the production, gathering, cooking, storing, and preservation, and chocolate

Water: for consumption, bathing, personal care, cooking, fire prevention, irrigation, alternate power source, and recreation

Shelters: homes, farms, community centers, specialized buildings for exploring passions (e.g. art room, machine shop, schools), recreation centers

Clothing and shoes: provide raw materials, creating threads, creating fabrics, clothing design, manufacturing fabrics for clothing and shoes, distribution

Medical care: all allopathic, holistic, homeopathic, and alternative methods

Dental care: all allopathic, holistic, homeopathic, and alternative methods

Personal care: creating soaps, cleansers, deodorant, combs, brushes, cloth for cleaning, razors, and chocolate

Sewage/compost/waste management

Basic transportation: carts, horses, mules, oxen, roads, Earth-friendly vehicles, environmentally-friendly fuels and energy sources

Education: teaching, writing, training, anything to do with the preservation and sharing of knowledge

Recreation and entertainment: art, music, poetry, writing, games, dancing, painting, sculpting, acting, athletics

Protection for the community: only for defense

Eldercare and childcare

Animal care and training

Of course, this is not a complete list. It is a sample of the basic ingredients for a working community. What else did you think of that would help a community grow? How would your passion help others?

KNOWLEDGE OF THE MASTERS

In the Hawaiian culture, if you happened to be a person who mastered a specific technique or skill, and you accepted the responsibility of being the *keepers of the secret(s)*, you were given the title of Kahuna. Kahu, in Hawaiian, means "guardian," and huna means "secret." It's been said that knowledge, through the passage of *mana*, was transferred from a Kahuna to a family member right before death in a practice called the hā ritual. This was a magical ritual that gave the recipient all the knowledge that the Kahuna obtained for his or her craft. There were Kahunas for boat building, Kahunas for fishing, Kahunas for medicine, weaving, prayer, and so on.

It would be great if we could all go to a Kahuna and request to have her knowledge instantly transferred inside of us, but we don't need to go to a faraway place to do this. We have so many talented and gifted people to learn from right in our own neighborhood. These people would be able to continue mastering their craft and pass along their knowledge while they are still alive. Talk about a great way to achieve immortality. If you want to live on for untold passages of time, pass along your knowledge and skills to as many people as possible. As they take your knowledge and incorporate it into their own, they will pass on both your knowledge and their knowledge to willing students. A part of your soul would live on longer than the souls of the great pharaohs of Egypt.

In a world driven by money, control, and power, knowledge and skills are kept secret because of competition and profit. It's an easy way to corner a market. Ask a company for their secret recipe and see what they say. Ego also keeps people from passing down skills and ability. There are people whose ego demands that they be the only one to have a unique skill or knowledge so they can remain special. The more people release ego, and with no monetary system, people will be free to pass down as much knowledge as possible. I look forward to the day when we can give our best inventions, medical discoveries, art, music, and creativity away for everyone's benefit.

While I was teaching band class, my goal was to have my students surpass my skill and perform to the best of their abilities. I was so proud of what they could do at such early ages. They were playing things that I never dreamed of playing, and they were not even in high school yet. They weren't my children, but I sure felt like a proud parent.

I know many teachers who also encourage their students to begin teaching others, even though they have not yet mastered their craft. If you really want to know whether someone understands something, have him teach a specific skill to another student. If my music students were able to effectively teach another student how to play a scale correctly, or to use a correct fingering to play a C on a clarinet, I knew they understood that skill or concept. It was instant success. Also, you don't have to wait to become a master before you can pass on your skills. I have a Master's Degree in Music Performance from The Florida State University, and I must tell you that music still kicks my butt to this day. I am an accomplished performer, but there is plenty of music out there that I have not yet played or mastered. Did I have to master all music to teach it? No, of course not. We wouldn't have many teachers at all if they all had to be perfect before they could teach. With less ego, you are no longer competing against others; you are only competing with yourself to reach your highest ability, while encouraging success in others.

CHAPTER TWENTY

A WORLD OF PEACE

IN THE LAST CHAPTER, I listed a number of passions and occupations to help inspire you to think in a way that is different from our current financial programming. I realize that viewing a world without money can be rather new for many people. Thinking of a passion that is not linked to money can also be fresh and novel. Let's go back a little ways to your childhood and examine how this programming began and how it can transform from money back to dreams again.

As a child, you probably heard messages from your parents and teachers to reach for the stars. You were told that anything is possible. Hopefully you were encouraged never to allow someone to steal your dreams. A bigger hope is that you clung to those words of wisdom like a dog holds onto its favorite chew toy. It never hurts to hear these inspirational words again. Hear them ring loudly in your mind as you read each sentence below. Let them reverberate for days to come.

"Reach for the stars! Dream again and again! Pursue your passions and don't hold back! Don't let anyone steal your dreams! Be happy! You can do it!"

Read them again before going on...

As you graduated from elementary school, moved on to middle school, then prepared for high school, you might have noticed how the programming began to shift from dreams to jobs. Once in high school or college, it was time to focus on a career path to earn money right after you received your diploma. You were trained to pursue a passion in the form of a career, not a passion that was free from financial obligation. Money and dreams began to conflict with each other considerably, and guess which one won most of the time?

Have you also observed how money has influenced many people to give up their dreams and settle for something less because they have to earn a paycheck? The great news is this: In this new community, the concept is completely reversed. There is no monetary system. There are no class systems or special privileges granted by noble birth. Everyone and everything has equal importance. In this society of peace, each individual is just as important as every cell and organ in the human body. You cannot decide to remove your heart and expect to live very long. You cannot take away food, water, or shelter, or the system begins to falter. You can see how each has its place of importance, and no one basic need or person has more value than another. This would be a land where the words *"All men, women, and children are created equal"* would have meaning again.

In our current system, value is created by the ego, and ego makes one job, one toy, one car, or one piece of food more valuable than another. Supply and demand can also be attributed to fear. People become afraid that this object might be the last one. They are afraid there will be no others to replace it; therefore, it must be valuable. As a result, fear and ego create supply and demand and value.

Countless people are ready to walk away right now from this financially driven system of slavery. Maybe you are one of them. I have heard from scores of others who have told me they are extremely excited about this community concept because people are born free from a monetary system and encouraged to live their dreams and share their accomplishments with others. People are not required to work, but are encouraged to succeed and produce. We know it is hard to live in peace and freedom if you are forced to live with the old laws of financial slavery. Given a choice, would you rather pursue a paycheck, or would you rather pursue all of your life's passions and share with your neighbors?

As you may have encountered in our current system, there are many people who are motivated by money. They create a dream job to generate untold riches. This becomes their passion because there were no other options presented to them. No fault there, and there shouldn't be any bad feelings toward these people, either. I still say, "Pursue money until you are tired of that lifestyle." Now that you have read this material, you have at least one other option to consider. Ask yourself this question: If money were no longer necessary, would you still pursue your current occupation with a passion? If you said yes, woohoo! You are living your dream, and I am happy for you. If not, you are one day closer to living your passion. Keep going!

Here is something else to consider for a world without money. If we can alleviate the need for a monetary or barter system, we alleviate numerous occupations that no longer provide a contribution to a society of peace. No more IRS! (Can you hear the cheers now? They are deafening!) No more banks, credit cards, or financial advisors. No more mortgages, Realtors, car salesmen, or salespeople of any type. No more frivolous lawsuits. No more insurance companies. No more commercials or advertising. People can go to a community center to gather the needed ingredients to make pies for you and your neighbors. There would be abundant amounts of fabric to sew wonderful designer clothing. There would be great pieces of artwork to brighten your home. People would be waiting and available to help you achieve your new project. Those who were working in occupations driven by money would now be able to pursue their dream and do other things that contribute to life.

If you took all these people and offered them a chance to use their skills in another way, some may stay and continue on their current path, but I foresee a mass exodus from the lifestyle of business suits, charts, graphs, and quarterly profit reports. I foresee hundreds and thousands, if not millions, of people changing overnight to live freely again. If you took only half of the population whose jobs were created because of money, and asked them to grow one edible plant instead of working in a monetary system, we would wipe out world hunger within one harvest. Is taking care of world hunger better than living for yourself? You have to make that decision.

As I have talked with various people about their passions, it seems that almost everyone has been forced to make a concession on their dreams to ensure enough income to survive in this financially driven system. Money conflicts with passions and desires, unless the passion is for money and control. If people give up their dreams because of a controlling financial system, it must have a huge impact on how well those people perform their jobs.

At the time I was writing this book, there was, and maybe still is, a great debate going on in our country about medical care and the rising costs of medical insurance. Some of our leaders welcome a socialized medical system, while others cringe at the very thought of it. I heard on one of the news channels that an unofficial survey of doctors showed a large number of physicians would walk away from their profession if this system passed through legislation. Some would walk away because they do not like the system and how long treatment could take for those in dire need. Others would walk away because their ability to create a large profit margin would be regulated. I can see it both ways. If a physician's dream was to create abundant wealth, who could blame him? We are brainwashed in this country to pursue wealth. It only takes a few people, though, to start a new trend of thinking without supply and demand, control, fear, and money. I'm cheering already for a world of peace where people pursue their passions.

Someone shared this thought with me. He said, "If doctors are working for money and huge bank accounts, are they really serving society as healers? Their true intentions of wealth would show in their work subconsciously. I would rather have a doctor that remains a doctor because he wants to serve others by helping them get better, and not because of a big paycheck." What do you think about this?

SIMPLE SHIFT IN EDUCATION

From the time I was a child attending school, to the time I was teaching in public schools, there has always been a huge concern from parents and students regarding the number of facts and figures that were required memorization in each class. If you were good at memorizing and could recall information at a pre-determined hour, while scribbling frantically to beat a time limit, you were considered a good learner. You were smart and a good student. You got A's on your report card, and you were admired for your effort and ability to memorize.

Another valid concern shared by teachers, parents, and students alike, is the fact that students today are being forced to pass a state or national standardized test. Teachers are judged on how well their students score on these tests. Students are judged based on their test scores and placed in remedial classes if they do not perform well. Superintendents are pressed to get good scores for funding from the state. And some parents are upset that most of the school year is being spent on preparation to pass a single test. (Not everyone is upset or feels that standardized testing is bad. I am only commenting on personal experiences and reports from colleagues and members of the community.)

At one of the schools I taught in, I was told by my administrators that I had to spend X amount of time during homeroom on math problems and English assignments to help students practice for these standardized tests, even though I was a band director. (Music and the arts were not included on these tests.) Now I was good with math, but my advanced math skills were a little rusty since I was not using my geometry theorems and calculus equations in everyday life, not to mention that the *new math* is not how I was taught in school. I also tested out of math in college, so the last math class I took was back in high school. My current professional hours and free time were spent mastering the craft of band directing and helping students become great musicians and great citizens. I am sharing this with you so you can see how much these tests influenced decision-making in our schools.

I knew then that these tests were not only about test scores—they were also about funding and money for the schools. Try to see this through the eyes of an administrator. Principals and superintendents need money in our financially driven society to run their schools. If you want more money, you need higher test scores. Higher test scores turn into bragging rights and advertisement to draw families into the community. More students equal more money in today's school systems. You can see how this could influence an administrator to have his or her teachers teach toward a test.

The major downside of focusing on these tests in our education system is that it removes the teachers' freedom to create curriculum and teach to their best abilities. Natural abilities are like water—they run best if given the freedom to exist and flow as nature intended. If you pool up water, stop it, or dam it up without freedom to move, what happens? Water becomes stagnant, and it grows old and lifeless. Have you ever smelled old stagnant water? It is smelly and nasty! Educators' natural skills are hampered and constrained when forced to teach in a completely structured environment.

This has a huge impact on the effectiveness of teachers and how well students are able to learn.

You may be asking why this happens. Let me explain. If teachers want to continue teaching and receive favorable reviews to keep their jobs, they are almost forced to teach to the test and follow district objectives and guidelines. If superintendents want funding from the state, they must do what the state and govern-mint tell them to do, so they are forced to give their students these tests. If corporations want more profit margins, they need higher-educated worker bees. They lobby the government officials and create new standards and tests for higher corporate earnings. Parents and others, who are also stockholders in these companies, press the CEOs to produce more dividends. It is a trickledown effect with a vicious, never-ending cycle. I can tell you firsthand that we were not free to pick curriculum, teaching schedules, or objectives outside what was defined by the govern-mint, state legislators, district administrators, and policymakers. My best talents were hampered by guidelines imposed by others.

If I had a choice, I would rather have spent all my time in homeroom helping my students learn lessons of life. I would have taught those lessons that promote self-governing, tolerance, patience, potential, and how to release fear. I did that in my classroom anyway, but not nearly enough time is spent on these important qualities. In my room, negative words were considered profanity. Words like *can't* were not allowed. If someone said, "Mr. Rhodes, I *can't* play this," the entire class would react in a positive way. You could hear them playfully respond, "Mr. Rhodes, did you hear her? She swore." After the supportive laughter died down, the students were encouraged to try, and try again, and try some more until they mastered their skill. Even if they were not able to do the task in class, they were encouraged to continue at home and come back to share their success.

Do you remember back to your days in school? How much time was spent on self-governing? How much time was spent on tolerance? How much role-playing was done to help people survive together in peace instead of living for one's self and memorizing facts to pass a test?

I will ask you these simple questions: Would you rather live in a society where people have a good high school education and know how to live together in peace and harmony, or would you rather have students with a college degree, master's degree, or multiple doctorates, who can memorize and spit out information like a digital recorder, but can't get along with their neighbor? Which is more important, cooperation and tolerance, or memorization? There is no right or wrong answer here. It is all completely personal and left to individual perception. I do not propose that we stop teaching facts and figures. I do not propose that we throw away all standards and memorization. I can only hope for a balance between the two. There are ways to teach and evaluate without tests and memorization. Can we as parents, teachers, and members of society be allowed to choose and encourage growth without the old standards of memorization that were dictated to our teachers by our state and local govern-mints? Could potential and exploration be the new measuring stick for students? Can we find ways of measurement that promote and encourage instead of creating fear and using structured timetables for learning? Yes, we can!

Currently, the govern-mint and states control how much time a child must spend in the education system. Parents are not able to focus on their children and spend enough time to teach important lessons of life because they are forced to work for a paycheck. Some parents are working two, three, or four jobs and never get to see their children. In addition, their children are required by law to be in school a certain number of hours and days, which drastically shortens the time they spend in a family environment. Teachers are not able to spend all their time teaching good citizenship because they are required to complete objectives in their course material so students can pass tests. I say again, no individual is to blame here. A simple shift in the system could create solutions rather easily. If the monetary system was removed, people would be able to spend more time in their passions and sharing lessons of cooperation. They would be able to spend more family time together, teach self-governing, and create peace within themselves and others. You can see how time and opportunity become massively abundant again by removing a mandatory monetary system.

Like all trends and identities, people will continue doing the same thing over and over again until they become tired of it. Let's hope for a peaceful transition when the time comes.

OTHER SHIFTS IN THE SYSTEM

Removing a monetary system is a huge step toward allowing people to pursue their passions and live in peace. But removing money will not take care of all the problems. If you remove money, someone who craves power will simply apply a new barter system to control the masses. Water, food, clothing, shelter, protection, and knowledge can all be used as the new wealth. Any natural resource could easily become the new five dollar bill. So what needs to be adjusted? Since I have mentioned it numerous times throughout the book, you have probably already figured it out.

If you remove money alone, the system might work, but other types of control will arise. Ego must be transformed from living for the self to living for others. When this is accomplished, the system has a better chance of working. However, if fear remains, the system can still collapse. Fear must be transformed into courage and love to help a society transcend to the next level. When a monetary system can finally be removed, and fear and ego have been transformed, you increase the chance that a community will flourish in peace. And if you give the community a binding belief system, especially if that belief system is peace, and not religion, you have created an even greater chance of success for all of humanity.

Fear and ego must be transformed or released in order to move in the direction we once lived before. Money and wealth were not always a part of everyday life. Many indigenous tribes survive to this day rather well without money. We seem to be moving in that direction again, as all things in history cycle. What was young becomes old. Those at the top also spend time at the bottom. No one system has survived as the dominating force. Living for the self has just about used up its time, and we are ready for a change. The change will be a time of living for others. We needed this present-day experience for a reference point. We needed to live this lifestyle so we could remember where we came from and where we are headed. We will now begin a new era where giving and sharing are the new passions. I enjoyed experiencing money and living for myself for a short while, so I can appreciate living for others even more.

POSITIVE PATTERNS

I have noticed a pattern that has repeated itself many times over in my life. As I grow near the completion of a project or presentation—such as this book—while doing further research to verify facts and content, I often come across records, articles, and personal accounts of those who had similar ideas and approaches. I also seem to find many more facts and figures that support my ideas. How refreshing is that? Well, not too surprisingly, it happened again while coming to the end of creating content for this book. I came across page after page on the internet and in numerous books that suggest alternative solutions for monetary control, barter systems, and nations without a single-role government. It is extremely encouraging to see so many people looking into possible solutions to help society move in a peaceful direction.

A few years back, when I first shared my ideas for a peaceful community, some of my friends smiled knowingly at me. I soon discovered that there were cities in existence that use commune principles for living, and that they thrive very well. It didn't surprise me, though, that I wasn't the first to think of this. Those who seek peace will invariably come up with similar solutions, and it was refreshing to know that I wasn't the only one. This was a huge benefit for me. I didn't have to teach more people about the concept. I didn't have to convince them that this type of system could work; it was already being done. That made my job that much easier. I can use my energies elsewhere to help others transform fear and refine my ideas of peaceful living.

When two people open up to each other, trust each other, and share many of the same interests, there seems to be a connection that transcends traditional needs of vocalizing thoughts and ideas. Many times my wife and I know exactly what the other is thinking without saying a word. If I had an ounce of gold every time one of us said, "I was just thinking the same thing," gold would become obsolete. We would own it all. We share a common bubble of thoughts and feelings. We are in each other's circle and we openly invite each other in. We are not afraid of knowing each other's feelings or thoughts, and that is very comforting.

To take this a step further, when a group of people think along the same lines, such as world peace, cooperation, or alternative governments without monetary systems, these people will also connect to a similar wavelength or thought pattern. Identical twins are a great example of this connection. As twins are created from the same zygote, they often share a very close bond and stream of thought patterns. When one twin starts a sentence, the other can pick up in the middle of the same thought and complete the sentence exactly as the first would have done. Twins can also sense the emotional states of their sibling, even when they are miles away. Some mothers have this connection with their children. A mother can pick up the phone and call her child living in another state and ask, "What's wrong? Is anyone hurt?" And the child replies that he was just injured—and then asks, "How did you know, Mom?"

I have heard stories of inventors and scientists on opposite sides of the state, country, and the world, coming up with the exact same idea for an invention or the same conclusion to an experiment at the same time. Is this simply coincidence, or are these people working on the same wave length and tapping into the same source of shared information?

I have experimented with a tuning fork on many different objects. I know that if you strike an A-440 tuning fork in a room, the other tuning forks tuned to A-440 in that room will also vibrate. This is called sympathetic vibration. I have taken a tuning fork, struck it, then placed it on the node of a singing bowl tuned to a B. The bowl instantly changed pitch and started resonating to an A. I used an A-440 tuning fork and changed a vibraphone note in the same manner. I also applied a tuning fork to the sarcophagus in the King's chamber in Egypt. The sarcophagus resonated to the A pitch. (It's not an exact A-440, but it was interesting for sure.)

This is not to say that A-440 is the pitch that all things resonate to. I am merely pointing out that one vibration can mesh with other vibrations very easily without regard to pitch or tuning. When a pitch has more things in common, such as vibration, resonance, and volume, then more attraction is created in that surrounding area to vibrate the same way. The more people resonate to peace, the more ideas they will share in common and create a stronger vibration of peace. This makes sense. As people are less resistant, they become open to more ideas. In musical terms, or terms of vibration, they become less resistant as their intensity, or amplitude, diminishes. This makes people a great example of a musical node. In terms of physics, the place with no amplitude (intensity), or very little amplitude, is called the node of a standing wave.

As the theory goes, all things in the Universe(s) are made up of vibration. Vibrations can communicate, entrain, form wonderful pleasing sounds of consonance, dissonance, and change with little effort when approached with the least resistance, or at the nodal point. Part of the underlying concept of string theory, although still a controversial theory for some, states that everything has a specific vibration. Each variation in vibration becomes a new building block, or roadmap, for subatomic particles.

There are also theories that the human body and internal organs resonate to specific frequencies. When using concentrated pitch, the body can heal itself faster, sometimes instantaneously, as the frequencies are focused toward the internal organ. This may sound far-fetched, but a mother's soothing voice can instantly calm a baby quicker than a rattle or a wooby blanket. Belief also contributes to the success of a healing modality.

As more people decide to live in a society of peace, my theory is that they will gravitate toward each other by a natural process of entrainment. They will seek each other out from the source of thought and emotion. These people seem to be the least resistant because they have shed their need for control, power, money, and greed. They have become the standing wave for a new era of cooperation. As they have less amplitude, the nodal point of their spirit will allow them an easier transition to cooperate with more people and work toward a peaceful solution.

COMBINING THEORIES

You may be familiar with other proposed systems besides our current economic and capitalistic democracy. There is the gift economy, in which services and goods are given without any expectation of a return in kind or in value. I use this analogy a lot when describing how well this system can work. If you give to your neighbors, and they give to their neighbors, and they give to their neighbors, eventually you will also receive gifts and services because you are also somebody's neighbor.

The main obstacle to this system is our old friends—fear and ego. Imagine this: You work really hard to create your best batch of canned peaches. You spend days, maybe weeks, in your kitchen preparing all the canning supplies, pealing peaches, and getting just the right amount of cinnamon and brown sugar into your mix. This is your tastiest batch ever. You poured your life into your work and you are very proud of what you've accomplished. Then, you give all the peaches away to your neighbors. If your ego creeps up, you might place a value on your services and skills. When it's your turn to receive from your neighbors, if you don't receive what you consider to be a fair return, your feelings become hurt. You become jealous or angry, which can build to resentment and hate. You would then have less incentive to give your best effort and share with everyone else in the future. You can see how important it is to work on transforming fear and ego before this society of peace can prosper. Once that is accomplished, our future children will be born into a place where value for monetary gains is no longer an issue. It will no longer be part of the genetic programming. This will solidify as new programming and become an accepted way of life for generations to come.

Another alternative is the free market system. In this system, there is no government intervention except to prevent force or fraud. There is no single monetary system, government regulation, or subsidization. Value is agreed upon by consent between the two parties engaging in commerce. Basically, it's still a bartering system, and bartering is about expecting something of equal or greater amount in return. You can see there is still a major challenge within this system because value is at the heart and core of this concept. You also have control built deep inside because of supply and demand. Supply and demand can easily be used as a means of power. As I have mentioned before, value, along with supply and demand, are created from ego and fear.

Albert Einstein is attributed with saying that the definition of insanity is doing the same thing over and over again and expecting a different result. We have been bound to a monetary system for over 5,000 years. If we want a change, if we dream of a change, if we expect a change, we might have to leave money, or value and ego, out of the picture.

Of course, there are other proposed systems of government and economic solutions. We could talk about laissez-faire, economy of the Iroquois, equal distribution of wealth, deregulation, and many more until the next major migration. Each has its place and possesses some positive qualities to use as a guide for the next evolution of humanity. Each type of government has become the building block for another. We are becoming increasingly freer with each new step we take. As we continue to learn about the successes and challenges of each system, we are able to take the best from each and implement it into a true society of peace.

WORDS OF HOPE FROM THE ELDERS

I have been a hunter-gatherer of knowledge from the moment I took my first breath. I think my first words were *why, who, how,* and *what.* In an effort to gather even more information about communal living and smaller communities, I traveled to a powwow to talk with some of the Native American elders. I wanted to hear how their grandfathers, and their grandfather's fathers, lived before times changed and their lands were taken away from them. I knew there were many things we could learn from their teachings and philosophies. I knew we could resurrect the good parts of the old ways and incorporate them into the new. While I spoke with each elder, I could feel that we shared a common bond as they expressed their interest to share knowledge and wisdom with the masses. Here is what they had to say.

Terry "Swift Bird" Fiddler, an expert at Native American dance, is a member of the Cheyenne River Sioux tribe. His wisdom and sincerity were truly inspirational as he answered my questions on the history of Native Americans and their tribal belief systems. Here is what he had to say.

"As native people, we have always been taught to look out for everyone, and we are taught to share everything we have, and to never keep anything for ourselves. And this goes against everything that is taught to everyone else. To accumulate wealth is a great thing in this country. But in our way, it was frowned upon when there were people out there who needed food or shelter. For our people to survive, these were the teachings that our forefathers had passed down to us. We were taught to take care of the people, our children, our women, the elders, and take care of them first before yourself. Those are some of the things that were taught as traditional values. In those teachings, there is a whole cycle of life that we call the circle of life. From the time you come here, to the time you leave, there's time that you need help. You need help to grow as a child, and you need help when you become old. We call it the sacred hoop."

Another elder and excellent dancer I spoke with was Allenroy "Northwind" Paquin, a member of the Jicarilla Apache Nation in New Mexico. I asked him to share some of his thoughts on the benefits of tribal living. I also asked him what he thought was important to emulate in a community of passion and peace. His answers were equally pleasing and wise. He stated, "Well, because tribes are usually such small communities, everyone knows each other." In regard to those who are not Native American, "...even if they are not tribal members, or are not the same tribe or nation, if they need help, we are willing to help them out. It's a connectedness that people are missing. It's that closeness, willingness to help each other, lend a hand, give some money, and to pray for one another. Tribal living, that grouping, is something that a lot of people are looking for. They want to be part of a family."

I asked him if there was a message that he wished to share with the entire world. He told me there were many, but he emphasized prayer: "There is power in prayer. Many of my prayers have been answered. My successes come from answered prayers." He continued by saying he wished we "had more acceptance of different people as a whole. Be open and have the willingness to accept people for their differences, for being different, and to pray."

I was blessed to meet these two great gentlemen.

PUTTING IT ALL TOGETHER

By now, you have been thinking of your passions. Your dreams will be coming to life very soon. Your dreams just got a huge shot of adrenaline and are surging in your soul. They have been incubating inside your mind and are ready to hatch and come out into the world. Embrace them. Cherish them. Use them to fuel your new direction in life. Use them to empower yourself and help others become empowered. Help a friend, a stranger, a loved one to find their dreams, and you will be living one of yours in turn. Your success and skills will be an inspiration to others. Success breeds success. As you inspire others, you will be inspired. Continue to find strength and courage within yourself. You have all the abilities you need. They are there. Resources and knowledge are abundant and at your fingertips. Don't let anyone steal your dreams. Reach for your star with confidence.

A good place to start is by placing yourself in the right environment for success. Share your dreams with those you know will support you. By combining positive thoughts with others in the beginning, you give more positive energy to your dreams so they can become a reality. Once the ball is rolling, then you can share your dream with everyone else if you wish. Do what you feel is best. Trust your instincts. Follow your inner voice. Nobody knows yourself better than you do. Is today the day to start your new life?

If you want to live in a community of peace and potential like the one I've shared in this book, let others know. The more people who know what you really want, the more they can help you. If more people know you want to live in a community where passions and peace are the binding belief system, those same peaceful, successful, and motivational people will gravitate toward you. You will be able to grow from the supportive energies of like minds. If you find you are tired of pursuing money and wish to live for others, let them know. The right situations will present themselves to you.

Start the process today. Write down your dreams. Carry them with you.

Pull them out in times of elation and sorrow. Let your dreams and passions become the light that brightens the way. Tell your subconscious what you want. Make it known to all parts of your conscious self. Pray with others to help everyone achieve their goals. Get active. Draw your dreams and passions. Paint them, record them, and cut out pictures of them. Turn your desire into a poem or a song. Sing life into your dreams every day. Do all that you can to make them come true. I believe in you. All it takes is a little support, a little nudge. I am behind your endeavors of peace and passion. It is time to start living again. It is time to bring a world of peace into action. It has started; now it is time for it to grow. It will grow within first. Then it will spread with the winds to the rest of the world.

MY FINAL THOUGHTS

There have been so many times in my life when I could have loved more, forgiven more, let go of more ego, transformed more fear into courage, and been kinder to my fellow man. As I focus on the now and the future, I can make conscious changes. We can always look at the past, but use it to learn from, not to dwell on and suffer over.

We have the freedom to change. We have the freedom to change our lives and be better. We have a new *Freedom Code* by which to live our lives. We can love, cherish, accept, and forgive. We can help, nurture, teach, and guide. We can allow others to live their lives and encourage them to hold onto their identities until they are tired of them. We can do better with our gifts and our unexplored talents. We can pursue more passions and create peace within ourselves. We can create instead of destroy. We can love instead of hate. We can encourage instead of kill. We can choose bravery instead of fear. We can inspire and be inspired. We can be more tolerant and patient. You and I *can* make a difference. You can make the difference. You are the difference. It only takes one step, one breath of motion to create your dreams. I am here for you in spirit through this book if you want to make a difference in yourself. I am here for you in the form of these inspirational words. I believe in you. I believe in your ability. I believe in your potential. I believe in your success. It is time that *WE ALL BELIEVE.*

Wish Granted!

SUGGESTED READING

Dunbar, R.I.M. "Neocortex size as a constraint on group size in primates," *Journal of Human Evolution* (1992): vol. 20, pp. 469–493.

Goswani, Amit, Goswani, Maggie, and Reed, Richard E. *The Self-Aware Universe: How Consciousness Creates the Material World*. New York, New York: Penguin Putnam, 1993.

Greene, Brian. *The Elegant Universe: Superstrings, Hidden Dimensions, and the Quest for the Ultimate Theory*. New York: Vintage Books, 2003.

———. *The Fabric of the Cosmos: Space, Time, and the Texture of Reality*. New York: Vintage Books, 2004.

Lopresti, Robert. *Which U.S. Presidents Owned Slaves?* <http://www.nas.com/~lopresti/ps.htm> Accessed: October 29, 2009.

Kaku, Michio. *Hyperspace: A Scientific Odyssey Through Parallel Universes, Time Warps, and the 10th Dimension*. New York: Anchor Books, 1995.

Long, Max Freedom. *The Secret Science Behind Miracles: Unveiling the Huna Tradition of the Ancient Polynesians*. Camarillo, CA: Devorss & Company, 1976.

Ranganathan, Vinoth K., Siemionowa, Vlodek, Liu, Jing Z., Sahgal, Vinod, and Yue, Guang H. "From mental power to muscle power; gaining strength by using the mind." *Neuropsychologia* (2004) 42970 944–956.

Talbot, Michael. *The Holographic Universe*. New York, New York: Harper-Perennial, 1991.

"The Constitution of the United States," Article 1, Section 3.

Tompkins, Peter, and Bird, Christopher. *The Secret Life of Plants*. New York, New York: HarperPerennial, 1973.

U.S. Public Law 103–150 (S.J. Res. 19), Nov. 23, 1993.

INDEX

ABOUT THE AUTHOR

MICHAEL RHODES has a B.S. in Music Education, an M.M. in Music Performance, over twenty years of classroom and individual instruction experience, over 400 hours of hypnosis training, is certified in Meridian Therapy, and he has over twenty years of practical experience with self-empowerment training.

Michael has given numerous lectures and workshops on the benefits of hypnosis, Sacred Geometry, quantum physics, Huna, and self-empowerment. He has also produced eleven published songs for percussion, royalty free hypnosis music, meditation music, and guided sessions on CD and .mp3 format.

Michael is a motivational speaker and is available for public speaking, group and individual hypnosis sessions, and guided meditations. He can be reached at www.AncientEldersPress.com and www.HTHypnosis.com.